Conference Interpreting

'Andrew Gillies' book offers a fount of useful, practical and fun exercises which students can do, individually or collectively, to develop specific skills. A great book for teachers and students alike to dip into.'
Roderick Jones, author of *Conference Interpreting Explained*

Conference Interpreting: A Student's Practice Book brings together a comprehensive compilation of tried and tested practical exercises which hone the sub-skills that make up conference interpreting.

Unique in its exclusively practical focus, *Conference Interpreting: A Student's Practice Book* is a reference for students and teachers seeking to solve specific interpreting-related difficulties. By breaking down the necessary skills and linking these to the most relevant and effective exercises, students can target their areas of weakness and work more efficiently towards greater interpreting competence.

Split into four parts, this *Practice Book* includes a detailed introduction offering general principles for effective practice drawn from the author's own extensive experience as an interpreter and interpreter-trainer. The second, 'language', section covers language enhancement at this very high level, an area that standard language courses and textbooks are unable to deal with. The last two sections cover the key sub-skills needed to effectively handle the two components of conference interpreting: simultaneous and consecutive interpreting.

Conference Interpreting: A Student's Practice Book is not language-specific and as such is an essential resource for all interpreting students, regardless of their language combination.

Andrew Gillies is a freelance interpreter working primarily, but not exclusively, for EU and European Institutions in Brussels, Paris and Munich.

Conference Interpreting

A student's practice book

Andrew Gillies

Routledge
Taylor & Francis Group

LONDON AND NEW YORK

First published 2013
by Routledge
2 Park Square, Milton Park, Abingdon, Oxon OX14 4RN

Simultaneously published in the USA and Canada
by Routledge
711 Third Avenue, New York, NY 10017

Routledge is an imprint of the Taylor & Francis Group, an informa business

British Library Cataloguing in Publication Data
A catalogue record for this book is available from the British Library

Library of Congress Cataloging in Publication Data
Gillies, Andrew, 1971–
Conference Interpreting: a Student's Practice Book / Andrew Gillies.
pages cm
Includes bibliographical references.
1. Translating and interpreting–Study and teaching. 2. Translators–Training of.
I. Title.
P306.5.G56 2013
418'.02–dc23
2012044243

ISBN: 978-0-415-53234-1 (hbk)
ISBN: 978-0-415-53236-5 (pbk)
ISBN: 978-0-203-11492-6 (ebk)

Typeset in Times New Roman
by Saxon Graphics Ltd, Derby

Printed and bound in Great Britain by
TJ International Ltd, Padstow, Cornwall

Contents

Part D: Simultaneous interpreting

Acknowledgements

I wouldn't have managed to complete this book without Tatiana's help and patience. Thank you also to all the interpreters quoted in this book for their wonderful ideas and to all the interpreter trainers with whom I have discussed, tested and tweaked these exercises. And to Cathy Pearson, who gave me a shove just when it was needed.

The publishers would like to thank St Jerome Publishing, *Le Monde*, The Guardian News and Media Limited, The Independent Print Limited, R.J.C Watt and Hasbro for permission to use their material. Every effort has been made to contact copyright holders. If any have been overlooked, the publishers will be pleased to make the necessary arrangements at the first opportunity.

Introduction

About this book

> Assuming Conference Interpreting is mainly a skill, very much like one of the more difficult sports, performed mainly by the interpreter's brain, it becomes important to realize that the most difficult exercises can only be performed by the interpreter if he can draw upon a solid reserve of automatic reflexes which allow him to free his mind for those parts of the interpretative process which need his fullest attention.
>
> Weber 1989: 162

Interpreting, despite the fact that it is often taught at universities, is not an academic subject; it is far more akin to a craft or a sport. One cannot learn to interpret by going to a lecture (or reading a book) and understanding an explanation of how interpreting works. Interpreting is a skill or, to be more exact, a combination of skills that one can explain and understand quite quickly, but which take far longer to master in practice. In practice, and through practice!

This book offers some guidelines for effective practice and a compilation of practice exercises drawn from conference interpreting literature and teachers. As such it is meant as a resource for students and trainers looking for practice ideas. Though the book is directed primarily at students and teachers of conference interpreting, it should also have much to offer those training for other types of interpreting – court, community, sign language etc.

There are a number of simple ideas underpinning this book. First is that mentioned above, that to learn to carry out a skill we must practise, repeatedly. Repeated practice of a skill allows us to internalize it, that is to say, arrive at a place where some part of what we are doing becomes automatic and we can complete the skill without giving it our full attention. This is particularly important in interpreting, because the mental capacity freed up in this way will not go to waste. It will be put towards the other skills that go to make up interpreting.

Second, complex skills can be broken down into their component parts, which can then be practised in isolation. Interpreting is a complex skill. It involves doing a number of different things at the same time, some of them relatively simple, some less so. In this book the skills that go to make up conference interpreting have been split up and exercises offered for each one. Each of these skills may well be new to the would-be interpreter and it is useful to learn, and practise, new skills one at a time, adding another only when the previous one has been mastered.

By practising each skill in isolation you can concentrate on achieving the necessary degree of internalization for it without the distraction of trying to complete the other tasks at the same time.[1]

Let me draw an analogy with swimming. A competitive swimmer under the instruction of a qualified coach will regularly swim with a float between their legs (thus immobilizing them) in order to concentrate on the arm movements alone. Similarly, they will hold the float in outstretched arms to focus on the correct leg movements. The techniques for turning around at the end of each length and breathing correctly are also practised in isolation. Only when adjustments to these elements have been made, and practised, in isolation will those same adjustments be introduced to the full stroke.

Isolating skills like this makes it possible to practise each one in a more focused way, allowing you to arrive at a stage where you have internalized the skill, that is to say, you can complete it automatically (without too much thinking about it). You can now direct the mental capacity thus freed up to one of the other tasks, until that too becomes automatic, and so on. Of course in practice the progression is never quite so deliberate and the isolation of skills never so exact and total, particularly for simultaneous interpreting. Nevertheless the approach is still sound enough to be used as a complement to your other work.

Third, you don't have to interpret to get better at interpreting. You will interpret, of course. But you don't have to, indeed you should not, *only* interpret. This is particularly true in the early stages, when interpreting will be far too difficult for you and therefore potentially discouraging. But it is also true while interpreting, when you come across particular problems that are difficult to address.

Fourth, a change is as good as a rest. We can practise the same skills in many different ways, or always in the same way. Using different exercises to practise the same skill can help bring a new angle to an old problem and therefore help us find solutions where perhaps we had become stuck in a rut.

Last, variety is the spice of life. Having a variety of exercises at our disposal will help us avoid boredom, keep us on our toes and as a result keep us motivated in our quest to master the complex skill that is conference interpreting. A quest that is likely to take several years.

The practice exercises included in this book have been suggested by interpreter trainers, interpreters and student interpreters; adapted from ELTA[2] classes; taken from conference interpreting literature; or, to a much lesser extent, invented by the author. Where an exercise has been taken directly from a published text, I refer to the author, year of publication and page number, for example (Kalina 2000: 179), and further information about that publication can then be found in the bibliography. In the case of exercises that are widely known, or have been 'invented' independently by various people and appear in a published text of which I am aware, the reference appears as follows: 'also Sainz 1993: 139'. Where the works of several authors are cited in the same place, they appear in chronological order according to the publication date. Unpublished exercises that I can attribute to individual teachers are annotated with the name of the teacher in question, for example, 'Poger'. There are no doubt also exercises that appear in conference interpreting literature that I have not read and are therefore not credited to any one author. My apologies to any author whose exercises are not properly credited to them here.

Where the original mention of an exercise was overly concise, I have elaborated, sometimes considerably, on the aims and instructions for that exercise. Where essentially the same exercise is described slightly differently by different sources, I have approximated the versions of that same exercise. And in some cases I have also suggested a number of variations on, or examples of, an exercise that the original source did not.

Not all exercises in works cited in this book have been included here. For example, where exercises were described unclearly in the original, or appear to relate to types of interpreting other than conference interpreting, they have not been included here. Also, where exercises in other works are self-contained examples (eg. 'translate the following idioms') that cannot obviously be repeated with other material, they have also not been included here.

In most cases I make no judgement on the effectiveness of any of the exercises, on some of which interpreter trainers have strong and differing views. Empirical evidence on the subject is, however, almost non-existent.[3] I simply suggest that you try the exercises out, and if they work for you then that is good enough. The exercises can be done by students alone or with the help of a teacher.

Some of the exercises involve more than one skill, so by changing their focus they can be used to practise different things. As such there is some repetition in the list of exercises. Each exercise is also described so as to be applicable immediately without reference to other exercises. There is therefore also some repetition between similar exercises or variations on a single exercise in any given part of the book.

The book does not address the principles of good interpreting (which are described elsewhere: Jones 1998; Seleskovich 1968 and 2002) but rather how to practise some of those principles that are generally held to be valid.

This book is loosely based on an earlier publication, *Conference Interpreting – A Students' Companion*, published in 2001 in Cracow, Poland. The fact that this work is unavailable outside Poland, and the need to thoroughly update and revise it, are behind this new publication.

How to use this book

This book is not intended to be read from cover to cover but used as a reference work to be dipped into as and when necessary. And the exercises are meant as a complement to your normal interpreting practice, not a substitute. Similar exercises are grouped together where possible, but that doesn't mean that you should do the exercises in the order they are presented here – this is not a course book. Nor should you try to do all of the exercises in the book – that's probably not even possible! Instead, you should work out, perhaps in consultation with a teacher, what skills you need to work on and then you can look up practice exercises for those skills here. Interpreter trainers looking for ideas to help students with a given skill can turn to the appropriate section of the book or check the index to find a suitable exercise. Where possible, similar exercises within each chapter have been grouped together, so do browse back and forth either side of the exercise you're looking at.

The exercises are not ranked by effectiveness. They are organised thematically and if you want an opinion on the effectiveness of any exercise you should speak to your teachers. Neither are they organized as being suitable for *beginners, intermediate* or *advanced students*, because these labels are difficult to ascribe reliably to interpreting students who will experience different problems at different stages of their courses. You might be relatively advanced in one skill while struggling with another, while your colleague who started at the same time as you has the opposite skill-set.

The four main sections of the book, A, B, C and D, are divided into a number of sub-skills. For example, Delivery, Analysis, Note-taking etc., so if you're looking for exercises to practise analysis in consecutive you should turn to section C, exercises C.26–C.69, where you'll find exercises designed to practise that specific skill.

Similarly, you'll find an index at the back of the book which lists all the exercises by skill targeted and which also tells you the type of exercise – spoken, text-based etc – and the number of people needed to do it.

Technical terms relating to conference interpreting are marked with an asterisk and explained in the Glossary at the back of the book.

Notes numbered in the text will be found at the end of each Part.

Notes

1   The isolation of component skills during practice and training is also advocated in Weber 1989: 162; Van Dam 1989: 168; Seleskovitch and Lederer 1989: 133; Moser-Mercer 1994: 66.
2   ELTA: English Language Teaching to Adults.
3   For a detailed description of the limited experimental data available see Pöchhacker 2004: 184.

Part A
Practice

How to practise

One cannot achieve a high level of competence in interpreting only by attending time-tabled interpreting classes. That's why students have to practise outside class time.[1]

Heine 2000: 214

A.1 Practise often

Practise often. Five days per week is a reasonable timetable. That's often enough to mean you never get out of practice, and you continue getting better. But practising a lot doesn't mean you're not entitled to some rest time.

A.2 Practise in short sessions

Be aware that practising twice for thirty minutes in one day, morning and then afternoon, may be better than one session of one hour. And that one hour per day for a week is definitely better than seven hours practice on one day and nothing for the rest of the week.

A.3 Don't only interpret

If you are a student interpreter, you probably love interpreting. And if you have the choice between doing any type of course work or practice and actually interpreting, you will choose interpreting every time. But practice does not have to be interpreting to be useful. So treat yourself to non-interpreting practice activities on a regular basis. You'll find plenty of them in this book.

A.4 Practise skills in isolation

It is possible to break interpreting down into its component skills and practise them in isolation, or practise some but not all of them at the same time. This is the concept underlying much of this book. So read on!

Source: Van Dam 1989: 170; Weber 1989: 164; Seleskovitch and Lederer 1989: 133; Moser-Mercer 1994: 66; Gillies 2001: 66

A.5 Practise with an aim

Set yourself an aim for each practice session. For example, 'Today (or this week) I'm going to concentrate on good delivery.' Early in the course the skills you practise should probably reflect the content of your lessons. Many courses, for example, teach delivery and memory skills first and, say, note-taking later. You can practise a new skill in each practice session or for a few days or weeks at a time. This also has the advantage of giving you interim goals to aim at and achieve. This allows you to see progress being made, which is likely to increase your motivation levels, not least of all because progress in interpreting as a whole is very difficult to see over short periods. You might notice an improvement between January and April, but it is unlikely that you'll see a tangible improvement in your work from one week to the next. However, if you practise delivery skills in isolation, for example, you can make significant and visible progress in a matter of days or weeks.

Source: Gillies 2001: 66

A.6 Think about your work

Take time out to think about your interpreting performance, and discuss it with others. Learning comes not only from doing, but from thinking about what you've done. Only you can actually learn, no-one else can learn for you.

A.7 Take a break

Stop practising if you are getting tired. If you recognise that you are tiring, then your interpreting has probably already been less than your best for 10–15 minutes. So stop!

This doesn't apply to class and exam situations, of course, where you will just have to battle through. That's also part of interpreting. But if you're practising, it's best to stop and come back to it when you've had a break.

A.8 Don't force yourself

Interpreting requires all your effort and motivation. Anything less than 100 per cent and you will not produce your best performance. So don't practise if you don't want to. And if you find that you don't want to practise all that often, then you know that interpreting isn't for you.

A.9 Start interpreting into your best language

Begin by learning to interpret into your best active language*. Later, when you are comfortable with that, and if you have a second active language, start practising interpreting into that language. Practise all of your language combinations.

Source: Déjean Le Féal; EMCI 2002: 28

A.10 Practise in groups

For most people, working in groups is more fun than working alone or in class. Groups should be of 2–4 people for consecutive*: you'll need at least one speaker and one interpreter; in consecutive the speaker can double as the audience. For simultaneous, groups should be of 3–6 people. You need more people for simultaneous because the speaker cannot listen to the interpreting as they can in consecutive. That means you'll need one speaker, one interpreter and one listener to make a group.

There are a number of advantages to practising in groups rather than alone or only in class time. Working with other students and preparing speeches for one another means that you will have plenty of practice material (speeches) to interpret and that they will be pitched at the right level of difficulty. Speeches that student interpreters give tend to be simpler in structure, logic and vocabulary than authentic speeches and this is as it should be for the first part of your course. Start simple and work up. Preparing and giving the speeches is also useful for you and shouldn't be considered simply an exercise in altruism. As you'll see in the exercises below, creating speeches is an exercise in understanding speech structure and note-taking, while giving a speech trains note-reading and public-speaking skills in isolation.

A.11 Shake it up

Don't always work with the same people when practising. Work with a variety of other students, not only your best friend on the course. That way you are also less likely to develop bad habits or get too used to the same speaker and speech type.

A.12 Listen to each other

One of the simplest ways to train your ability to listen to, and monitor, your own interpreting performance is to listen to and assess those of your fellow students. It's easier because when you are interpreting and trying to listen to yourself you're doing several things at once, including monitoring your performance. Here you are only listening and assessing, not interpreting as well.

Always listen with particular criteria in mind; for example, is the delivery good, do the main points make sense, is the language register appropriate? And try to listen for only one or two of these criteria, and not always all of them at once.

Listening to others is also useful because most students make similar mistakes and a limited number of types of mistakes. So the person you're listening to probably has some of the same interpreting problems as you.

Obviously, simultaneous interpreting can and should also be practised alone from recorded material (and with a dictaphone to record yourself); consecutive can also be practised in this way if needs must. But the reactions of others, and the opportunity to listen to their work yourself, are invaluable.

Source: Heine 2000: 223

A.13 Be a listener

The temptation with simultaneous is for lots of people to interpret the same speech, and no-one to listen to the interpreting. Resist it! Don't all go into the booths and interpret just because booths are free. Listeners can listen to only the interpreter, or to the interpreter and original speech simultaneously; both are valid and useful exercises.

A.14 Work with listeners who need interpretation

Very often we practise with people who have the same language combination as we do. And that means that their assessment of your interpreted version of a speech is influenced by their knowledge of the source language and/or their understanding of the original speech. That's often very useful of course, but you need not always work with a listener who understands the source language.

It is very useful to have a 'real' listener who 'needs' the interpreter to understand the speech. Afterwards ask them simply whether they understood what was being said. Their questions about what was not clear are often extremely helpful in highlighting the major problem areas, as opposed to the minor errors that listeners who understand both the source and the target languages tend to highlight.

A.15 Get non-interpreters involved

You needn't work only with your classmates. Other people – family, friends, anyone who can be roped in to listen – will do. These listeners will often be more demanding and perhaps more perceptive in their analysis of your work than you are. At the very least they will offer a different point of view on it. Whether it's fellow students or other people who are listening, the fact of having someone listen to you is important. Interpreting is about communicating between people, something one can forget when practising alone from recorded speech after recorded speech.

Practice material

The type of speech you use to practise interpreting can make, or break, your interpreting practice. Interpreters don't (barring rare exceptions) interpret newspaper articles or PhD theses, nor music lyrics or poetry; they interpret spoken discourse in certain very specific contexts. You should seek to use the same types of speeches and recreate the same types of situations.

Similarly, a speech that is too difficult is not useful. It will demoralize you and not give you the opportunity to work on the skills you are learning. A speech that is too easy, on the other hand, will not push you to improve. Don't just try to interpret the first thing that you lay your hands on. Think about the material you practise with – for your own sake and that of your fellow students!

A.16 Use appropriate types of speeches

Be aware that the type of speech that we are asked to interpret consecutively is different to that which we are asked to do simultaneously. Take this into account when looking for speeches and the texts of speeches. Debates in national parliaments, for example, are never interpreted consecutively, whereas ceremonial openings of new buildings often are. If possible choose the type of speech that might have been interpreted in consecutive; for example...

> After-dinner speeches at banquets or to open receptions are a classic example ... the opening of a cultural event held at a centre like the British Council or Goethe Institute. ... the opening of a French supermarket in Poland, or the launch of a German boat in Korea. It could be a foreign winner of an award making an acceptance speech in their own language, or a composer's 70th birthday at the Philharmonic.
>
> Gillies 2005: 3

The texts of these speeches can often be found on the websites of government ministries, companies or associations. Speeches by ambassadors or embassy staff are particularly well suited since they are very often given by a person of one nationality to those of another, and some type of communication between cultures is being attempted. Try to avoid speeches of more than two pages of A4, which is already quite a long speech.

If you're looking for speeches on national ministry websites you'll find that it is often not the minister themselves, but the lower ranking ministers, under-secretaries etc., who give these sort of speeches.

When preparing speeches yourself, try to mimic these situations and types of speeches.

Example

> Members of AustCham, ladies and gentlemen,
>
> It is a great pleasure to be here this evening, almost 25 years to the day since I arrived in Hong Kong as a young diplomat for language training before I started my first posting at the Australian Consulate-General in Hong Kong...
>
> F. Adamson, Australian Ambassador to China
> Speech to China-Australia Chamber of Commerce
> 27th October 2011
> http://www.china.embassy.gov.au/bjng/01112011speech.html

Source: Gillies 2005: 3

A.17 Use speeches of the right level of difficulty

Material used for practice should be appropriate for the stage of the course and for interpretation purposes. By this I mean that debates in national parliaments are not suitable for the first week of a course, indeed the first half of the course, because they are too difficult and too fast. News broadcasts, which many student interpreters seem to fall back on, are not suitable for interpretation at all. They bear little relation to what is interpreted by working interpreters in that the content varies wildly every 60 seconds; it is written language being read out; it's extremely dense, much denser than the spoken word, because news programmes are trying to pack as much as possible into a limited time slot. Be aware also that most of the authentic recorded speeches available on the internet are far too difficult for all but the later stages of your course. Don't hesitate to ask your teacher for their opinion about the degree of difficulty of the material you're using for practice. And in all things start with the simple and work upwards.

Graduation of speech difficulty according to Seleskovitch and Lederer

The following classification of difficulty might serve as a general guide:

- narrative speech on a familiar topic
- argumentative speech on a familiar topic
- narrative speech on a new topic
- argumentative speech on a new topic
- stylistically sophisticated speech on a familiar topic
- stylistically sophisticated speech on a new topic
- topic requiring preparation
- descriptive speech requiring terminological preparation
- rhetorical speech

Seleskovitch and Lederer 1995: 53

Graduation of speech difficulty according to Lederer

Subject progression:

- practical
- abstract
- expressive

Speech type progression:

- narrative
- argumentative
- descriptive
- expressive

Lederer 2001: 177

Examples

One of the best places to find a 'narrative on a familiar subject' is in a fairytale. Get someone to tell a fairytale that the listener does not already know. (This works best if you are lucky enough to be in a very multi-national group with different traditional fairytales.) The 'interpreter' listens and then retells the story. Of course, you will quickly run out of material and you'll need to move on to more conventional 'narratives', like events in the news.

The following speech, on the Deepwater Horizon oil-platform disaster in 2012, might be considered a 'narrative on a familiar subject' according to the Seleskovitch and Lederer scale above, or as 'practical' and 'narrative' according to the Lederer scale. 'Narrative' because it tells the story of events and the President's movements; 'familiar' because anyone reading the newspapers in 2010 would have seen countless articles on this subject; and 'practical' because it describes events in straightforward, non-abstract terms. So this speech could be considered as relatively easy practice material.

> Good evening. As we speak, our nation faces a multitude of challenges. At home, our top priority is to recover and rebuild from a recession that has touched the lives of nearly every American. Abroad, our brave men and women in uniform are taking the fight to al Qaeda wherever it exists. And tonight, I've returned from a trip to the Gulf Coast to speak with you about the battle we're waging against an oil spill that is assaulting our shores and our citizens.
>
> On April 20th, an explosion ripped through BP Deepwater Horizon drilling rig, about 40 miles off the coast of Louisiana. Eleven workers lost their lives. Seventeen others were injured. And soon, nearly a mile beneath the surface of the ocean, oil began spewing into the water.
>
> Barack Obama, US President
> 15 June 2010
> http://www.whitehouse.gov/the-press-office/remarks-president-nation-bp-oil-spill

The following speech, on the other hand, could be considered difficult because, according to the Seleskovitch and Lederer scale above, it is 'high register' and/or 'expressive rhetoric'. According to the Lederer scale it would also be difficult because it is 'abstract' and 'expressive'.

> We gather every year in Heerstraße, and in Commonwealth Cemeteries across the world, to remember those who fought and fell in combat.
>
> We gather today in solemnity and with dignity to contemplate the sacrifice of those who went before, a sacrifice which ensured that we meet today in freedom and with hope. In this cemetery are interred the remains of soldiers, sailors and airmen from the United Kingdom, Canada, Australia, New Zealand, South Africa, undivided India and Poland. We honour their memory.
>
> Simon McDonald, British Ambassador to Germany
> 13 November 2011
> http://ukingermany.fco.gov.uk/en/news/?view=Speech&id=691522882

If you find yourself getting into difficulties with a certain type of speech, for whatever reason, go back to a simpler type and start again from there. Be considerate also of your fellow students. When preparing speeches for each other for practice sessions, think about whether the speech is reasonable or not, because unreasonable is also unhelpful.

Likewise if your colleague has asked to concentrate on one skill in isolation, for example good intonation during delivery, then a slower speech will be more useful than a very fast one. If you want to experiment with a longer time-lag* or new ideas for reformulation, a simpler speech will be more helpful.

A.18 Use speech transcripts

Many of the exercises described in the following chapters can be done with the spoken word or with the text of a speech. So I consider the transcripts of speeches as much a part of practice material as spoken speeches themselves. You will probably do more exercises from texts in the early part of your course than later.

Try to use the texts of speeches that were actually spoken rather than newspaper or magazine articles, which have a different structure and purpose. But be aware that written speeches are often written down *before* they are spoken, not afterwards! As such they can sometimes be dense and difficult.

The texts of these speeches can often be found on the websites of government ministries, embassies, companies or associations.

A.19 Use appropriate texts for sight translation

If you're doing any of the exercises in this book that involve sight translation, be aware that in the course of an interpreter's work not all texts are equally likely to be translated on sight. Newspaper articles, literature and dialogue, for example, are very rarely translated in this way. Formal statements, resolutions and press releases, on the other hand, are. Use these types of text when practising. You can also ask your teachers what other types of text they sight translate when working.

That is not to say that you won't be asked by your teachers to sight translate other types – with good pedagogical reasons – but in your own practice stick to those types of text most often translated on sight in the real world.

A.20 Prepare and give speeches yourself

The best way to guarantee suitable speeches in the early part of the course is to prepare them yourselves or have your teacher do it. Your teacher is unlikely to have time to prepare speeches for all your practice sessions, so the sooner you get into preparing them yourself the better.

Use a speech transcript as a starting point, noting down the main arguments and points. Add some of your own information, from your preparation, and then put the transcript away and give the speech from your notes. You will most likely have a much simplified version of the original that will make ideal practice material for your colleagues.

A.21 Prepare two-column structure maps

Aim: to create speaking notes for practice.
You will need: a piece of paper, a speech transcript.

Take the transcript of a short speech, or part of a speech (not longer than one page of A4), and lay it out next to a blank page of A4 on which there is only a vertical line about a quarter of the way across, dividing the page from the left.

In the left-hand column created on the blank page note what you think is the function of that part of the speech. (For a more detailed description of structure maps see C.44 and C.45). In the right hand column note a minimum of information that will help you to recreate the speech. When you've done that, put away the original speech and try to recreate the speech from the structure map.

Example

I want to make one very simple point in this speech. To the police, housing officers, local authorities – we've listened, we've given you the powers, and it's time to use them.

You've got new powers to deal with nuisance neighbours – use them.

You've got new powers to deal with abandoned cars – use them.

You've got new powers to give fixed penalty fines for anti-social behaviour – without going through a long court process, use them.

The new legislation, the ASB Unit in the Home Office, this Action Plan we launched today has been two years in the making. In this time, I have visited many estates and talked to local people about their concerns. Two things emerged. First, ASB is for many the number one item of concern right on their doorstep – the graffiti, vandalism, dumped cars, drug dealers in the street, abuse from truanting school-age children. Secondly, though many of these things are in law a criminal offence, it is next to impossible for the police to prosecute without protracted court process, bureaucracy and hassle, when conviction will only result in a minor sentence.

Hence these new powers to take swift, summary action. The FPNs were piloted in four local areas. Over 6000 fines were issued. The only complaint of the police was that the powers weren't wide enough. So we have listened, we have extended the powers, extended who can use them, and made them from early next year when the Bill becomes law, nation-wide.

Tony Blair, PM of UK
October 2003

What is he going to say?	Police, etc Use new powers!
List of new powers, 1	noise
new power 2	cars
new power 3	anti-social
background	2 years preparing law, new ASB unit, Action plan
2 points, 1	ASB big concern
2	police helpless cos red tape light sentences
Therefore...	new FPNs = swift action
...conclusions	4 pilots 6000 fines
	extended powers!

A.22 Prepare speaking-notes on a single page

Aim: to create speaking notes for practice.
You will need: a piece of paper.

In preparing speeches that you will give for interpreting practice, set yourself the task of preparing your speaking-notes on a single piece of paper (not bigger than A4!). This limitation will force you to think more about what you are going to say and to speak more freely when you deliver the speech.

Source: Walker, D.; Nolan 2005: 298

A.23 Prepare speeches in consecutive note form

Aim: to make preparation time more efficient.
You will need: speech transcripts, a note-pad.

Prepare speeches for lessons and practice sessions in consecutive note-taking style and use those notes to give your speeches. These notes will not correspond exactly to what might have been noted from a spoken speech (the role of memory will be different if we prepare hours/days in advance, for example); however, it can still be a very useful exercise. You can use either speech transcripts as a starting point, or prepare a speech of your own from material you've researched.

By preparing speeches in this way you will be practising note-taking techniques (i.e. brevity and clarity of our notes, familiarizing ourselves with the use of diagonal notes or margins, for example) but without the time pressure associated with note-taking from live speeches. When giving the speech to colleagues you are practising note-reading and delivery, while hopefully those interpreting the speech have a well delivered, fluent speech to practise from. In this way you are using your practice time more efficiently.

Example

> Ladies and Gentlemen. Let me warmly welcome our distinguished Chinese guests to Austrade's Business Club Australia, a hub for business meetings throughout the Olympics. Let me also congratulate China on the terrific start to the Beijing Olympics – the events have been sensational, the facilities are fantastic, and China's friendliness and warm hospitality will ensure that these will be a great Olympic Games...
>
> Australian Minister for Trade, Simon Crean
> 11 August 2008
> Beijing

I

<u>hi</u>

ZH °
(to Austrade Bus. Club)
(Olympic hub)

_____

+   I

congrat

ZH/
(Olymp start)

_____

events
facilities

<u>✓</u>

_____

ZH friend [ns]
Hosp

→

<u>✓ games</u>

_____

A.24 Prepare technical speeches

Aim: to acquire the semi-technical terminology that educated native speakers have in a broad range of subjects.
You will need: at least one other person.

Prepare speeches in which you explain technical issues. To do this you will have to research the subject and understand it, and all the other students will benefit from the speech you give. If several students do this, then you'll have practice material to interpret from and you'll all save a lot of time researching. Below is an example of (part of) a speech you could easily prepare on a fairly technical subject without too much difficulty.

Example

> Good morning, today I'd like to spend a few moments talking about how crude oil is refined and the multitude of products that the resulting products go to make up. You might think oil is used only to make fuels, like kerosene, petrol and fuel oil, but you'd be very wrong, as I will explain later.
>
> I don't want to talk about extracting the oil from the ground, that's the subject for a different debate, but only about refining and the first major step in the refining process is fractioning.
>
> Crude oil is not a uniform substance, it's actually made up of many different hydrocarbons (molecules made up exclusively of hydrogen and carbon atoms) with a variety of properties. Before we can make useful products out of them they have to be separated from one another. One of the different properties these different hydrocarbons have is a different boiling point, and this means that they can be separated from one another by fractional distillation, 'fractioning'. The crude oil is pumped over a heating installation and then into the bottom of a fractioning column...
>
> Sources: Howitworks.com, Wikipedia, OSHA Technical manual, BP.com

Source: Martin and Padilla 1989: 245

Preparation

The techniques of interpreting and understanding the words you hear in a given speech are two distinct elements of what you are trying to learn to do: be a conference interpreter. The best way to concentrate on practising the techniques is to eliminate, as far as possible, the problems of understanding the vocabulary and understanding the concepts that will come up. In other words, prepare the topic so that you know what is being talked about and you aren't surprised when interpreting by the technical terms relating to that field. How to deal with terms you have never heard before is of course a technique in itself, but you should try to limit the number of unpleasant surprises you get in any speech.

Preparation will also serve to widen your general knowledge and exposure to the language, two elements discussed elsewhere in this text that are useful for student interpreters.

A.25 Read around your subject

Aim: to prepare class-specific terminology and knowledge.
You will need: some preparation time.

Read articles on the same topic in both languages. The Internet is full of how-it-works websites, encyclopedias, newspapers and magazines to help you. Thus you will avoid literal translations and see how similar ideas* are expressed in two (or more) languages without language interference*.

In interpreting, forewarned is forearmed. If you've seen something before, because of your preparation, then it will be much easier to interpret.

A.26 News round-up

Aim: to become familiar with current affairs.
You will need: at least two other people.

Each week one or more students prepare newspaper cuttings of the week's main or interesting news. Each topic should be covered in an article in each of the relevant languages. Photocopies of the compilation are distributed to all students. Sharing the workload means more efficient use of time.

Reading about the same events in different languages will increase familiarity with the political and economic terminology whilst avoiding the pitfalls of literal translation. This exercise is not so much a preparation exercise for a specific topic, but for all topics.

A.27 News round-up presentation

Aim: to make preparation time (and knowledge gathering) more efficient by pooling resources.
You will need: at least two other people.

Once or twice a week one person presents a summary of the main news of the past few days. Tasks can be divided up within the group. For example, one person could present the news from each country, or alternatively one person could present national news, one Asian news, another European news etc.

Reading the newspapers won't immediately appear to be improving your general knowledge, but it's a habit worth getting into. The benefits will come after a year or two of regular reading, when you find that you can name the ministers or describe political issues from other countries, which you wouldn't have been able to do before. By sharing the workload in the way described in this exercise you take some of the hard work out of that reading.

A.28 Pool your resources

Aim: to make preparation time more efficient by pooling resources.
You will need: at least two other people.

Topic preparation takes up a lot of time: reading around a subject, identifying the main issues, making a useful but brief list of important terms. It all takes time and it seems as if you just don't have enough free time to do everything your teachers are asking of you. Get together and pool your resources, so that one or two people take responsibility for preparing the ground on a given subject and present their results to the group. One idea is to create a cyclical topic preparation system for classes or practice sessions like the one below.

Example

Week 1
- students (and teacher) agree on subject areas for interpreting classes and practice in 2 week's time.
- 2 students read around the subject and prepare articles / vocabulary before the next practice session.

Week 2
- the same students hand out prepared texts and vocabulary to the others who read it before week 3.

Week 3
- all students are prepared for the subject of the week's lessons/ practice sessions.

By repeating the three stages each subsequent week with different students and subject areas, we arrive at a well-prepared subject area for each week's practice and/or lessons. You will also find yourself cooperating with and checking each other's preparation; these are useful habits to learn. Also, your reaction to how your colleagues prepare will help hone your own preparation strategies. What did you find useful and less useful in their presentations, for example? (The timing mentioned above can be changed to suit your needs.)

Source: Gillies 2001: 70

A.29 Brainstorm

Aim: to anticipate language that will come up in practice.
You will need: two other people.

If you have chosen a topic for the speeches for your practice session, start the session with a quick round-up of vocabulary and expressions you would expect to encounter. Try to come up with collocations and whole phrases rather than only individual words.

A.30 Brainstorm without a pen

Aim: to recall and speak terms and expressions in advance of needing to do so while interpreting.
You will need: a subject, at least two other people.

If brainstorming with colleagues, try not to write anything down during the session. At the end of the brainstorming session, try to write down as many of the terms, expressions and information items as possible.

In this exercise the aim of the brainstorming session is not to create a list of words or phrases on a piece of paper, but to activate them in the interpreter's mind so that they can be recalled and used more quickly when interpreting. Trying to recall them at the end of the brainstorming session mimics the recall powers you will have to apply in the booth, and repeats, in a shorter time period, the brainstorming session itself. This repetition, and even the mechanical mouthing of the words to yourself, will help activate them.

A.31 Improvise from prepared information

Aim: to activate the terminology and concepts and actively speculate on what the speaker might say.
You will need: a subject you've prepared, at least two other people.

Take a topic that has been prepared and on which you have read a good deal of material. Before the speaker starts giving the speech (or you start looking at a text for sight-translation), get the interpreter(s) to pretend to be the speaker and improvise for a few minutes on the topic.

Source: Béziat

A.32 Read around both sides of the argument

Aim: to identify the language elements that are characteristic of a given view point.
You will need: at least two articles or speeches representing opposite views on the same subject.

If you're preparing for a class or a meeting in which two sides of an argument are likely to be aired, it's useful to know not only the factual case that representatives of each side put forward, but also the type of language they use to express those arguments. As the interpreter you'll have to speak for both sides. What you will sometimes find is not that the two sides simply disagree on a given point, but that they address entirely different subjects in their arguments.

Example

Until now, the growth of the UK's offshore wind energy capacity has been slower[1] than anticipated because it is more costly than experts originally predicted …

Offshore wind power is a much less developed technology than onshore wind. A total of 1371 offshore turbines are now installed and grid connected in European waters, spread across 53 wind farms in 10 countries. This installed capacity produces enough electricity to cover just 0.4%[2] of the EU's total annual consumption. The UK is by far the largest market with 568 installed offshore turbines and a further 665 under construction. But in terms of actual energy output[2] for offshore, we are still building the equivalent of the UK's first conventional power station …

The 15 new potential offshore sites will destroy[4] forever the beauty of the Berwickshire and East Lothian coastline, the Firth of Forth, the Moray Firth, the Northern Isles, the rugged[4] coast of Sutherland, the Western Isles, the Firth of Clyde and the Solway Firth. A monstrous[4] array of turbines stretches from Lochboisdale in South Uist to Tobermory in Mull, completely engulfing[4] Tiree and Coll, stretching for more than 60 miles and appearing on the Marine Scotland plans as almost double the size of the Outer Hebrides.[4]

Struan Stevenson
9 August 2012
http://www.struanstevenson.com/media/speech/offshore_windfarms_in_scotland

Offshore wind – a crucial tool in the race to cut our carbon emissions

Wind power is the fastest growing[1,3] energy technology in the world. It has proved that renewable energy is ready and able to match conventional energy technologies euro for euro, kilowatt for kilowatt. The industry has now developed technology of sufficient size, reliability and efficiency that it is ready to unlock the vast offshore wind resources[3] that exist around the world. In Europe alone, the North and Baltic seas boast massive wind resources that have so far remained largely unexploited.[2]

The 'repowering debate' in Europe has already begun. Roughly two-thirds (100GW) of the overall installed coal-fired generating capacity within the 25-member EU is provided by power plants that are over 20 years old.[3] This means that between 75 and 100 coal-fired plants will retire[3] within the next two decades. Europe's power sector must seriously consider offshore wind farms, as offshore wind is ideally positioned to replace this retiring[3] capacity. The wind industry itself is ready, but only if supported by European energy policy. Greenpeace is therefore calling for a drastic policy shift.

Greenpeace brochure
http://www.greenpeace.org/international/Global/international/planet-2/report/2006/3/offshore-wind-implementing-a.pdf

The numbering in the text above refers to the following points:

1. The two sides may simply say the opposite to one another.
2. Both sides use figures to promote their case – absolute figures suit the anti camp on the left, relative figures suit the pro camp on the right. Similarly, the anti camp compares wind energy to other capacity (it's a small part), whereas the pro camp highlights the potential!
3. The pro camp, on the right, portray young and modern being better than old, ageing and unchanged.
4. The anti camp, on the left, is very emotive about the impact on the environment.

A.33 Create a debating society

Aim: to practise speaking in a formal register in your active languages; practise expressing views you do not hold personally.
You will need: at least two other people.

Meet up with fellow students and debate issues that might be debated at the sort of international meetings at which interpreters work. Pick a subject in advance and assign speaking roles to each other; for example, for and against the death penalty, or environmentalist and climate change sceptic. Debating from a point of view that differs from your own is particularly useful. Interpreters, like lawyers, are called upon to advocate views that may be diametrically opposed to their own, but they still have to do their job to the best of their abilities!

This exercise is a great warm-up for interpreting on the same subject later the same day.

Source: De Clarens 1973: 123

A.34 Know thy speaker 1

Aim: to anticipate opinions and issues that will come up in a speech.
You will need: a recording of a speech by a well-known speaker, or one person playing their role; information about when and where the speech was originally given.

A lot of your practice will involve giving speeches for one another, but you may also be practising from recorded speeches from the internet, invited speakers, or mock conferences. Whenever you are interpreting a named speaker, ask yourself (and answer) the following questions before the speech starts. In order to make this a habit, ask yourself the same questions whenever you are listening to anyone speak, be it radio interviews, TV discussions or a special announcement made at your school.

- Has the speaker written anything on the topic before?
- Does the location have anything to do with promoting literature on the topic?
- Is the speaker linked to any special causes, events, etc.?
- Where does the speaker generally voice his/her opinion?
- Is the speaker in any way related to the place housing the event?
- Will the location influence the speaker's words in any way?
- Why has this person been chosen for this occasion?
- Is the occasion incidental or of relevance to the location?

Source: Monacelli 1999: 17

A.35 Know thy speaker 2

Aim: to anticipate opinions and issues that will come up in a speech.
You will need: a recording of a speech by a well-known speaker, or one person playing their role; information about when and where the speech was originally given.

Before you start interpreting any speech, ask yourself the following questions:

- Who is the speaker?
- What is his nationality?
- What is his cultural background?
- What is his 'thought-world'?
- What is he hoping to get out of the conference?
- What is the position of his government on this issue?

Source: Namy 1978: 28; Nolan 2005: 19

A.36 Work with real documents

Aim: to extract important information from large quantities of documents.
You will need: real meeting documents.

Ask your teacher to supply copies of a set of meeting documents (which they have permission to distribute in this way). Some groups in some institutions, like the EU and UN, and many national parliaments, publish meeting documents online and you'll be able to access them directly, but it's often helpful to have documents from a teacher who can give you the background information to a given meeting.

You may also find annotating paper documents easier than annotating digital ones, but of course annotating .pdf documents will save you a lot of printer-ink and paper!

What you'll notice is that the documents, reports etc., on a given subject may stretch to tens or hundreds of pages. So you won't be able to read it all. Ask your teacher for tips on how to skim-read documents like this. For example, you might read the contents page first to get an overview of each document. Or you might flick through looking at only the titles on each page.

Give yourselves a fixed time-limit to go through a large document or pile of several documents, for example 15 minutes only. You won't just be reading for terminology, but also to get an idea of what the document is trying to say, and to whom. Highlight the most important messages, illustrations and terms. Compare with colleagues. Why did you highlight what you did?

Source: Makarova 1994: 201

A.37 Sight translation*

Aim: to activate* topic-specific terminology and idiom; practise doing two things at once in preparation for interpreting.
You will need: a speech transcript on the same subject as the speeches you will later interpret.

If you can find the text of a speech on a subject similar to the one you are going to interpret, then doing a sight translation of that text is an excellent way to prepare. It will give you an opportunity to practise actually using the expressions and terminology that you have collected while preparing. It may sound trivial, but it is much harder to work out, or recall, and then use a translation or expression a first time, than at any subsequent time. Consequently it is better to make sure that the 'first time' is not in the booth, but part of your preparation.

Feedback

Feedback from classmates helps not only in identifying and tackling problems. It can and should encourage [students] and even help to reduce excess stress and frustration where necessary.

Heine 2000: 223[2]

Most of your interpreting practice will be in groups with other students, not in a classroom with an interpreter/teacher. It's worth, then, taking a moment to think about the way in which you comment on each other's interpreting performances.

A.38 Focus on technique issues

Feedback has at least two distinct functions: to assess the performance; and to help the interpreter improve that performance for next time. The latter is far more useful; and as students who are not yet qualified and experienced interpreters, the former is almost impossible. If you want to improve for next time you'll need, together with your teachers and training partners, to identify why you are having problems – that is to say, address technique issues.

In practice this means that you shouldn't simply list lots of minor errors. Try instead to prioritize and comment on areas of the interpreted speech where there were more serious communication problems. This is particularly important in the early part of the course. Try to identify not only that there were problems with the interpreting, but why there were problems. Knowing which mechanisms are causing errors is far more useful than knowing what the errors themselves were. In other words, being told that you have made a mistake will not, per se, make you do it better next time. Being told why you made a mistake might.

When you know why you've made a mistake, interpret the relevant sections of the speech again and try to correct the problem. If you can't work out why you're having problems yourself, or with other students, ask your teachers. When you've identified the problem area, find an exercise in the index to this book that will help you practise the skill you're having trouble with.

A.39 Structure your feedback

Going through a list of points in chronological order may be the most obvious way to conduct feedback, but it's not necessarily the most useful. Before you start giving feedback to another student, spend a few moments looking at your notes and ranking the points in order of importance. When you give feedback, address the most important points first. For example: three main points first, hopefully related to technique; then some minor points; at the end, return to the main points and repeat them. Make sure that the interpreter tries to improve on them when they next interpret.

When you make that last set of comments at the end of practice sessions, don't introduce new comments that will be forgotten between now and the next practice session; recap on the most common or important problems.

A.40 Be positive

Don't only comment on or correct mistakes when giving feedback. Make a point of highlighting things that went right as well!

Source: Harmer 1990: 239

A.41 Be disciplined about time management

Don't get into never-ending discussions about an interpreting performance or the meaning of a given phrase. Time is of the essence. If you're working in groups, set yourselves a time limit. For example, for a 10-minute interpreting performance the feedback should last no longer than 10 minutes. This means that you waste less time and do more practice. It also has the beneficial side-effect of focusing the assessor's mind on the main points that need to be made.

A.42 Use a feedback template

One way of making sure that feedback is consistent and useful is to use a template for your assessments. The table below is based on one suggested by Anne Schjoldager for the evaluation of simultaneous, but you should add, amend and customize this as you and your teachers see fit, or take another template entirely.

You could either create one table per practice session, with room for more detailed comments, or you could create something like the table below and assess several performances on a single sheet. This makes it possible to pick up on recurring traits in your work. For example, the interpreter below seems to have a habit of adding fillers.

Example

Assessment criteria	1	2			
1. Coherence and plausibility					
Does it make sense as a whole?	yes	yes			
Were there any non-sequiturs?	no	yes			
Are there unfinished sentences?	no	yes			
2. Faithfulness					
Are there serious omissions?	no	no			
Are there unjustified changes?	no	yes			
Are there unjustified additions?	no	yes			
3. Delivery					
Can everything be acoustically understood?	yes	yes			
Are there fillers?	yes	yes			
Is the intonation unnatural?	no	no			
Are there too many corrections?	no	yes			
Is the interpreter convincing?	yes	yes			
4. Language					
Are there mispronunciations?	no	yes			
Are there grammatical mistakes?	yes	yes			
Is there source language interference*?	yes	yes			
Is the language un-idiomatic?	no	no			

Source: adapted from Schjoldager 1996: 190

A.43 Write feedback down

If you're the interpreter, write down what is said to you about your interpreting performance. Memory is a fickle friend and we tend to remember what we want to remember. And that may not be the same as what we need to remember!

A.44 Keep a logbook

One way of getting the most out of feedback is to record the comments made about your interpreting performances by your teachers and fellow students. The first step to solving problems is to be aware of them. Keeping a record is the only sure way of remembering and comparing your performances over the year or two of your course.

Make a distinction between issues of vocabulary and interpreting technique. Items of vocabulary tend to come up very rarely, and are therefore less useful per item. Technique issues will recur with greater regularity and are thus much more useful to you. One suggestion would be to note technique-related comments at the front and vocabulary at the back of the same book. Alternatively you could keep a book for each. As time goes by you can flick through the pad seeing how the same problems recur, or what progress is being made (as comments note change over time). It can also be used in the booth to remind you of certain do's and don'ts.

Source: also Sainz 1993: 139; Gillies 2001: 68

A.45 Record your work

Record all your interpreting work! And listen to at least some of it each week. And then correct it!

Memory is not always reliable. After the event we may 'forget' the things we less like to hear and remember only the things we like to hear. In this way your subconscious could stop you dealing with a technique problem for quite some time. Recording yourself whenever you work will add a little more pressure and motivation to succeed. Practising with no apparent pressure on, you can let down your guard and relax, something interpreters should never do while working.

A.46 Analyse problems encountered

Knowing you are doing something less than well is a good start. But you also have to do something about the problem. So stop and think about the mistakes you make and the problems you have when interpreting. What caused your difficulties? Be aware of why something is difficult or easy. Isolate problem constructions, record examples and practise interpreting them (for example, the 'involved sentences'[3] for which German is notorious). This applies both to consecutive and simultaneous interpretation.

A.47 Use Post-it notes

Feedback and comments from teachers or other students are all very well. But can you actually remember them, and more importantly put them into practice, in the booth or as you are about to start a consecutive?

Write down on a Post-it note or a piece of paper, in one or two words, a reminder to yourself of the element of technique that you want to work on. Attach it somewhere prominent (to you) in the booth. For example, you might write 'ERR' to remind you not to say 'er' or 'um', or perhaps 'WAIT' to stop yourself jumping in too early in simultaneous.

In consecutive, fold across the last page of your notepad, as in the illustration below, and then return to the front of the note-pad. You can use the protruding bit of page to note these reminders without interfering with your note-taking and page-turning.

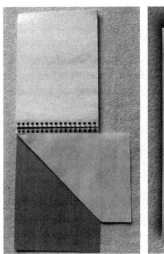 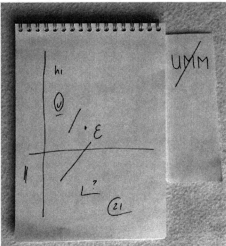

A.48 Rehearse

Don't be afraid to interpret the same speech twice, once before and once immediately after feedback. In that way you can apply the suggestions made during the feedback session. This is why feedback at the end of a session is less useful (see above), because you won't be able to act on it for hours or days, until you next interpret.

Immediate repetition makes it easier to correct errors of technique mentioned in feedback, because everything is fresh in your mind and specific examples of a problem can still be recalled.

NB If you interpret the same text several times, remember – the aim of this is not to get a word-perfect interpretation but rather to highlight difficulties and think carefully about how to avoid falling into the same traps next time round.

Source: also Lederer 2001: 174

A.49 Collect solutions

In any language there are lots of common expressions and ideas that do not lend themselves readily to translation into other languages. Try to find good versions of these sort of expressions in your active languages and make a note of them. For example, all Polish parliamentary speeches begin 'Wysoka Izbo!' (literally 'Exalted Chamber'). Since we don't address buildings in English and you don't want to have to think about what a better version might be every time you hear it, you could note a version in your logbook – for example, 'Honourable Members of the House', which is how British MPs begin their speeches. Regular consultation of your logbook and re-reading of these solutions will soon see them committed to memory.

A.50 Look for learning strategies

Your interpreting school will be the central point of your studies, practice and learning, but that doesn't mean that it should be the exclusive source of inspiration for you. Different people learn in different ways, and learning is not always linear. Learning how you learn best can help you get the most out of your studies.

Search for study strategies in libraries and online. Good learning abides by certain principles that are independent of the subject being learnt, so check out what is out there.

Notes

1 'Die Regulären Dolmetsch-Lehrveranstaltungen … reichen nicht aus, um eine hohe Dolmetscherkompetenz zu erreichen Aus diesem Grunde müssen die Student selbstständig weitertrainieren.' Translation from the German by Andrew Gillies.
2 'Die Rückkopplung seitens der Kommilitonen kann nicht nur helfen, Mängel zu erkennen und Probleme zu überwinden, die kann und sollte auch Mut machen und ggf. auch beim Abbau von übermässigem Stress und Frustration helfen.' Translation from the German by Andrew Gillies.
3 'Schactelsätze'.

Part B

Language

In this part the activities will help you to improve your knowledge of your languages and your language skills, focusing on:

General knowledge
Improving your passive languages
Improving your active languages

> The vocabulary of a language is boundless and one must continually work to expand one's knowledge of it.
>
> Seleskovitch 1968: 133[1]

> In practice it is essential to radically separate exercises aiming at perfecting language skills and exercises calling on translation skills.
>
> Pergnier and Lavault 1995: 7

At advanced levels, where grammar has been more or less mastered, the main difference between foreign students and native speakers is that the latter have been exposed to their language for many years, over thousands and thousands of hours. As a result they have a wider cultural and contextual understanding of the language, a wider vocabulary and a command of a wider range of registers. Constant contact with the language and the subjects that are discussed in that language means that native speakers have a huge head start on foreign learners.

Students of foreign languages therefore have considerable ground to make up, and this can only be done by maximizing language exposure. For students of interpreting this will often include at least one year living in the country concerned, but even this pales into insignificance next to the twenty-five or more years an adult native speaker has spent immersed in their language. We must, therefore, continue maximizing language exposure wherever we are.

All of the exercises listed in this part of the book are meant as a complement to long stays abroad in the country or countries where your languages are spoken, not a substitute for them.

General knowledge

You may be surprised to see 'general knowledge' in a section on language enhancement. But at the advanced levels of language knowledge at which you are now operating, the two overlap and intertwine. Think about the following for a moment: when you don't know a word in a foreign language there is a tendency to consider it a vocabulary issue; but when you don't know a word in your own language, you are more likely to talk about a shortfall in your general knowledge. And what happens if you have worked in, say, a hospital in your foreign language, but not in your own language? You know technical terminology in the foreign language that you don't know in your own. General knowledge and language knowledge are very much part of the same process.

Translating terms from one language to another is one thing, but the ideal for the interpreter is to thoroughly understand a given subject so that they can speak fluently and idiomatically about it in their active language(s)*. No-one can be an expert in every domain but that doesn't excuse us from not trying.

Having a broad and thorough grounding in general knowledge also has other advantages that are useful for student (and practising) interpreters. Knowing what we are talking about when we are interpreting (because of broad general knowledge) also makes the interpreting easier. Instead of using up mental capacity working out conceptually what the speaker is talking about, you can devote it to analysing the linguistic elements and transforming the message into the other language.

General knowledge is also a large part of the answer to a commonly asked question, 'How do you interpret jokes?'' Knowing why a joke is funny, or why a speaker would tell that sort of joke, or simply knowing the actual joke already, is all part of the thorough knowledge of language and culture that student interpreters should aspire to.

This whole section on language, covering passive and active languages and general knowledge, should be considered part of learning to interpret in both consecutive and simultaneous modes.

You will never stop playing catch-up with native speakers when it comes to cultural background knowledge. The ideas below will all help to make up the shortfall. Making tangible progress in catching up will take years, but if you can get into good habits now, you will see progress over the years. That's what this section is about.

B.1 News round-up

Aim: become familiar with current affairs.
You will need: at least two other people.

Each week one or more students prepare newspaper cuttings of the week's main or interesting news. Each topic should be covered in an article in each of the relevant languages. Photocopies of the compilation are distributed to all students.

Reading about the same events in different languages will increase familiarity with the appropriate terminology whilst avoiding the pitfalls of literal translation. You will also be improving your general knowledge in the process.

Sharing the workload means more efficient use of time.

B.2 News round-up presentation

Aim: to make current affairs preparation more efficient by pooling resources.
You will need: at least two other people.

Once or twice a week one person presents a summary of the main news of the past few days. Tasks can be divided up within the group. For example, one person could present the news from each country, or alternatively one person could present national news, one Asian news, another European news etc.

Reading the newspapers won't immediately appear to be improving your general knowledge, but it's a habit that is worth getting into. The benefits will come after a year or two of regular reading, when you find that you can name the ministers or describe political issues from other countries that you wouldn't have been able to before.

B.3 Question the implicit knowledge in newspaper articles

Aim: to demonstrate that we know less than we think. .
You will need: a topical newspaper article, a couple of other people.

Read a newspaper article. Now try to ask apparently straightforward questions about what the author of the article assumes his reader knows.

Example

Syrian crisis needs Arab solution, says Russia

Russia has put itself at the centre of efforts to resolve the deepening Syrian crisis, calling for an 'Arab solution' to the uprising against Bashar al-Assad's regime as more civilians were killed in a government assault on the city of Homs.

Three days after Moscow infuriated western and Arab countries by vetoing a UN resolution on Syria, Russia's foreign minister, Sergei Lavrov, flew to Damascus to hear Assad pledge a referendum on a new constitution and request that Arab League monitors – withdrawn last month – return to Syria . . .

On Tuesday, six Arab Gulf states and Tunisia followed the US and several European countries in recalling their ambassadors, a deliberate signal of mounting international alarm at a crisis which many are already describing as a civil war.

Assad promised to 'stop violence regardless of where it may come from'. But the regime's actions belied this statement. Syrian state media reported a determination to continue fighting 'armed terrorist gangs', amidst mounting evidence that most casualties in Homs are civilians. Hundreds are said to have died since shelling began on Friday. At least 95 people were killed there on Monday and nine more on Tuesday, the Syrian revolution general commission reported.

The *Guardian*, 7 February 2012
Copyright Guardian News & Media Ltd 2012

Now ask yourself these questions, none of which are answered in the text but form the background to it.

- Why might an 'Arab solution' be more desirable than any other?
- Why did Russia and China veto a UN Security Council resolution calling on Assad to give up power?
- Are there actual reasons that are different to their stated reasons?
- Why did Arab League observers leave Syria?
- How did President Assad come to power in Syria?
- Does Syria have a parliament? Is it a democracy?
- What ethnic groups are there in Syria? Which one does Assad belong to?
- What countries is Syria traditionally allied to? And to which is it hostile?
- Is Homs historically significant in the context of anti-government protest in Syria?

Source: Lederer 2001: 233

B.4 Swot up from school books

Aim: to acquire the general knowledge that educated native speakers have in a broad range of subjects (from the viewpoint of that country).
You will need: school textbooks (for 14–16 year olds) in the language in question.

Read up about subjects that you are familiar with in your own language but not in your foreign language – be it geography, industrial processes, chemistry, sport etc. Start with school textbooks for 14–16 year olds. These are semi-technical, but clearly written and you should be able to get the technical vocabulary very quickly as you recall the same things from your own time at school.

Source: Guichot de Fortis 2009: 6

B.5 Read specialist magazines

Aim: to acquire the general knowledge that educated native speakers have in a broad range of subjects (from the viewpoint of that country).
You will need: a specialist newsagent, a specialist magazine, internet connection to look up terms, a notepad.

Buy specialist magazines (*Aeroplanes Today!*; *Potholing Weekly*; *Market Gardeners' Monthly*; *Trainspotter* etc.). They will all have explanations of how things work, as well as a good selection of semi-technical terminology. The most useful terms will be those that come up several times in one edition; look up and note these. Don't worry about terms that appear only once.

If you buy several specialist magazines on the same subject over a period of 3–6 months, the terminology and subjects that are repeated will give you a sound grounding in that subject area. This exercise will not only give you a broad range of vocabulary in semi-technical subjects but may also help to cultivate the curiosity that is important for interpreters. Read a few of this type of magazine and you may well find yourself developing a real interest in areas you thought you would find boring!

Example

Source: Walker 2005

B.6 Prepare technical speeches

Aim: to acquire the semi-technical terminology that educated native speakers have in a broad range of subjects.
You will need: at least one other person.

Prepare speeches in which you explain technical issues. To do this you will have to research the subject and understand it, and all the other students will benefit from the speech you give. If several students do this, you'll have practice material to interpret from and all save a lot of time researching. Below is an example of (part of) a speech you could easily prepare on a fairly technical subject without too much difficulty.

Example

Good morning, today I'd like to spend a few moments talking about how crude oil is refined and the multitude of products that the resulting products go to make up. You might think oil is used only to make fuels, like kerosene, petrol and fuel oil, but you'd be very wrong, as I will explain later.

I don't want to talk about extracting the oil from the ground, that's the subject for a different debate, but only about refining, and the first major step in the refining process is fractioning.

Crude oil is not a uniform substance, it's actually made up of many different hydrocarbons with a variety of properties and before we can make useful products out of them they have to be separated from one another. One of the different properties these different hydrocarbons have is a different boiling point, and this means that they can be separated from one another by fractional distillation, 'fractioning'. The crude oil is pumped over a heating installation and then into the bottom of a fractioning column ...

Sources: Howitworks.com; Wikipedia; OSHA Technical manual; BP.com

Source: Martin and Padilla 1989: 245

B.7 Understand rather than translate

Aim: to facilitate concentration on meaning rather than terminology.
You will need: reference works in two languages.

When preparing a technical subject, don't simply read through the foreign language text noting down all the words you don't know and looking for translations of them in bilingual dictionaries. Instead, look them up in mono-lingual dictionaries and reference works (encyclopedias) and read the description/explanation. Now you understand what the word refers to, you will be able to paraphrase it intelligently even if you never find an exact translation.

You probably want a translation all the same. If you find a possible translation, look it up in a mono-lingual reference work and see if the definition matches the foreign-language term you looked up a moment ago.

Source: Lederer 2001: 238

B.8 Wiki-parallels

Aim: to avoid dictionary translations and get into the habit of understanding words in context.
You will need: internet access.

Wikipedia now exists in many languages. If you look up an expression in one language you'll most likely be offered links in the left-hand menu to many other language versions. The advantage of this is that there will be a full explanation of the term in question in both languages, which you can compare to be sure that one is really a good translation of the other.

If the term you are looking for is medical or botanical you can check that the Latin term is the same in both entries; this can often be a useful check that the two entries really are talking about the same thing.

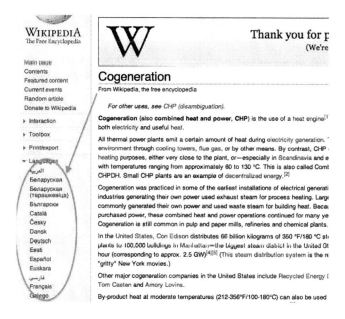

B.9 Research your speaker's people

Aim: to give you a broader understanding of how the speakers you'll be interpreting might see the world.
You will need: someone to recommend an interesting book to you.

There are many books about any nation's people – the English, the Germans, the French and so on. Some are written by 'foreigners' looking in, some by their own compatriots. They can offer you some useful insights. For example, *The English* by Jeremy Paxman; *Was ist Deutsch* by H-D. Gelfert; *Polskę da się lubić* by Stefan Moeller.

B.10 Trivial Pursuit

Aim: to become familiar with those facts and figures known to native speakers of the language you are working with.

You will need: Trivial Pursuit or similar quiz game, at least one other person, preferably someone from the country in question.

Play Trivial Pursuit and similar quiz games using versions of the games purchased in the countries where your B and C languages* are spoken. You'll notice that the questions are not the same in each country and you will be amazed at how much worse you are than native speakers. That difference is equal to the amount of general knowledge that you have to try to catch up with and that you're missing because you didn't grow up in that country.

However, try not to be disheartened by this. Remember, no-one gets that many questions right in their own language version of Trivial Pursuit either.

Example

The questions D, H, and SL below are very much directed at French players and will be much more difficult for anyone who hasn't grown up in France or surrounded by French culture.

(D) Which business funded Les Chaussettes Noires (a French rock group whose name translates as *The Black Socks* and who were sponsored by sock-maker Stemm)?

(H) The battle of Agincourt was part of which war? (Agincourt was a battle between the English and the French in 1415; it features prominently in the history books of both those nations, but not elsewhere.)

(SL) In which sport would you use a chistera? (A chistera is the scoop-like racket used for launching the ball in the Basque sport of pelota. France, like Spain, has a Basque region and as such this sort of thing is much more likely to be familiar to French speakers than, say, American, English or Russian speakers.)

TRIVIAL PURSUIT © 2012 Hasbro. Used with permission

B.11 Read books

Aim: to catch up with native-speakers' life experience in a language.
You will need: some free time and some books.

General knowledge is closely tied to our own life experience. If you've worked in a print shop you will know more about printing than most people. If you've had a baby you'll know a lot of baby-related stuff you didn't know before, both medical and non-medical. But we can't all have experienced all of these things in our own lives, certainly not before we start studying to become an interpreter. Reading books is a good substitute (though not a perfect one) for life experience. It doesn't have to be great literature, trashy spy novels are just as valid. If you read a couple of books on a subject in a year, you will have encountered the important terms and concepts in the subject area so often that you won't forget them for a while.

Source: Poger

B.12 The picture you can't see

Aim: to demonstrate the usefulness of general knowledge to the interpreter
You will need: at least one other person, a speech based on a picture / image.

Ask a speaker to choose a picture of a scene, object or machine with which you're not familiar and to give a speech describing the contents of the picture in some detail. The picture should be visible to the speaker and the audience, but not to the interpreter. Interpret the speech simultaneously.

Afterwards, look at the picture and discuss your version with your listeners.

Now interpret the same speech again, this time with the picture visible. Or, alternatively, interpret a new speech, again based on a picture, but this time with the picture visible to the interpreter.

You can do the same exercise with a speech on a subject the interpreter knows about, and one that they don't.

These exercises underline the importance of knowing what you are talking about. You can get all the words right when interpreting, but when you see the picture you'll realize that much of what you said was not quite right (or even very wrong), simply because you couldn't see the picture.

B.13   Word association

Aim: to improve knowledge of basic facts.
You will need: at least one other person.

In a group of two or more try to recall groups of associated words. For example, between five and seven rivers, capital cities, world leaders. You can either go round the group in turn or each person could try to come up with a series of associated words in one go. Doing this exercise at speed will also provide practice in the rapid reaction times that interpreters need.

Source: Heine 2000: 218

B.14 Acronym testing

Aim: to improve knowledge of basic facts.
You will need: at least one other person.

In groups of two or more, one student gives an acronym or initialization (for example, UNESCO or OSCE), the next must immediately give the full title in the same language (or, to make it a bit more difficult, in a different language). This can be done into or out of your native language. What you don't know, you will learn from your partners.

Source: Zalka 1989: 186

B.15 General knowledge collocation

Aim: to practise using general knowledge to reconstruct missing parts of the original.
You will need: a speaker, a list of collocations of proper names.

Have the speaker of speeches used in practice mumble a few words incomprehensibly, or cough over one half of a collocation. Using your general knowledge, fill in the gaps. This can be done with both consecutive and simultaneous speeches. Do this exercise first as a monolingual exercise, for instance from English to English, and then later from one language to another.

For example, 'cheddar cheese' would be halved to 'cheddar *cough*' and the interpreters would be required to complete the gap. Other examples of the type of collocation with which speeches could be liberally sprinkled are: Amnesty International, Buckingham Palace, Hereditary Peers, London Eye, Scotland Yard.

Source: Szabó 2003: 87

B.16 Re-introducing context

Aim: to activate general knowledge, practise analysing what is implicit in what is explicitly mentioned.
You will need: at least one other person, and a series of newspaper headlines (preferably current).

One person presents a newspaper headline. The others must then expand on the headline by adding in as much historical and contextual information as they can and by making explicit anything that is implicit. At first this can take the form of a group brainstorming session, but later each person should be able to do this immediately in the form of a presentation or speech. Prompt each other with questions if necessary.

Example 1

Having turned a blind eye over many years the US is now pursuing doping in sport seriously.

Despite the use of performance enhancing drugs in athletics particularly, but also in other sports like cycling, being an open secret, in the past the US authorities have not dealt with the issue as a criminal matter. This has now changed with a number of high profile police raids and a statement from the police outlining their current (new) approach. The IOC has long been accused of ignoring the issue, but the establishment of WADA, the Anti-doping agency, with American support seems to herald a new approach.

Example 2

You can also ask yourself, or each other, questions to prompt more information.

Bhopal victims will be paid compensation

Q: What happened in Bhopal? (Where is Bhopal?)
A: In 1984, in Bhopal in India, there was a chemical disaster, the Union Carbide chemical plant explosion, which killed thousands immediately and tens of thousands in the years that followed.

Q: Why is compensation an issue so long afterwards?
Because the owners refused to accept responsibility for the accident. Victims will now receive compensation for their injuries and the loss of loved ones. It is a major step forward for campaigners who see this not only as a victory against Union Carbide, which has long refused to pay compensation, but also as a precedent in similar campaigns against large multi-nationals who are rarely held to account for acts of environmental pollution.

Source: Kremer 2005: 787

B.17 What's in a name?

Aim: to cultivate active curiosity and general knowledge.
You will need: to open your eyes, a notebook.

As you walk around the town you live in, look up at the street names and the names given to public buildings and spaces. They are very often named for historical figures and events. Do you know who that person is or was, or what that event is? Don't just be content with knowing the name of the street, building or square; find out what that name signifies. In this way you will find out a lot about local historical figures and events – which is obviously most useful if you are living in a city where one of your working languages is spoken – but also about world events, because some figures and events feature in towns all over the world. Doing this regularly may also help cultivate the intellectual curiosity that is important for interpreters.

Example

Boulevard de Sébastopol in Paris
Sebastopol, now Sevastopol, is a Ukrainian Black Sea port founded in 1783 and besieged for 11 months during the Crimean War by French and British forces.

Rue Jarry in Paris
Alfred Jarry was a playwright living at the turn of the twentieth century, known for his absurdist writings, most particularly the play *Ubu Roi*.

Improving your passive languages

While speaking your language actively in conversation clearly has a role to play for anyone learning a language, and particularly for student interpreters with 'B*' languages, it is not a substitute for expansive language exposure. 'Language exposure' means reading in, and listening to, the foreign language. It fulfils different learning needs from, say, conversations with native speakers. Given the possibilities afforded by the internet, a lack of contact with native speakers is no longer an excuse for inadequate language exposure.

Language exposure is contact not only with the vocabulary, grammar and idiom of a language but also, by default, with the subject matter that is most talked about in that country. In this way you will be quietly improving your general knowledge as you go.

It is always difficult to find time for the amount of language exposure required, which may require hundreds of hours just to maintain your standard. But it is worth finding time. Get into good habits, like listening to the news over breakfast, or taking a newspaper to read or podcasts to listen to on public transport.

The exercises in this section are meant as a complement or follow-up to an extended stay (9 months or more) in a country where your languages are spoken, not as a substitute. You should probably be spending a couple of hours a day on the reading and listening exercises provided here as language exposure, not including classroom or practice time.

B.18 Get the news in multiple formats

Aim: to become as familiar as native speakers with the content and style of news.
You will need: the newspapers, perseverance, some free time.

Read quality newspapers (online or in hard-copy) on a daily basis. Listen to the radio and watch TV news broadcasts.

The educated native speakers that we would like to emulate will often hear or see the same news in several different formats each day. It's an area where they get a lot of repeated language exposure. Repetition will pay off in terms of comprehension and remembering what you've heard.

B.19 Read different papers

Aim: to become as familiar as native speakers with the different styles of different media in different countries.
You will need: the newspapers, perseverance, some free time.

Don't always stick to the best-known papers, as each paper tends to have its own limited style and lexicon. Every now and again read something that you might never have thought of reading, such as a local newspaper from New Zealand, or *The Times of India* etc. Shake things up a bit. Notice how a perspective on world events changes when you're reading a newspaper from the other side of the globe. Similarly, don't always read only the headlines. Try reading the middle pages and the editorials as well. This particularly applies to those reading online, where the less important news is much harder to find.

B.20 Reading for register

Aim: to become as familiar as native-speakers with the different registers encountered by the native-speaker in daily life.
You will need: the newspapers, some free time.

Don't read only the major newspapers. Vary what you read. For example, try periodically to read any, or all, of the following: tabloid newspapers, quality literature, junk fiction, popular culture magazines, medical magazines, political party brochures. What are the stylistic and lexical devices that mark out each of these registers?

B.21 Read specialist magazines

Aim: to acquire the general knowledge that educated native speakers have in a broad range of subjects (from the viewpoint of that country).

You will need: a specialist newsagent, a specialist magazine, internet connection to look up terms, a notepad.

Buy specialist magazines (*Aeroplanes Today!*, *Potholing Weekly*, *Market Gardeners Monthly*, *Trainspotter* etc.). They will all have explanations of how things work, as well as a good selection of semi-technical terminology. The most useful terms will be the ones that come up several times in one edition; look up and note these. Don't worry about terms that appear only once.

Buy several specialist magazines on the same subject over a period of 3–6 months and look back at previous notes to see which of those concepts and terms occur in several different issues/magazines. This repetition of core terminology and concepts will soon give you a sound grounding in the terminology and issues in that subject area.

Example

Source: Walker 2005

B.22 Copy out what you've read

Aim: to anchor passive language in your memory.
You will need: books, newspapers, something to write with.

Don't content yourself with just reading to improve your passive language knowledge. Copy out for yourself some of the more interesting parts of what you read (or hear). This active reproduction of the language heard will anchor it more effectively in your memory.

Source: Seleskovitch and Lederer 2000: 318

B.23 Read about your language(s)

Aim: to learn more about your language and how it works.
You will need: books like the ones mentioned below.

Read books not just 'in' your languages but also 'about' your languages. For example, *The English Verb* by Michael Lewis; *Metaphors We Live By* by Lakoff and Johnson; or *Mother Tongue* by Bill Bryson, to name just a few about the English language (see Bibliography).

B.24 Make friends with dictionaries

Aim: to increase your vocabulary,
You will need: two dictionaries, a monolingual and a bilingual one,

Look up any word or expression that you see twice and don't know. Even better, look it up in a couple of dictionaries, one bilingual, one monolingual.

B.25 Use Wikipedia as a multi-lingual dictionary

Aim: to avoid dictionary translations and get into the habit of understanding words in context.
You will need: internet access.

Wikipedia now exists in many languages. If you look up an expression in one language you'll most likely be offered links in the left-hand menu to many other language versions. The advantage of this is that there will be a full explanation of the term in question in both languages, which you can compare to be sure that one is really a good translation of the other.

If the term you are looking for is medical or botanical you can check that the Latin term is the same in both entries; this can often be a useful check that the two entries really are talking about the same thing.

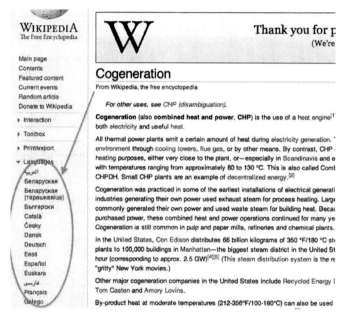

B.26 Listen to talk radio

Aim: to increase exposure time to a language and the issues its speakers discuss.
You will need: radio or internet radio, headphones or speakers.

Listening to foreign language radio, by radio or online, will allow you to listen for hours a day while doing other things (cooking, travelling, ironing etc). Listen to news or talk radio, not music channels. You'll soon become very familiar with the recurring themes that interest or occupy the minds of the media's listeners, as well as the vocabulary and idiom in which they are described.

Podcasts of the same programmes are equally useful, although you should beware of one thing: we tend to choose which podcasts we download and listen to. Live radio has the advantage of making us listen to things we might not have chosen to listen to.

Don't just listen to news shows. Hour-long discussion shows on a single subject are a great way to get a thorough introduction to a subject area and its terminology.

B.27 Watch popular TV

Aim: to increase exposure time to a language and the issues its speakers discuss.
You will need: internet TV or a satellite dish and TV.

If you can buy a small satellite dish to receive TV in your working languages, or if you can find channels that broadcast on the internet, then watch them. Don't just watch news programmes. Watch the programmes that the locals are watching! That includes day time TV, chat-shows and soap operas (though it's probably a good idea to give preference to locally produced programmes rather than those that have been imported and dubbed). The benefits of watching what some people consider low brow TV are sorely underestimated, but it's just as useful as reading the classics of literature. Popular culture is still culture.

B.28 Use the internet in other languages

Aim: to increase exposure time to a language and the issues its speakers discuss.
You will need: internet TV or a satellite dish and TV.

Keeping up with the news has never been so easy, but often we gravitate towards our own language online. Make a point of searching in other languages online, as well as reading and listening to them.

B.29 Change your settings to 'other language'

Aim: to increase exposure time to a language.
You will need: a computer and its software.

Most of us have our operating system and software set to communicate with us in our A language. But we spend so much time in front of a computer each day that it's a wasted opportunity for language exposure. Change the settings so that all the menus, messages etc. are in your foreign language. That constant contact with the language, without any great effort but over months and years, will pay off.

B.30 Listen to pop music and read the lyrics

Aim: to familiarize yourself with contemporary culture and lyricism.
You will need: an internet connection, possibly a native-speaker.

The internet makes it possible to listen to contemporary (and less contemporary) pop music and find the texts of the lyrics. This gives you the chance to understand and enjoy songs that are acoustically often difficult to decipher. It's also an enjoyable way of tackling language in verse.

It's quite possible that you'll still need a native-speaker to help you understand some of the texts, but verse, poetry and songs are like that. They often need a bit of explaining.

Source: Walker 2005

B.31 Use your school's facilities

Aim: increase language exposure and make the most of what's around you.
You will need: to know what facilities your school has.

Use your school's facilities to the full. If the school has a satellite dish, record radio and TV programmes in your working languages at the school and listen to them in the train, car or at home etc. Copy recorded materials or ask native speakers on the staff to make speeches for you.

B.32 What's on!

Aim: to take in some local culture and make the most of what's around you.
You will need: a 'What's On' guide or the local newspapers, an open mind.

Scour the 'What's On' pages in the press for visiting speakers at universities or colleges, book readings, films in their original version etc. Anything that is happening in your working languages, or relates to the countries in which they are spoken, can be useful.

Source: Gillies 2001: 62, Lomb 2008: 158

B.33 A change is as good as a rest

Aim: to avoid boredom and maximize exposure time to the language.
You will need: a book with lots of different exercise ideas!

When you start getting bored or tired of your work on your passive language*, don't force yourself to continue. But don't stop altogether either. Try something different: instead of listening to the radio or podcasts, pick up a book. Or instead of reading current affairs magazines, watch some TV. A change is as good as a rest.

Source: Lomb 2008: 159

Improving your active languages

Don't forget, your native language is one of your active languages* and can always be improved! So these exercises are not just for improving an active foreign language, but for all your active languages. This is particularly important for students living abroad who risk losing touch with their first language.

One thing you will notice consistently through this section is that the exercises rarely focus on grammar or vocabulary alone. Language learning enhancement at this level is often addressed by learning to use chunks of ready-to-use bits of language – not words alone, but words in their grammatical, syntactical and lexical contexts. This approach has been advocated in both the world of English teaching (Lewis 1997) and in some parts of the interpreting world (EMCI 2002; Lomb 2008) for some time.

The exercises below will also help improve your passive language* knowledge.

B.34 Write in your language(s)

Aim: to achieve a level of automatism, through repeated practice, in the formulation of good quality language, and activation* of high register language.
You will need: perseverance.

Write in all your languages! E-mails, a diary, letters, short stories – make a point of writing and crafting language. Writing allows you to reassess your own competence and gauge what you need to do to improve. Checking and thinking about what you write will help you to improve your spoken language, and some of what you have written will be recalled and used when interpreting.

Source: Pergnier and Lavault 1995: 7; Gethin and Gunnemark 1996: 198

B.35 Become a watchful reader

Aim: to identify quality language use with the aim of later imitating it.
You will need: time and perseverance.

In order to write well you should first study the writings of others. Become a 'watchful reader', a reader who is able to read a variety of material and discern how form is at the service of content; a reader who can identify which style best suits which message and who can identify the way different stylistic devices are used in different types of text.

Source: Pergnier and Lavault 1995: 23; Lederer 2001: 148

B.36 Create topic files

Aim: to create a reference collection for important subject areas.
You will need: an organized filing system (digital or paper).

Make up files of newspaper articles/information on topical issues. These should contain complete texts rather than vocabulary lists (vocabulary out of context is not helpful and can be misleading).

You can refer back to these articles whenever you need to reactivate the terminology for a given subject area. The example here shows a paper version of this idea, but you can, of course, also do this on a computer.

B.37 Parallel texts

Aim: to see how the same information is expressed and addressed differently in different languages.
You will need: texts about the same events in two different languages – major news events are the easiest examples.

Read and compare articles on the same topic but written independently in both languages. Find examples of the same thing being described in both texts. Make a note of the two versions. In this way you avoid literal, or dictionary, translations because you can see how similar ideas are expressed independently in two languages without interference* from the source language, something that the interpreter must always seek to avoid.

When doing this exercise you should choose two texts from people or organizations with comparable political points of view, bias, or lack of bias. If you compare a left-wing text with a right-wing text the corresponding terms and expressions are likely to be politically different and therefore dangerous for an interpreter.

Example

The two articles overleaf appeared on the same day in July 2012. The expressions which correspond to one another, as independently drafted descriptions of the same phenomena, are numbered and in bold and underlined.

French automaker Peugeot to shed 8,000 jobs[1]

French automaker PSA Peugeot Citroen has announced to **slash 8,000 jobs**[1] and close a major **plant**[2] outside Paris as it struggles with mounting losses, in a move that could spark more **restructuring**[3] and political tension in austerity-strapped Europe.

The Aulnay plant near Paris, which employs more than 3,000 workers, **will stop making cars**[4] in 2014 as Peugeot reorganises its under-used domestic production capacity, the company said on Thursday.

Aulnay, which builds the Citroen C3 subcompact, will become the first French car plant to close in more than two decades, challenging new Socialist President Francois Hollande's pledge to revive industrial production.

"I know how serious these measures are for the people concerned, and for our entire company," Chief Executive Philippe Varin told reporters. "But a company can't preserve jobs when it is burning 200 million euros ($245m) a month in cash."

...Jean-Marc Ayrault, the French prime minister, said the government was studying the closure plan, which he called a "great shock", but stopped short of condemning it, which incurred the wrath of the CGT, France's biggest industrial union.

Peugeot said another plant in the western city of Rennes will shed 1,400 workers as it shrinks in step with demand for larger cars such as the Peugeot 508 and Citroen C5.

Some **3,600 non-assembly jobs**[5] will also be scrapped[1] across the country.

La suppression de 8.000 emplois[1] chez PSA crée un choc sans précédent

Le groupe Peugeot-Citroën a annoncé hier l'arrêt de la production à Aulnay-sous-Bois, première fermeture **d'usine**[2] en France depuis vingt ans. Les politiques et les syndicats montent au créneau[6].

Comme pour tenter de préparer les esprits, Arnaud Montebourg avait déclaré mercredi qu'il redoutait « *un choc pour la nation* ». La formule n'était pas excessive. L'annonce, hier, par PSA de la suppression de 8.000 postes en France a provoqué un véritable séisme, suscitant la colère des syndicats et de la classe politique. Le groupe Peugeot-Citroën ne s'est pas contenté de dévoiler un énième plan de départs volontaires. Il a fait part de sa décision **d'arrêter la production automobile**[4] dans l'usine d'Aulnay-sous-Bois et de réduire la voilure à Rennes. Corollaire de la baisse des effectifs dans la production, **les fonctions administratives seront également touchées, à hauteur de 3.600 postes**[5]. Ces départs pourront se faire sur la base du volontariat, mais jusqu'à mi-2013 seulement...

...Les précautions verbales du président de PSA, Philippe Varin, n'ont pas suffi à éteindre l'incendie. « *Personne ne sera laissé au bord du chemin* », a-t-il garanti, tout en précisant que la moitié des 3.000 salariés d'Aulnay pourraient être reclassés à Poissy. Ce dernier a également promis de « *revitaliser* » Aulnay. Pour apaiser les inquiétudes grandissantes sur l'usine de Rennes, le dirigeant s'est engagé à lui affecter un nouveau véhicule.

Unions decry[6] decision

Combined with France's share of 6,000 European job cuts announced last year, the latest measures **will reduce Peugeot's 100,000-strong domestic workforce**[1] by close to 10 per cent, excluding subcontractors and service providers.

Workers at Aulnay downed tools after the announcement, halting production. Hundreds gathered under protest banners at the main entrance to the plant, the biggest industrial employer in the depressed, multiethnic Seine-Saint Denis district northeast of Paris.

...Peugeot's global **sales fell**[7] 13 per cent to 1.62 million light vehicles in the first six months – contrasting with a more modest 3.3 per cent decline reported by Renault and a 10 per cent gain for the Volkswagen brand...

Still, the French automaker's plans could prompt **restructuring**[3] moves by rivals, analysts say, as the European industry battles overcapacity estimated at 20 per cent.

Renault and Fiat are also **reducing headcount**[1], while GM's Opel division plans to close its Bochum plant in Germany by 2017.

Al Jazeera
http://www.aljazeera.com/news/europe/2012/07/20127121546390440.html

PSA justifie ces décisions par la dépression du marché automobile européen, où **les volumes ont chuté**[7] de près de 25 % depuis 2007. Dans ce contexte, la situation financière du groupe s'est brutalement dégradée depuis un an. Philippe Varin a évoqué un « *rythme de pertes intenable* », écartant toutefois le risque de faillite grâce à une « *sécurité financière de 9,5 milliards d'euros* ». « *Mais cette réserve n'est pas infinie* », a-t-il prévenu. Malgré ces difficultés, une aide financière de l'Etat semble écartée. « *Ce n'est pas à l'ordre du jour, a-t-il déclaré. Notre préoccupation est de remplir les usines du groupe. Injecter de l'argent n'est pas ce qui permettrait de les faire tourner.* »

...Le ministre a été chargé de présenter le 25 juillet un « *plan de soutien* » à l'industrie automobile. C'est à cette date que PSA doit annoncer les deux autres volets de son **projet de redressement**[3] – Investissements et baisse des prix des véhicules -ainsi que ses résultats financiers pour le premier semestre 2012...

Les Echos 13th July 2012
http://www.lesechos.fr/entreprises-secteurs/auto-transport/dossier/0202171808246/0202171808457-la-suppression-de-8-000-emplois-chez-psa-cree-un-choc-sans-precedent-343994.php

B.38 Sight translation* to activate* new language

Aim: to activate expressions in your active languages*.
You will need: speech texts that you have studied for good useable language.

Once you've identified and noted expressions in your B language*, using exercises like 'Parallel texts' above, try doing a sight translation of the same or similar texts from your A into your B language*. In this way you will practise quickly recalling and using the expressions you've just identified.

B.39 The language of death

Aim: to identify the language elements that are characteristic of a given register.
You will need: several short texts exhibiting a specific language register.

Some registers in the language are very specific and relatively limited in scope. As such they can be analysed and copied very easily in order to improve your active language skills. For example, interpreters are regularly called upon to interpret announcements of death or disaster. In these announcements, or formal statements, speakers re-use a number of standard expressions and stylistic devices. The same goes for crime reporting, medical procedures, cinema and theatre reviews, horoscopes, biblical references and more. So although the example in this exercise deals only with the language of death, you can do this exercise, with the appropriate texts, for any register.

Collect 10–20 short examples of a type of register. Below are just a few examples of English-speaking politicians talking about deaths. Even in this limited selection some of the similarities are striking. Look for collocation, stylistic devices and any other recurring elements.

Example

> Mr Roche, EU Council, 30th March 2004
> The KFOR international peacekeeping force has been strengthened significantly in response to the violence. I pay tribute to the efforts of all who worked hard to stabilise the situation and to restore calm in Kosovo. I would also like to offer my condolences and those of the Council to all who have once again suffered loss of life, injury and loss of loved ones.

> Neena Gilla, MEP, 3rd December 2008
> Mr President, on behalf of the Delegation for relations with India, may I firstly give my sincere condolences to the families and friends of all those who were killed in last week's horrific terrorist atrocities in Mumbai and wish all those injured a speedy recovery. My sympathy also to colleagues and officials of the European Parliament caught up in these horrific and outrageous attacks. I have written to the Indian Prime Minister and the Chief Minister of Maharashtra to express our sympathy.

Pat Cox, President EP, 8th March 2004
It is my sad duty today to express, on behalf of this House, our condemnation and our grief at the terrorist attacks in Baghdad and Karbala last Tuesday, 2 March 2004, aimed at the Shiite community as they celebrated the festival of Ashoura. At least 170 innocent people were killed and almost 400 injured in those attacks.
    As the European Parliament, we offer our sympathy and sincere condolences to the families of the victims and to the Iraqi authorities. We condemn those behind indiscriminate and criminal terrorist attacks, which struck at a time of traditional, peaceful and religious celebration. I ask you, colleagues, to join with me now in a minute of silence.

David Martin, Vice President of EP, 4th December 2003
Colleagues, we have waited until the Chamber is full as I am sure you will all wish to join with me in paying tribute to the Spanish citizens who were killed in Iraq last Saturday, 29 November 2003.
    Given the gravity of the situation, and given that we all wish to pay our respects – both to the individuals involved and to their families – I would ask you to join me now in a minute's silence in honour of the Spanish citizens who were killed in Iraq.

William Hague MP, 29th February 2009
I join the Prime Minister in paying tribute to Lance Corporal Stephen Kingscott and Marine Darren Smith, who were killed in Afghanistan, and to Private Ryan Wrathall, who died in Iraq. Whenever we read out such names, it is a reminder that whenever death comes, or however it comes, it is a devastating loss to the families involved.

Tony Blair, Prime Minister, 8th June 2005
Before I list my engagements I know that the whole House will want to join me in conveying the condolences of the House on the death of the hon. Member for Cheadle, Patsy Calton. Our thoughts and prayers are with her and her family at this time.

Source: also Alexieva 1992: 227; Visson: 1999: 138

B.40 Parallel texts for political standpoint

Aim: to see how the same information is expressed and addressed differently depending on the author's political/ geographical standpoint.
You will need: texts about the same events in two publications of opposing political leanings – major news events are the easiest examples.

Read and compare articles on the same subject matter in left-wing and right-of-centre newspapers. Find examples of the same thing being described in both texts and make a note of the two versions. How does the language they use to describe the same events differ? Certain groups have very particular ways of talking about some things, for example, right-wingers about immigration, or communists about the rich. As an interpreter you will have to speak on behalf of people of all political hues. This is a good way of arming yourself with the necessary registers to do so.

If you're preparing for a class, or a meeting, in which two sides of an argument are likely to be aired, and which you will have to interpret, it's useful to have a look at publications that represent both sides of that argument, or different ends of the political spectrum, to get an idea of how some of the same things are expressed differently by people representing the two sides. This is useful for all your active languages.

In the example below, two newspapers, one with a predominantly left-of-centre readership and another with a predominantly right-of-centre readership, report on the same welfare reforms. In bold, and numbered 1–6, are expressions describing the same thing slightly differently.

In addition to corresponding expressions you'll also find expressions that set the tone for the article in one or other, or both, texts. These can also be useful as you prepare. To illustrate this in the texts below, the negative expressions related to claiming social security benefits in the *Mail on Sunday* are underlined.

Example

Housing benefit for under-25s could be[1] scrapped, PM to announce	**Cameron to axe[1] housing benefits for feckless under 25s as he declares war on welfare culture**
…The government wants to cut as much as £10bn from the **welfare budget[2]** by 2016, and is looking at setting regional benefit levels and cutting benefits from striking workers. Cameron and the Treasury set the £10bn target for new welfare **cuts[3]** in last year's autumn statement and the PM will go into detail in a speech on Monday… he will propose that 380,000 **people under 25 are stripped of housing benefit[4]** and forced to join the growing number of young adults who still live with their parents. He will make exemptions for those that have been victims of domestic violence. The savings – which will mean an average loss per person of around £90 per week[5] – are likely to be in the order of £1.8bn.	Radical new welfare cuts targeting feckless couples who have children and expect to live **on state handouts[2]** will be proposed by David Cameron tomorrow. His bold **reforms[3]** could also lead to 380,000 people under 25 being stripped of housing benefits and forced to join the growing number of young adults who still live with their parents. In a keynote speech likely to inflame tensions with his deputy Nick Clegg, the Prime Minister will call for a debate on the welfare state, focusing on reforms to 'working-age benefits'. Among the ideas being considered by Mr Cameron are:

Labour accepts that the housing benefit budget is out of control and last week the party welcomed proposals of cuts from the left-of-centre thinktank the IPPR, but in the context of a massive housebuilding programme.

...Cameron also wants more done to cut jobseeker's allowance for those refusing to seek work actively. The government has already tightened up requirements in this area, but the PM wants to go further. 'We aren't even asking them, "Have you got a CV ready to go?"' Cameron said.

He is also looking at restricting child benefit to those who have more than three children and forcing **a small minority of unemployed people**[6] – an estimated 5,000 to 10,000 – to take part in community work if they fail or refuse to find work or training after two years.

The *Guardian*, 24th June 2012
http://www.guardian.co.uk/society/2012/jun/24/housing-benefit-under-25s-welfare

Copyright Guardian News & Media Ltd 2012

– **Scrapping most of the £1.8 billion in housing benefits**[4] paid to 380,000 under-25s, **worth an average £90 a week**[5], forcing them to support themselves or live with their parents.

– Stopping the £70-a-week dole money for the unemployed who refuse to try hard to find work or produce a CV.

– Forcing a hardcore of workshy claimants to do community work after two years on the dole – or lose all their benefits.

...

He also favours new curbs on the Jobseeker's Allowance, demanding the unemployed do more to find work. He said: "We aren't even asking them, 'Have you got a CV ready to go?'" A **small minority of hardcore workshy**[6], an estimated 5,000 to 10,000, could be forced to take part in community work if they fail or refuse to find work or training after two years.

Mail on Sunday, 23rd June 2012
http://www.dailymail.co.uk/news/article-2163773/David-Cameron-axe-housing-benefits-feckless-25s-declares-war-welfare-culture.html

© Associated Newspapers Ltd 2012

1. In the *Mail on Sunday*'s text this is definite, thus reinforcing a positive impression.
4. The *Guardian* relates this to people, 'people ... stripped of', whereas the *Mail on Sunday* dehumanizes the process by relating it to the payments 'scrapping ... benefits'.
5. As in 4. The *Guardian* seeks to talk about the 'loss to...' people, and the *Mail on Sunday* about the money involved (abstract), 'benefits ...worth'.

Source: Gillies 2001: 62

B.41 Magic Bag

Aim: to practise using different registers.
You will need: at least two other people.

This exercise is best suited to your A language.

Create two piles of cards, one with a list of subjects to be discussed and the other with a list of potential audiences (for example, international business people, students, press, TV talk-show etc.). Put the cards in two separate bags. One person picks one card from each pile, or bag, so that they have a subject and an audience. They then give that speech to that audience. The others in the room have to guess, from the language register used by the speaker, what type of audience the speaker was trying to address.

Source: Szabó 2003: 120

B.42 Use concordance software

Aim: to identify stylistic and lexical devices specific to certain registers of language.
You will need: concordance software.

Concordance software is a statistical tool that, amongst other things, can show you how many times a word or expression comes up in a text and the context in which it comes up. For an interpreter this means that you can use concordance software to analyse the terminology of documents and subject areas – useful terms will come up more often than they do in normal speech. This is particularly useful for some of the huge documents created by official bodies. No-one expects you to read and analyse several 200-page documents before each class!

You can also use concordance software to analyse and imitate language register – registers are often identifiable by certain (types of) recurring expressions.

In the example below, a European Commission Green Paper on online gambling has been put through the concordance software. In the left-hand column you can see the number of times each word comes up in the text. Obviously, many of these will be of no interest; short words like 'the' and 'and' come up dozens or hundreds of times. Some words will only come up once, and they probably aren't of much interest to us either. The most interesting for us are those in-between and you can quickly scroll through the whole alphabetical list, pausing to note anything of interest.

In the example on the next page we can see a selection taken from this document, and the terms 'benefit', 'benevolent', 'betting', 'blacklisting' stand out. By clicking on any of these terms the software will then show us the context in the right-hand columns in the following order: what comes before the word; the word;

and then what comes after it. This will help you understand the term better and use it correctly if this is one of your active languages. In the example below you can see that we have an interesting range of collocations for the term 'betting'.

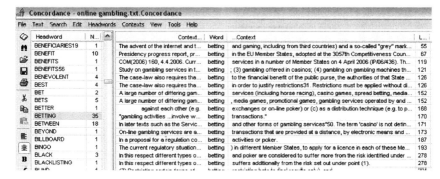

Find out more about concordance software at http://www.concordancesoftware.
co.uk/
European Commission Green Paper on Online Gambling
http://eur-lex.europa.eu/LexUriServ/LexUriServ.do?uri=COM:2011:0128:
FIN:EN:PDF

Source: Lewis 2000: 40

B.43 Activating grammatical structures

Aim: to consciously examine target language usage in order to understand and internalize grammar structures.
You will need: texts containing certain specific elements of language.

If you are having trouble using a particular grammatical structure in a foreign language, for example, the present perfect tense or the definite article in English, try identifying examples of where it is used in, say, newspaper articles or books, and ask yourself at each instance why the native speaker uses one form rather than another. Native speakers are not born with intuition for those bits of their language that defy clear rules, they have just seen so many examples that they get it right. All you need to do is see as many examples as a native speaker has.

Source: Walker 2005

B.44 Vocabulary ball

Aim: to activate* terminology in a broad range of subjects in a given language.
You will need: at least two other people, and a ball.

Pick a subject, perhaps the subject of the day's lesson. Throw the ball to someone. That person must improvise for 1 minute, spitting out as much vocab and idiom related to the subject as possible (and catch the ball).

Source: Llewellyn-Smith

B.45 Talk to native speakers

Aim: to activate* or maintain active language skills.
You will need: at least one native speaker of the language in question, possibly some money.

For those of you who aren't living in a country where your foreign languages are spoken: as far as is affordable, take conversation lessons or seek out contact with native speakers. Two lessons per week with two different people would be a good start. If money is short, look for people who are happy to speak your language with you half the time in exchange for speaking theirs the other half of the time. Having or making native-speaker friends is obviously a very good idea. Don't be shy! Spending time with people only because they are native speakers may sound mercenary but you may make new friends. If not, at least your foreign language skills will improve.

Source: also Gillies 2001: 62; Lomb 2008: 158

B.46 Talk to yourself – the internal monologue

Aim: to maximize time spent producing the active language*, rehearse good language that you might later use when interpreting.
You will need: nothing at all.

Switch your internal monologue (how we talk to ourselves in our minds) to the foreign language. This will maximize time spent producing your B language* and is almost as effective as actually talking to native speakers.

Most people instinctively think they must talk to native speakers and be corrected by them. However, native speakers (particularly of English) will not correct all or even a majority of mistakes and will very rarely correct stylistic errors. There is also plenty of literature to be found on the ineffectiveness of any such correction: see, for example, *Correction – a positive approach to language mistakes* by Bartram and Walton; and *The Lexical Approach* by Michael Lewis.

Source: Déjean le Féal 1976: 51; Gillies 2001: 63; Lomb 2008: 77

B.47 Listen to yourself live

Aim: to improve pronunciation.
You will need: a speech to interpret or to give.

Listen, not to recordings of yourself, but to yourself as you are actually speaking, be it your own speech, or shadowing* speeches or interviews. It's important to be able to hear, as you speak, whether what you're saying is correct or not. Correct any mispronunciation immediately. This immediate correction is likely to be more effective than a later correction from a recording, detached as it is from the original mistake.

Source: Gethin and Gunnemark 1996: 68

B.48 Record yourself 1

Aim: to identify, and later eliminate, those mistakes that you recognize when listening but still make when speaking.
You will need: digital voice recorder.

Record yourself speaking your B language*. Listen and analyse your language use. Alternatively, ask a colleague to listen and analyze for you.

You will notice some of your own mistakes while speaking but you will find more when listening to a recording of yourself.

B.49 Record and transcribe

Aim: to identify, and later eliminate, those mistakes that you recognize when listening but still make when speaking.
You will need: digital voice recorder.

Record yourself speaking, or interpreting into, your 'B' language. Write a transcript of what you have said. Check it for mistakes and write a corrected version alongside. Repeat at regular intervals.

Example

Your first version	Your own correction
However, the Rhine valley is the location for US military bases, military camps ever since the second World War and all you can see around these camps are concrete walls and wire fences, which is the reason why the people living in the area are so mad about this.	However, since the second World War, we see US military bases there. The bases are surrounded with concrete walls and barbed-wire fences. And all this infuriates local residents.

You will be much more critical of your 'B' language performance when reading a written version than you would be if (indeed, when) you were speaking. Consequently you will notice more errors or stylistic flaws. By doing this regularly you will eliminate those that recur.

This exercise will weed out those mistakes that you recognize as mistakes in the written version of your speech. However, as a non-native speaker there are probably mistakes you don't recognize. Add a third column to your table above and get a native speaker to first underline mistakes so you can try to correct them yourself, and if that doesn't work, ask them to actually correct your version.

Example

Your first version	Your own correction	Native-speaker correction
However, the Rhine valley is the location for US military bases, military camps ever since the second World War and all you can see around these camps are concrete walls and wire fences, which is the reason why the people living in the area are so mad about this.	However, since the second World War, we see US military bases there. The bases are surrounded with concrete walls and barbed-wire fhences. And all this infuriates local residents.	However, since the second World War, there have been US military bases there. The bases are surrounded by concrete walls and barbed-wire fences. And all this infuriates local residents.

B.50 Record yourself 2

Aim: to avoid making the same mistake repeatedly by having pre-prepared solutions.
You will need: a small notebook.

In the heat of interpreting battle, some of the language we produce is not nearly as good as we'd like. Record your interpreting performance. Afterwards, ask yourself how you would have said the same thing better, or differently, if you hadn't been under the pressure of interpreting. Make a note of the new solution. This way you'll have it ready for next time.

B.51 Your favourite mistakes

Aim: to eliminate recurring mistakes in your active languages.
You will need: a small notebook.

Make a note of the stylistic or grammatical mistakes that you make most frequently. Refer to this list from time to time. Repeated, conscious attempts to eliminate these errors will help, and keeping a record is one way of doing this. You won't stop making these mistakes immediately, but as you are repeatedly reminded of the problem you will slowly learn to avoid them.

Source: Gethin and Gunnemark 1996: 150

B.52 Reading aloud

Aim: to force yourself to enunciate grammatical structures and lexis that you would not normally use.
You will need: good quality written material.

Practise reading aloud a variety of texts, including narrative fiction, dialogue, news reports and technical manuals. Record yourself and listen critically to your enunciation and intonation.

 This exercise is one that reflects professional reality for interpreters, who are occasionally called upon to read out pre-prepared translations. Language teachers will tell you that the written word can interfere with otherwise good pronunciation, and that is a difficulty to be overcome here.

Source: Van Hoof 1962: 107; Pergnier and Lavault 1995

B.53 Total reading

Aim: to force yourself to recall and enunciate grammatical structures and lexis that you would not normally use.
You will need: a good book.

Read a text. At the end of each sentence repeat the same sentence verbatim without looking at the text again.

Source: Déjean le Féal 1976: 44

B.54 Total listening

Aim: to force yourself to recall and enunciate grammatical structures and lexis that you would not normally use.
You will need: a recorded speech.

Listen to a speech. Pause the recording after each sentence and repeat that sentence without listening again.

Source: Déjean le Féal 1976: 44

B.55 Inversion of form

Aim: to shift one's attention while listening.
You will need: a recorded speech.

When listening to a speech, deliberately concentrate on the 'little words' (for example, the prepositions), instead of on the major word types (nouns, verbs and adjectives) that transmit most of the information of a speech.

Source: Déjean le Féal 1976: 44

B.56 Shadowing*

Aim: to force yourself to enunciate grammatical structures and lexis that you would not normally use.
You will need: a recorded speech.

Shadow interviews or speeches in your active languages. Shadowing is an excellent way to improve an active language* because it draws attention to every single word of what is said, in particular structure words that the listener usually doesn't even register when listening, and which are therefore particularly difficult to get right. Copy the speaker's sentence intonation as well as pronunciation.

While shadowing is now generally discredited as an exercise for training to interpret, its usefulness as a way of improving pronunciation and intonation in a foreign language is not disputed.

Source: Guichot de Fortis 2009: 4; Déjean le Féal 1997: 621

B.57 Paraphrasing

Aim: to develop language flexibility in a B language*.
You will need: recorded spoken material.

Listen to interviews or speeches in your B language* and then paraphrase them, again in your B language. It's often easy to say something in one way in your B language*, but more challenging if you are obliged to find another way of saying the same thing.

B.58 Paraphrase a single sentence

Aim: to develop language flexibility in a B language*.
You will need: a sentence taken from a speech.

Take any sentence in your active language(s), preferably from a speech that might be interpreted, and paraphrase it into as many versions as you can. Your target in a B language* should be 10 different versions, 12 would be excellent. In your own language more than 15 versions is a minimum.

If you like a bit of pressure or competition you could do this as a group, with each person taking turns to give the next version.

Example

> The strength of our institutions has maintained Britain's reputation as a world leader in science, engineering and design.
>
> Giles Paxman
> British Ambassador to Spain,
> 5th June 2012
>
> 1. The robustness of our institutions has kept Britain's reputation as a global leader in science, engineering and design.
> 2. It's thanks to the strength of our universities that Britain has kept its reputation as a world leader in science, engineering and design.
> 3. Britain continues to be known as a pioneer in science, engineering and design because it has such sound universities.
> 4. Britain's continuing reputation as a world leader in science, engineering and design is based on the excellence of our institutions.
> 5. etc.

Source: Van Hoof 1962: 114; Guichot de Fortis 2009: 4

B.59 Semantic dictation

Aim: to produce high quality B language* without the time pressure associated with speaking.
You will need: at least one other person, a two-minute speech.

One person reads out a two-minute passage or, preferably, speaks for a couple of minutes in the listeners' B language*. Ideally the speaker is using their A language*. The passage might be a short description of an individual or, later, a longer chronological narrative. The others listen, and when the speaker has finished they write down a version of what they have heard in the same language. The end result should be somewhere between a half and a full page of A4.

Writing in your B language* will give you the time to craft a correct version with fewer mistakes than you would make under the time pressure of interpreting. This exercise can also be used as an introductory exercise for consecutive interpreting.

Source: Tryuk 2002: 56

B.60 Blind drawing

Aim: to demonstrate the need for precision of expression, and practise it.
You will need: a map, diagram or the like, one other person.

This exercise will work with pretty much any picture, but start with a map, a diagram of a machine or a geographical feature. One person can see the diagram, the other cannot. The person who can see the diagram describes it in their B language* to the other person, who must try to recreate the diagram by drawing what they hear.

You'll initially get something very different to the original diagram, but you'll soon learn to express with considerable accuracy all of the 'information' contained in the picture. This is useful for interpreters, who should not assume that just because they have said the same thing as the speaker, their listeners will have understood what the speaker meant.

B.61 Learn by heart 1

Aim: to transfer new high-quality language straight into your active language store.
You will need: a little time each day, some high-quality source texts.

Learn by heart, and practise reciting, 2–6 lines of well-written text in one of your active languages every day. Each day check that you still know all the texts from previous days. This may sound ambitious but it won't actually take more than 10 minutes per day, and after a week you will find yourself using the new structures and expressions when you speak your B language*.

This exercise will contribute very quickly and effectively to improving your active language in at least three ways: by immediately moving first, entire phrases (highlighted in the example below) and second, collocation pairs (underlined in the example below) from your passive to your active knowledge of a language.[2] Because you've learned the passage below by heart, it will be no problem to use only the highlighted/underlined parts in your own speech when appropriate.

Example

> During the last few days concern has been expressed in the media and in this House about possible exposure of United Kingdom forces to Depleted Uranium in the Balkans. It is suggested that some UK service personnel may have become ill as a result. This afternoon I will set out our position on depleted uranium, and list the steps we intend to take.

Third, as demonstrated in the following example, you can use the same syntactic constructions, which should be more stylish and interesting than those you can produce yourself, but substitute different content words (highlighted).

Example

> During the last few days surprise has been expressed by journalists and doctors about possible exposure of NHS radiologists and nurses to X-ray radiation in hospitals. It is suggested that some NHS medical staff may have become ill as a result. This afternoon I will set out our position on X-ray exposure, and list the steps we intend to take.

In a short time you will have a large body of good quality language that can be recalled instantaneously.

Source: Gillies 2001: 63; Lomb 2008: 163; Guichot de Fortis 2009: 7

B.62 Learn by heart 2

Aim: to transfer new, high-quality language straight into your active language store.
You will need: a little time each day, some high-quality source texts.

Choose an outstanding speech in the target language and memorize a sentence a day, writing it down and repeating it aloud as many times as necessary until it can be reproduced without conscious intellectual effort. Stop only when the entire speech has been internalized. In this way, it is again possible to appropriate some small part of the cadence and genius of the new active language.

Source: Guichot de Fortis 2009: 6

B.63 Write and learn speeches

Aim: to transfer new high-quality language into your active language store.
You will need: a little time.

Write model speeches for yourself and memorize the structures in them so that they come to mind instantly when required.

Source: Déjean le Féal 1981: 89; Nolan 2005: 9

B.64 Create a debating society

Aim: to practise speaking in a formal register in your active languages; to practise expressing views you do not hold personally.
You will need: at least two other people.

Meet up with fellow students and debate issues that might be debated at the sort of international meetings at which interpreters work. Pick a subject in advance and assign speaking roles to each other, for example, for and against the death penalty, or environmentalist against climate change sceptic. Debating from a point of view that differs from your own is particularly useful. Interpreters, like lawyers, are called upon to advocate views that may be diametrically opposed to their own, but they still have to do their job to the best of their abilities!

Source: de Clarens 1973: 123

B.65 Impersonate

Aim: to practise using native-speaker intonation patterns; to transfer new high-quality language straight into your active language store.
You will need: audio or video recordings of comedians, politicians etc.

Learn off by heart and mimic 1–2 minute extracts from interviews, speeches and stand-up comedians in your active languages. Repeat not only the same words but copy the speaker's sentence intonation and pronunciation. Learn one or two per week and each week check that you still know all the extracts from previous weeks.

Learning by heart and imitating will help you to develop the correct sentence intonation and rhythm when speaking your active languages. Both are very difficult to learn and often give away foreign speakers who otherwise have a very good command of the language.

In addition, learning extracts by heart will help, as in 'Learning by heart 1' above (B.61), in moving words, structures, and here also intonation patterns, directly from your passive to active language knowledge.

Comedians are mentioned here because they often use a more marked intonation for comic effect and this will be easier to copy. Also, to sound really authentic you will probably have to feel as if you are exaggerating the accent when you speak. – but in fact it will not be as over the top as you think.

Source: Gillies 2001: 63; Heine, 2000: 217

B.66 Poems and songs

Aim: to practise using native-speaker intonation patterns; to transfer new, high-quality language straight into your active language store.
You will need: a collection of poetry.

Do not be shy of learning by heart poems or songs in the language you're working to improve. Good diction plays a more significant role in speech performance than the mere articulation of individual sounds. Verses and melodies impose certain constraints. They set which sounds must be long and which must be short. The rhythm inherent in them guides speakers and helps them avoid the intonation traps of their native language.

Source: Lomb, 2008: 163

B.67 Re-enact comedy sketches

Aim: to improve intonation and delivery timing in active languages,
You will need: a film recording of a great comedy sketch,

Find a filmed recording of a comedy sketch, the better-known and funnier the better, and its transcript. The sketch should involve 2–4 people and not be longer than 3–4 minutes. You can use part of a longer sketch instead, of course. Assign one role to each member of your group. Together, watch the sketch several times, making sure you know why it's funny. Now rehearse the sketch together, repeating the script and imitating the intonation and body language of the actors/comedians in the original. Give yourselves 30 minutes to rehearse and then perform the sketch for other colleagues. Intonation and timing are always fundamental to good comedy, so if your colleagues don't laugh, you probably haven't got them right. If you can imitate the experts in this way you may also be able to apply some of this good intonation to your own active language production.

Some British examples of the type of sketch that is well-suited to this exercise are: *Monty Python*'s 'The Four Yorkshiremen'; *Not the Nine O'clock News*, 'Python Worshippers'; and John Bird and John Fortune, 'Subprime'.

B.68 Recording vocabulary

Aim: to collect vocabulary in context and in a format that is readily useable.
You will need: a system.

How to record vocabulary: don't make lists!

Record vocab in topic-based groupings, using images. Record words in context, not alone. The meaning of words is clearer if they are recorded in context and the words will be easier to recall.

For those with a visual memory the very fact of noting related terms and expressions side by side on the page will mean that recalling one of them helps to recall those that were around it on the page, or noted at the same time.

Source: Lewis 1993: 126

B.69 Collect vocabulary in collocation

Aim: to collect vocabulary in context and in a format that is readily useable.
You will need: a notebook.

Don't collect new vocabulary in lists, but collect it in context with other words that it can be used with. In this way you have ready phrases to use, rather than single words.

Example

(re-)draft table withdraw vote on sign	controversial compromise far-reaching	amendments

Be aware of the methods for vocabulary recording that are out there and which ones work for you. For example, you might have a look at Lewis & Wilberg's seminal students' book *Business English*, in which they offer a whole range of ways to record vocabulary more effectively. Have a look also at *Teaching Collocation* by the same author. Details in the bibliography at the back of this book.

Source: Lewis 1993: 126; Lomb 2008: 140; EMCI 2002: 60; Walker 2005

B.70 Create a collocation dictionary

Aim: to collect vocabulary in context and in a format that is readily useable.
You will need: a separate notebook.

Create a collocation dictionary for your active language. That is a collection of pairs of words that are often found together. For example, in English the phrases 'a heated debate' or 'untold suffering' are used in preference to the many other pairs that would be technically correct, for example, 'an angry debate' or 'grave suffering'. If you are to be convincing in your active languages you too must use them.

B.71 Become a label spotter

Aim: to demonstrate, and familiarize yourself with, the breadth of a language's everyday vocabulary.
You will need: a big store.

Go to a large local DIY store, major department store, home-fittings store, or similar. You'll notice that every product has a little sign in front of it on the shelf telling you exactly what it is. Do you know how to say that in your active languages? And if so, do you know what verb goes with that object in the most common collocations? (For example, 'to operate an orbital sander', 'to fold away a sofa-bed'.)

In practice this is easier if you are in a country where your A language* is not spoken, because you'll see the product, know what it is in your own language and won't have to look anything up.

If you're in the country where your A language* is spoken and need to find out what a product is called in your other active language*, you can look it up online. This is best done by taking a smart-phone with you to the store and comparing the product with pictures of similar products in a similar store in a country where the other language is spoken. Don't use any translations you find online. Trust the pictures and the descriptions of the products!

Source: Woodman

B.72 Look up only what crops up (several times)

Aim: to make dictionary use more time-efficient.
You will need: reference works.

Some people might suggest looking up everything you're not sure of in a dictionary or, even better, in a couple of dictionaries – one bilingual, one monolingual. You could also look in a collocation dictionary. It might be a bit more time-efficient, however, only to look up words that you come across two or more times in quick succession, because if a word is coming up frequently then it's probably important, and the fact that it is recurring means it's more likely to be fixed, by repetition, in your memory. How many words do we look up and then forget? A lot.

B.73 Use Google images as a picture dictionary

Aim: to avoid dictionary translations and interference* between languages.
You will need: an internet connection.

Try looking up non-abstract technical terms in your foreign languages, not in a dictionary but in Google images. A picture will appear. Now you know what the thing is, but can you name it in your own language? If you can, this exercise will help you to avoid using or finding overly literal dictionary translations. If you can't, it's not a gap in your terminology that you have, but in your general knowledge!

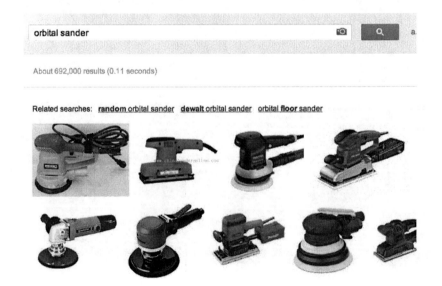

B.74 Wiki-parallels

Aim: to avoid dictionary translations and get into the habit of understanding words in context.
You will need: internet access.

Wikipedia now exists in many languages. If you look up an expression in one language you'll most likely be offered links in the left-hand menu to many other language versions. The advantage of this is that there will be a full explanation of the term in question, in both languages, which you can compare to be sure that one is really a good translation of the other.

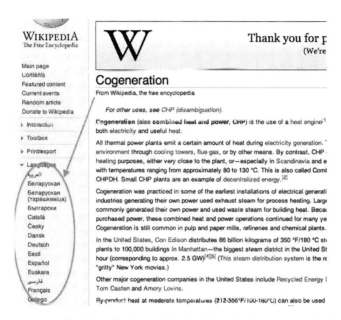

If the term you are looking for is medical or botanical you can check that the Latin term is the same in both entries; this can often be a useful check that the two entries really are talking about the same thing.

B.75 Read and record interesting terms

Aim: to increase the lexical and stylistic range of your active language.
You will need: a small notebook.

Spend about 15 minutes each day reading one article carefully and making a note of all the words and expressions that you wouldn't have used yourself. Try to use these words and expressions when writing or speaking your foreign language.

Source: Pergnier and Lavault 1995; Walker 2005; Guichot de Fortis 2009: 6

B.76 Stock expressions

Aim: to avoid overusing certain common expressions.
You will need: a notebook

Make lists of stock phrases* and of synonyms for frequently recurring words. Making the list will itself help you to recall these expressions when interpreting. And having them in a list to recall will help you to avoid overusing certain simple but common expressions, for example 'I think' or 'I agree'. You can then concentrate your efforts on translating the more original parts of the speaker's message, rather than spending time and effort on the mundane.

Example

Thank you very much
I'm very grateful for
Let me express my gratitude to

I agree
I share that view
I concur
I see it the same way

I think
To my mind
If you ask me
In my opinion

We all know that
It will come as no surprise that
I'm sure you're aware that
It's common knowledge that

B.77 The rise and fall of the synonym

Aim: to avoid overusing certain common expressions.
You will need: a notebook, a financial newspaper.

Take a stock market report in a financial newspaper and mark all the synonyms for 'rise' and 'fall' when referring to price. Because financial newspapers do a lot of reporting about the rise and fall of the stock markets, you'll find they are particularly rich in synonyms for certain frequently occurring expressions, including 'rise' and 'fall', as you can see in bold in the example below.

Note the expressions and try to use them where appropriate in your interpreting.

Example

Market Report: FlyBe falls to earth with profit warning

With London this weekend bidding farewell to thousands of athletes, one company happy to see them go will be FlyBe. Punters were pushing over each other to reach the emergency exit yesterday after the regional airline said the Olympics were partly to blame for its latest woeful update.

Since floating in 2010 at 295p-a-pop, the group has **shed more than three quarters of its value** following a number of profit warnings. Yesterday it was **nose-dived again**, **plummeting** 10.75p to 64.5p on the small-cap index after admitting its revenues for the year would be worse than previously thought.

...

Meanwhile, Liberum Capital's Peter Hyde – saying the update highlighted 'weakening UK demand' – said he 'would be taking profit' in FlyBe's rival easyJet, which **slipped back** 1.5 points to 555.5p.

The FTSE 100 narrowly failed to stretch its winning run to a sixth session, **creeping down** 4.4 points to 5,847.11, as Chinese trade figures proved worse than expected. Nonetheless, the top-tier index has still **added 220 points** over the past fortnight.

The appointment late on Thursday of Sir David Walker as Barclays' new chairman was well received, as the bank closed in the gold medal position after **advancing 4.45p to 183.4p**. Shore Capital's Gary Greenwood was certainly impressed – the analyst said the City grandee 'ticks all the right boxes', adding that he struggled 'to see how the board could have found a better candidate for the role'.

At the other end, Bunzl **was knocked back 54p to 1,112.5p** after UBS's Shang Liew recommended selling the plastic bag supplier, noting the stock **had jumped** by more than two-thirds over the past year.

...

A **20 per cent increase in the value** of Hugo Boss over the first-half of the year prompted SVG Capital – whose biggest investment is the German fashion house – **to tick up 4.3p to 264.8p**, with the private equity firm's **asset values up 12.3 per cent** in total.

Meanwhile, the news it had paid €10m for a 22 per cent stake in PIXmania, giving it full control of the electricals website, **saw** high street chain Dixons Retail **move 0.27p higher to 16.27p**.

Down on Aim, Mercury Recycling **was pegged back** 0.25p to 5.5p after saying it had received a letter 'from lawyers…'

Toby Green, *The Independent*, 11th August 2012
© The Independent
http://www.independent.co.uk/news/business/sharewatch/market-report-flybe-falls-to-earth-with-profit-warning-8031766.html

B.78 Crosswords

Aim: to practice rapid synonym activation*.
You will need: quick crosswords.

Do quick crosswords† in your active language(s). Buy a thesaurus and use it. The ability to find synonyms quickly is essential for the interpreter and this is a useful way to get regular, enjoyable practice.

† In British English, crosswords are divided between 'cryptic' and 'quick'. The latter require only that you come up with a synonym for the clue given. That's all you need. The former are considerably more complicated.

Source: Walker 2005

Across
3. talent that needs training
4. interpreting but not from in the meeting room
6. writing memory prompts
7. etc…

Down
1. following
2. substitute
3. father of consecutive note-taking
5. interpreters' workplace
8. etc…

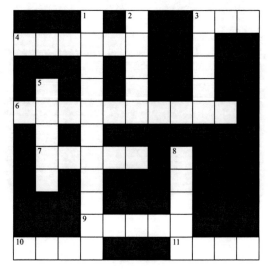

B.79 Link memory

Aim: to add technical terminology to your active vocabulary.
You will need: an illustrated technical dictionary.

Learn and practise the 'link' method of memorizing things (see exercise C.82). Now open a technical picture dictionary in your foreign language at five chosen sections and alternately 'link' items from the different sections. With 15 minutes work you can get 20 or more words a day into your active vocabulary like this. It is particularly effective for technical vocabulary (ie. machine parts) that is otherwise difficult to learn and that you may need to learn in a hurry.

The link method involves imagining a visual image of an object, larger than life and surreal if possible. Then 'link' it to a similarly unusual visual image of another object, and another, and another. It is extremely difficult to forget lists of words learned in this way. For more details on memory techniques like these, see Daniels, Lorayne and Lucas in the Bibliography.

B.80 Inter-language memory association

Aim: to add technical terminology to your active vocabulary.
You will need: a list of related terms you wish to learn.

Regardless of how obscure or entirely unlike any other word a technical term may be, you can remember it by associating it in your own mind with something that sounds similar, or looks similar in another language you know. Anything goes, because it is your memory that you have to inspire to remember things. For example, picture a man standing in the freezing cold and snow in front of a painter's easel dabbing the canvas with a lemon. Ridiculous enough to stick in your mind? Now note that 'dab' is the English name for a fish that in French is called 'limande' (which is close to the English 'lemon'), and that in Polish this fish is 'zimnica' ('zimne' is Polish for cold). For someone who knows these three languages those prompts are enough to recall the correct term. You can do the same for dozens of other fish, birds, animals, crop types, or indeed any group of terms that you need to learn in a hurry.

The British illusionist and memory expert Paul Daniels, best known for his TV magic shows in the 1980s, actually brought out a language course called the *Magic Language Memory Method* that was heavily reliant on this method of recalling vocabulary, and other memory specialists have described the same technique.

Source: Daniels, Lorayne and Lucas 1974: 45; Walker 2005

B.81 Cloze* exercise

Aim: to develop linguistic flexibility.
You will need: at least one other person.

One person reads aloud, or speaks, and then pauses mid-sentence. The others try to arrive at the largest number of grammatically sound alternative versions of the rest of the sentence. This will test the flexibility of your use of your active languages. It will also be useful later in the booth, where making it to the end of a sentence, whatever is going on around you, will be an imperative.

Example

[The relationship between China and Australia] is broad-based, strong and valued by both countries. Both countries see tremendous potential for…

> F. Adamson, Australian Ambassador to China
> 27th October 2011

[The relationship between China and Australia] is broad-based, strong and valued by both countries. Both countries see tremendous potential for…

… further exchanges.
… further cooperation on environmental issues.
… an acceleration of trade cooperation over the next few years.
… further engagement, particularly in the services sector.

Source: Visson 1999: 126; Kalina 2000: 180; Nolan 2005: 24

B.82 Synonym association

Aim: to increase flexibility in language use.
You will need: at least two other people.

Play word association games with your fellow students in your active languages. One person says a word, a second must offer a synonym or associated word as quickly as possible. A third person then does the same on the basis of the second person's offering.

B.83 Taboo

Aim: to practise language flexibility.
You will need: a set of the game Taboo, or make your own.

In this game, one person has a card with a word on it. They have to describe that word and the others have to guess what it is, or you have to get them to say it. But also on the card is a list of terms that are 'taboo', that is to say, which you cannot use in your explanation. Those terms are the ones that are most commonly used to describe the word.

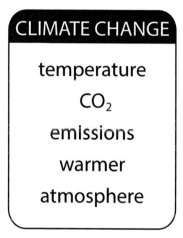

CLIMATE CHANGE

temperature

CO$_2$

emissions

warmer

atmosphere

This exercise is great practice for paraphrasing, either in your A language*, or your other active languages.

Source: Interpreter's Launchpad

B.84 Definition matching

Aim: to highlight subtle differences between similar terms.
You will need: some preparation time, at least two other people.

Take three words of similar meaning and one definition. Match the correct definition to the appropriate word, for example, country, nation, state. This could take the form of multiple choice, or a group exercise prepared by students for each other or by the trainer for the students. If students are doing the preparing, this exercise is an excellent way of highlighting such subtle differences in the meaning of important concepts.

The interpreter must be able to rapidly access a very exact linguistic version of the ideas he or she wishes to communicate. Done at speed, this exercise can help.

Source: Zalka 1989: 186

B.85 Terminology Bingo

Aim: to train for rapid translation of terms with no obvious counterpart in the target language*.
You will need: at least 3 other people, a list of 36 terms that have no obvious counterpart in the target language.

Create a grid of 6 by 6 boxes. In each box write a technical term or proper name that is difficult to translate into your B language* and distribute the grid to the whole group. The terms are called out in turn and participants must offer a B language* version (refereed by the others). If your version is acceptable then circle the box on your grid; the others must cross out that box on their grids. The aim is to get a row of four circled boxes.

Example

have a quorum	standing committee	immunity	roll-call vote
committee of inquiry	equal opportunities	bill	point of order
subsidies	transparency	budget discharge	waiver
table a proposal	eligibility	postpone the vote	Court of Auditors

Source: Szabó 2003: 105

Notes

1 'Le vocabulaire d'une langue est illimité et sa connaissance doit constamment être complétée.' Translated from the French by Andrew Gillies.
2 See the Gravitational Model of linguistic availability in Gile 1995: 212–23; and see also Lewis, *The Lexical Approach*.

Part C

Consecutive interpreting

This section suggests practice activities for some of the main elements of consecutive interpretation technique:

- Delivery
- Active listening and analysis
- Memory
- Note-taking
- Reformulation
- Self-monitoring
- Split attention

Delivery

However ambitious it may seem, your goal as a student interpreter is to speak, when interpreting, like a competent public speaker giving their own speech. The details of what exactly that means and how it is to be achieved will be part of your interpreting course, though you will also find pointers online. Here are a few exercises to help you achieve that goal.

Most of the exercises in this section are aimed at improving your speaking technique, rather than physiologically training up the parts of the body involved in speaking. The latter are the preserve of professional voice coaches and here I have neither the space nor the expertise to go into all the possible exercises they might recommend. If exercises C.1 and C.2 appeal to you, you will find references in the bibliography to guide you towards more voice training exercises. Alternatively, find a voice coach, or suggest to your interpreting school that they hire one to come and give your class some training.

C.1 Breathe

Aim: to slow down your breathing to promote better voice quality, and relax.
You will need: space to stretch your arms.

Stand with your feet about 50cm apart, leaving enough space around you to extend your arms, with shoulders relaxed, but not hanging down! Your chest is open, the ribcage in a natural position. Your hands are touching each other in front of your belly, palms facing upwards. Breathe in, lifting your arms gradually out to the sides until they are level with your shoulders. This movement should make you breathe in. When breathing out, let your arms gradually go back to the original position. Repeat ten times.

Take a deep breath, lifting your arms to the side again, and think you are breathing into your belly and your lower back. Your lungs need space to expand, that is why they push out your belly. Now bring your arms to the front but keep them at the height of your shoulders and form a circle with your thumb and index finger, as if you are holding a thin rubber band. Now exhale slowly, pulling this imaginary rubber band with your index finger and thumb until your arms are back out at 180°, level with your shoulders, and you run out of breath. This will help you control the amount of breath you exhale. Exhale very slowly as you are pulling the ' 'rubber band' and try to resist as long as possible. Exhale on a long 'sssss' or 'fffff' sound. Notice that 'fff' will make you exhale faster then 'sss'. Try to control the amount of air you exhale.

Voice coaches will ask you do this same exercise exhaling while you make a series of different sounds – p, t, k or h-h-h, or prrrr and brrrr. If you're interested in more of the same, check the bibliography or consult a voice coach.

Source: Mühle

C.2 Face massage

Aim: to improve diction and relax the face and parts of the body involved in speaking.
You will need: space to stretch your arms.

Massage your face, the underside of your jaw and the jaw muscles. Pull on your lips. Scrunch the face together and then stretch it apart. Pull funny faces (gurn)! Pull your hands down the front of your face, pulling your mouth open, relaxing the lower jaw and making a 'ha' sound as you do.

A lot of tension resides in the face, which can affect the quality of your voice and your stress levels.

Source: Mühle

C.3 Just a Minute 1

Aim: to practise public speaking under time pressure.
You will need: at least two other people.

'Just a Minute' is a UK radio game show in which one person must speak on a given subject, without hesitation or repetition, for 60 seconds or more. The speaker doesn't know in advance what the subject is. For this exercise, the subject is suggested by the others in the group and they then assess the speaker's performance according to a set of public-speaking guidelines you have been working with as part of your course.

Can you speak fluently and confidently on any subject at a few seconds' notice? This exercise will help you to sound confident even when you are not.

C.4 Just a Minute 2

Aim: to practise public speaking under time pressure.
You will need: at least two other people.

When you are comfortable with the Just a Minute exercise above (C.3), extend the time in which the speaker has to improvise towards 2 minutes and then add the following element to the exercise.

One of the people listening shows a card with a word or concept written in large letters on it. The person speaking must coherently incorporate the word/ concept on the card into the improvised speech.

A further stage is to show the card only to the speaker and not to the other listeners. The listeners must try to guess what was on the card from the speaker's intonation. If the speaker has mastered the art of controlled public speaking, they will not give away which word was on the card by, for example, sounding hesitant or smiling when they include that word in their improvised speech.

C.5 Talking to a mirror

Aim: to raise awareness about how you appear to others when speaking.
You will need: a mirror.

Practise speaking in front of a mirror. Check for twitches, gestures and the like. What impression do you make on the listener? If you or your school have a video camera, try using that too. If your mobile phone has a video camera, then use that.

Source: Heine 2000: 217

C.6 Tell it to grandma

Aim: to rediscover your natural speaking ability.
You will need: a speech.

Pick a topic or listen to a speech and then imagine you are explaining it to your grandmother or a relative from abroad who might not be familiar with the subject matter. You'll have to explain and communicate the subject more naturally, paying less attention to the detail of the information and more attention to making sure the listener understands what you're saying. This is communication!

C.7 Observe and copy

Aim: to improve your speaking skills by imitating the experts.
You will need: access to professional speakers' speeches or performances.

Observe professional speakers in, for example, national parliaments; note and try to emulate how and when they pause for breath, their rhythm and other oratorial techniques.

Source: Heine, 2000: 217

C.8 Write and deliver speeches

Aim: to practise debating skills and defending opinions that are not your own.
You will need: at least one other person.

Write and deliver speeches commenting on articles reported in newspaper articles, or imagine that you are trying to persuade a government official to change a certain rule. Record yourself or ask a colleague to listen. Are you convincing?

Source: Nolan 2005: 9

C.9 Defend controversial viewpoints

Aim: to practise debating skills and defending opinions that are not your own.
You will need: at least one other person.

Think up a controversial statement designed to spark a lively debate (if not within your group, then in society as a whole). Speak defending first one side of the argument and then the other. You can also do this exercise in groups for more realism.

Example

Bull-fighting is a perfectly valid form of sport that involves minimal suffering for the animal, who also has a fair chance to win the bout.

Complete disarmament is a utopian ideal that will never be achieved and we shouldn't even aspire to.

Students should pay for their tuition, rather than be subsidized by the government.

Source: Nolan 2005: 9

C.10 Create a debating society/role play

Aim: to practise speaking in a formal register in your active languages; to practise expressing views you do not hold personally.
You will need: at least two other people.

Meet up with fellow students and debate issues that might be debated at the sort of international meetings at which interpreters work. Choose a controversial topic and then assign a speaking role (and point of view) to each person in the group. For example, 'nuclear power', with speakers in the following roles: an environmentalist opposed to nuclear power; a representative of the nuclear industry; a government official arguing nuclear energy is the best environmentally sustainable energy source. Each speaker then goes away and prepares their speaking part and you all meet together again for the 'debate'.

If you want to make this exercise more realistic, you can base the roles on real people who represent the different points of view and research online for what they might say. So in the example above, a debate on nuclear power, you might assign the following roles: Executive Director of Greenpeace (Kumi Naidoo) and the CEO of Areva (Luc Oursel).

Interpreters, like lawyers, are called upon to advocate views that may be diametrically opposed to their own, without betraying those differences in their speech.

This exercise is a great warm up for interpreting on the same subject later the same day.

Source: also de Clarens 1973: 123

C.11 Impersonate

Aim: to practise using native-speaker intonation patterns.
You will need: audio or video recordings of comedians, politicians etc.

Learn off by heart and mimic 1–2 minute extracts from interviews, speeches and stand-up comedians in your active languages. Repeat not only the same words but copy the speaker's sentence intonation and pronunciation.

If you are not a natural speaker, or if you have very little experience of speaking in public, then this exercise will help to develop the correct sentence intonation and rhythm when speaking your active language(s).

Source: also Heine, 2000: 217; Gillies 2001: 63

C.12 Turn up the volume

Aim: to explore the boundaries of the acceptable in public speaking.
You will need: a small audience.

When practising public speaking, try varying the speed and volume of your speech. Learn through your own experience what your voice and brain are comfortable with and at the same time what your audience is comfortable with.

Source: Heine, 2000: 217

C.13 Reading aloud

Aim: to force yourself to enunciate grammatical structures and lexis that you would not normally encounter.
You will need: good quality written material.

Practise reading aloud a variety of texts, including narrative fiction, dialogue, news reports, and technical manuals. Record yourself and listen critically to your enunciation and intonation.

Apart from forcing you to use grammatical structures and vocabulary that you might not otherwise use, this exercise also reflects professional reality for interpreters, who are very occasionally called upon to read out pre-prepared translations. Language teachers will tell you that the written word can interfere with otherwise good pronunciation, and that is a difficulty to be overcome here.

Source: Van Hoof 1962: 107; Pergnier and Lavault 1995

C.14 Giving speeches for each other

Aim: to practise public speaking to an audience.
You will need: at least two other people.

Giving speeches to one another in practice groups is a great way to practise your public speaking skills and make sure everyone has plenty of practice material to interpret from. Apply the principles of good delivery that you have learnt as part of your course, other reading, or experience elsewhere. See also exercises A.20–24.

C.15 Napkin speeches

Aim: to get used to, and practise, speaking freely and at length on any subject.
You will need: a paper napkin, or a small piece of paper (5cm x 7cm).

One person prepares a speech of 20 minutes, to be delivered in three parts. The speaker is allowed only a paper napkin or one small piece of paper for any notes they may require. Learning by heart is not allowed.

Source: Lederer 2001: 176

C.16 Record and transcribe

Aim: to make yourself aware of the unnatural intonation that interpreting causes, and correct it.
You will need: a voice recorder, a speech to interpret from.

Record your interpretation and, for at least part of it, make a transcript in which you space out the words on the page proportional to the time between them as you spoke them. For example,

Example

> 'Thank .... you Mr Chairman I'd .... just .... like .... to come in on this .... point if I may. We in Sweden .... are particularly concerned by .... the .... issues raised in .... this .... document.'

This exercise will show you whether or not your intonation within sentences is natural. Putting the pauses in the wrong places in a sentence, or using the wrong intonation, is not only unpleasant for the listener but can, as you see in the example below, change the meaning of a given sentence or pair of sentences. (This is particularly true in non-inflected languages like English, but also in others.)

Imagine a listener hears the following from the interpreter.

Example

> 'This document has ..... been adopted by the Secretariat the Executive Committee and the Congress ....'

The meaning seems entirely clear. But what the listener only discovers later is the next part of the sentence...

> 'This document has .... been adopted by the Secretariat the Executive Committee and the Congress .... will vote on it when they next convene.'

Listeners can't see the actual punctuation. They hear it, from the interpreter. What the speaker really wanted to say was:

> 'This document has been adopted by the Secretariat. The Executive Committee and the Congress will vote on it when they next convene.'

Listeners will initially be unaware of the full stop and understand the remark to mean that the Executive Committee and Congress have also approved the document. This is very wrong, as we see from what follows. By the time the interpreter and/or the listener work this out and try to correct it, the damage has already been done.

C.17 Intonation is meaning

Aim: to demonstrate that in some languages intonation can make a huge difference to the meaning of the same words when spoken; to practise doing this yourself.
You will need: copies of the sheet below, a group of people.

Hand out a copy of the sheet below to everyone in the group. Divide up into pairs, with one person going into the booth, or playing the role of the interpreter. That person then has to read out the words in the left-hand column in such a way that they are understood to mean one of the three or four options in the right-hand column. Don't do them in order! The person listening must guess which of the options in the right-hand column the interpreter is trying to say.

Thank you Italy	1. Thank you to Italy
	2. Thank you. Italy has the floor next.
	3. Thank you. Italy do you wish to take the floor?
This is a great report	1. For our opponents
	2. But we need a plan, not a report
	3. But this other report is complete rubbish
	4. Well done, rapporteur.
Thank you	1. It's you, not me, who deserves the thanks
	2. You're annoyed, not grateful to receive this
	3. I'm grateful for this
	4. Thank you? I ought to hit you.
Is he all right?	1. She's OK, but what about him
	2. Surprised by bad news
	3. Deeply concerned to know what might have happened
	4. Querying whether he really is OK

These are just four examples. There are many more that you can create for yourselves.

C.18 Film or record yourself

Aim: to make yourself aware of how you appear to other people when you're speaking.
You will need: a video camera.

There is nothing like seeing yourself on film or hearing your own voice played back to you. It may not be pleasant, but if you are preparing to inflict yourself on paying customers you should be prepared to watch yourself working. Do you look and sound like a professional speaker? Why not?

It's a good idea to keep some of the very first films you make so that you can look at them a few months later, compare them with newer films, and see that you really have made some progress.

Source: Schweda-Nicholson 1985: 149

C.19 Create a real client

Aim: to recreate a situation in which the interpreter is genuinely communicating with an audience that hasn't understood the original.
You will need: at least two other people.

Often when you're practising you will find yourself in a situation where everyone in the room speaks both the target and the source language. This means that they listen differently to the interpretation from a real client who is dependent on the interpreter.

So when you're practising consecutive in groups of 3 or more with other students, nominate a speaker, an interpreter and then a 'client'. Send the 'client' out of the room so that they cannot hear the original speech, but call them back to listen to the interpreter's version. (They can either just listen to it, or interpret it consecutively using the first interpreted version as their original. It's best, though, to start off just listening.) Afterwards the 'client' should ask the interpreter questions wherever they are unsure about what they have just heard. Often, the interpreter will be able to answer the 'client's' questions, or clear up their queries. If they can't, ask the speaker to repeat that part of the original.

This exercise reminds us that consecutive is a communicative exercise, not a purely intellectual one like a crossword.

C.20 Stand in a corner

Aim: to practise projecting your voice.
You will need: a largish room, at least one other person.

If you have a problem making yourself heard, or you are softly spoken, try moving as far away in the room from your practice partners as you can and interpreting from there. In this way you are forced to project your voice further than you normally would. Classrooms tend to be much smaller, and often quieter, than the rooms and spaces in which interpreters really do consecutive, so it's a good idea to learn to project your voice.

C.21 Speak outdoors

Aim: to practise projecting your voice over background noise.
You will need: a park and good weather, or a station, and at least one other person.

Try doing some speaking practice or consecutive outdoors in a park, or perhaps a quiet station. Can you make yourself heard over the background noise?

Classrooms tend to be much quieter than the rooms and spaces in which interpreters really do consecutive, so it's a good idea to learn to project your voice over background noise.

C.22 Sight translation* with a time limit

Aim: to practise fluent delivery and voice projection under pressure.
You will need: a stop watch and timer, a text to sight translate.

Start by sight translating a text as per usual. Time how long it took. Now sight translate the same text again but set the timer for 2/3 of the time you took for your first effort.

Source: Van Hoof 1962: 115

C.23 Note-reading practice

Aim: to practise reading back notes.
You will need: a speech transcript.

Take notes from the transcript of a speech. Do it relatively quickly, without going back over the speech time and time again, but more slowly than if you were listening to the speech. When you've finished, read back the speech from your notes. Make sure that you are maintaining eye contact with your audience, as well as sticking to all the other principles of good delivery that you've learnt. In this way you can practise your note-reading and delivery without quite so much pressure.

C.24 Note-reading according to Jones

Aim: to practise simultaneously reading ahead in your notes without interrupting your interpreting.
You will need: speech transcript, notepad.

Take notes from the transcript of a speech. Do it relatively quickly, without going back over the speech time and time again. When you've finished, read back the speech from your notes. Try to apply the technique described by Roderick Jones below and you'll immediately see how your attention is divided between the tasks of talking, reading ahead and recalling what you've read.

There is a specific technique that interpreters can try to develop, and which can be compared to a pianist reading music while playing but not sight-reading. The pianist who has practised a piece is in a similar situation to the consecutive interpreter: essentially they know what they want to play but the sheet-music is there to remind them. The pianist looks at the opening bars and then starts playing, and continues reading ahead of the notes they are playing, their eyes on the music always being a little ahead of their fingers on the keyboard. Similarly the interpreter should look at the first page of their notes then start speaking while looking up at their audience. As the interpreter moves towards the end of the passage they have looked at, they glance down at their notes again to read the next passage. In other words they do not wait until they finished one passage to look again at their notes, which would mean that the interpretation would become jerky, reading then speaking, reading then speaking. Rather the interpreter, while still talking, is already reading ahead, preparing the next passage, thus providing for a smooth, uninterrupted and efficient interpretation.

Source: Jones 1998: 64

C.25 Try different equipment

Aim: to find out what works for you.
You will need: a variety of pens and pads.

Try taking notes on a variety of different size notepads – A4, reporter's pad, passport-sized pad, tall thin pad etc. – with a variety of different types of writing implement: thin felt tip, fat felt tip, rollerball, biro, pencil etc. Find out which you are most comfortable writing with, on what size pad, and which combination is easiest to use when reading back your notes. Although most teachers recommend a reporter's notepad and a biro – and this works best for most people – it may not be the case for you.

Active listening and analysis

Active listening and analysis mean listening to how a speech is built up, what it is really about, what are the main points and what the speaker is trying to say. It is also about listening to all of a speech, not drifting off in the middle and not missing a single word of what the speaker says. In this part of the book we again isolate a skill and practise it on its own. Practising the analysis of texts without the time pressure of interpreting can help automize the analysis task before you try doing the same thing in the heat of the interpreting action.

Many of the analysis exercises below can be done first as reading exercises from the transcripts of speeches, then from the spoken word. For what sort of texts to use, see exercises A.16–24 in 'Practice Material' above.

C.26 Concentrate!

Aim: to develop focus and stamina in your concentrated listening.
You will need: a speech recording or news broadcast.

When listening to a speech or news broadcast in the foreign language, concentrate on 'hearing out' every single word/syllable without allowing your attention to wander to, say, your plans for the weekend.

It is difficult to concentrate as intensely as the interpreter does and requires some practice. It is all too easy to listen inattentively to a language when we understand it well and/or to allow our attention to drift to other subjects. This exercise should help you balance that out, which is useful at an early stage in your course.

C.27 Train your concentration

Aim: to listen without distraction.
You will need: a TV, or some kids.

Increase your concentration levels by listening to and/or shadowing a speech recording while there's a lot of background noise. For example, while your kids are watching cartoons in the background, or outdoors in a park. Can you listen properly despite the background noise?

Classrooms tend to be much quieter than the rooms and spaces in which interpreters really do consecutive, so it's a good idea to learn to listen despite background noise. This exercise will increase your ability to concentrate deliberately on what you need to concentrate on without being distracted by what you don't need to listen to.

Source: Sherwood-Gabrielson *et al.* 2008: 224

C.28 News summaries

Aim: to practise summary skills and information ranking.
You will need: newspapers.

Increase your analytical skills by reading a newspaper or magazine. After finishing each article, try to summarize what you read in a single sentence. Start in your A language*, then try it in all your active languages. When you're comfortable with that, move on to listening to radio and TV news broadcasts and do the same after each item of news.

Interpreters need to understand the underlying, basic message a speaker is trying to get across. After all, can you really say you've understood something if you are not able to summarize it?

C.29 Text summaries

Aim: to prioritize main points from subordinate information.
You will need: a speech transcript (around one page of A4).

Read all or part of the transcript of a short speech in a limited time (for example, two minutes for half a page of A4). Even better, get someone to read it out for you. Summarize the content orally without looking again at the text. This exercise can be done source language into source language and then later into a target language.

Like consecutive proper, this exercise lets the interpreter see/hear the whole speech first, before anything is interpreted. This reinforces the task of analysis because the interpreter must understand the whole, rather than just its component parts.

Source: Visson 1999: 125

C.30 Speech summaries 1

Aim: to break down a speech into manageable sections.
You will need: at least one other person.

Listen to a speech. How many points did the speech contain? Summarize it orally immediately afterwards in your own words, first in the same language then in a target language. Start off summarizing very briefly and in later sessions include more detail.

Speeches are never uninterrupted streams of information. They are always made up of sections, either those the speaker put in place when writing, or those the listener and the interpreter define for themselves to make comprehension easier. Looking for, and finding, these sections can be very reassuring as they break down a speech into much more manageable parts.

Source: also Gile 1995: 212; Alexieva 1992: 222

C.31 Counting on your fingers

Aim: to identify links and the points they join.
You will need: at least one other person.

One person gives a relatively straightforward speech. The others count the logical links* in the speech on their fingers. Then one person gives a brief summary of the speech, counting off each link on their fingers as they go.

Speeches are never uninterrupted streams of information. They are always made up of sections. It is often logical links that create the bridge between these sections. Looking for, and finding, these sections can be very reassuring as they break down a speech into much more manageable parts.

Source: Lederer 2001: 169

C.32 Speech summaries 2

Aim: to prioritize main points from subordinate information.
You will need: a short (3–4 minutes) practical presentation.

Get a short video or audio presentation on a semi-technical subject such as repairing an appliance or an explanation of a scientific process. Listen without taking notes and try to recall and repeat the main points. (You'll find good examples at http://www.khanacademy.org/ or on similar sites.) Repeat this exercise, but this time allow yourself to jot down a few key words. Again reproduce as much as possible.

Notice how easy this is for a technical area you are already familiar with, and how much more difficult for one that is unfamiliar.

Source: Mikkelson 2000: 91

C.33 Speech summaries 3

Aim: to prioritize main points from subordinate information.
You will need: at least one other person.

Listen to a speech. After the speech, but before the interpreter gives their consecutive interpretation, ask the interpreter to give a summary of the speech in one or two sentences, answering these four questions: who, when, why, what? Then interpret the speech consecutively as per usual.

After all, can you really say you've understood something if you are not able to summarize it?

Source: Brehm

C.34 Speech summaries 4

Aim: to identify the main points of a speech independently of the register used by the speaker and/or their ability to present points in a clearly organized manner.
You will need: a speaker able to make simple points in complicated language and/ or in a deliberately disorganized way.

One person prepares a speech that contains several simple points of content but which is delivered in a high language register and/or in a poorly organized way. The interpreter must listen and give back a summary of only the main points of the speech.

Source: Van Hoof 1962: 106

C.35 Structured speeches 1

Aim: to get into the habit of analyzing speeches on more than just a linguistic level.
You will need: pre-prepared speeches.

Write short speeches with simple structures: for example, for/against/conclusion; past/present/future; etc. The listeners have to guess the structure of the speech as they listen. Listeners, notice how knowing the structure also helps to remember the speech.

Start with simple structures and move on to more complicated speeches and/ or analyses thereof. For example, a more complicated structure might be: three points in favour, the last divided into two sub-points; two points against, both divided into two examples; three points in conclusion, and so on.

C.36 Five-point speeches

Aim: to identify the main points of a speech.
You will need: a speaker.

One person prepares a short speech containing, say, five clear points. The listener agrees to note only five words while listening to the speech and interpret on the basis of those notes.

The other person must listen and analyze in order to decide which five words best represent the core points of the speech (which they then note). If you can't recreate most of the speech from your five-word notes, then you probably didn't choose the right words for you.

C.37 Interpret film plots

Aim: to demonstrate that understanding is the key to remembering and reproducing.
You will need: at least one other person.

One person relates the story of a film or book which the 'interpreter' at least has not seen. It should take about 10 minutes and be in the speaker's A language*. The interpreter interprets into their A language.

Source: Lederer 2001: 169

C.38 Monolingual interpreting

Aim: to practise analysis in isolation from language comprehension.
You will need: a speaker with the same A language* as you.

Interpret not from one language into another but into the same language (for example English into English). In practice this means paraphrasing the original, not parroting it. In doing this you have removed the element of linguistic comprehension of the original speech. Any failure to get across the message of the original will most likely be due to a failure to understand and analyse the structure, or note it effectively.

C.39 Chop up into sections

Aim: to identify the major sections of a speech.
You will need: two speech transcripts, at least one other person.

Using word-processing software, remove the paragraph divisions from the text of a speech. Even better, get another student to do it for you, and you for them, so that neither of you has seen the original layout of the speeches that both of you will be working with. Read through the unbroken text and hit the Return key twice every time you think the speaker has moved on to a new section (chunk) of his speech. This exercise is also called 'chunking'.

At first, speeches may sound like uninterrupted streams of words, but you will see that actually they are always made up of smaller, deliberately separate sections. These sometimes equate to paragraphs in a written text, but not always.

Example: before chunking…

Ladies and Gentlemen, Many thanks for inviting me here this evening. I have been asked to talk about 'Germany and Britain: Meeting the Economic Challenge Together'. I think the 'together' important. There is a great deal that we could do together and that we can learn from each other. As you would expect, I shall paint a positive picture. But there is one aspect which causes some concern. To be provocative – I fear that Britain and Germany have somehow drifted apart. Not so much at government level, where quite the contrary has happened, as I'll explain in a minute. But at a personal level. Twenty years ago, German was a major language in British schools and many school children would visit Germany on regular exchanges. Spanish has now overtaken German, and young people in Britain have less exposure to Germany as a result. The British Army on the Rhine was in those days some 65,000 strong. If you include families, relatives etc., that gave many more thousand British people reason to visit Germany. The army is now around 20,000: so again a fall off.

British Ambassador, Sir Peter Torry
British Chamber of Commerce in Germany
January 2004

Example: after chunking

Ladies and Gentlemen, Many thanks for inviting me here this evening.

I have been asked to talk about 'Germany and Britain: Meeting the Economic Challenge Together'. I think the 'together' important. There is a great deal that we could do together and that we can learn from each other. As you would expect, I shall paint a positive picture. But there is one aspect which causes some concern.

To be provocative – I fear that Britain and Germany have somehow drifted apart. Not so much at government level, where quite the contrary has happened, as I'll explain in a minute. But at a personal level.

Twenty years ago, German was a major language in British schools and many school children would visit Germany on regular exchanges. Spanish has now overtaken German, and young people in Britain have less exposure to Germany as a result. The British Army on the Rhine was in those days some 65,000 strong. If you include families, relatives etc., that gave many more thousand British people reason to visit Germany. The army is now around 20,000: so again a fall off.

When you compare your work on this exercise with others, you may well find that you mostly agree but that you've divided the text a sentence earlier or later in some places. That's because there is often a sentence that serves to lead into the next part of the speech. For example, 'But there is one aspect which causes some concern' in the example above. Whether we consider this sentence as the first sentence of one section or the last of the preceding section is not important; this sentence's purpose is to create a transition between two sections (and therefore belongs to both sections).

C.40 Jigsaw puzzle

Aim: to get you thinking about how and why different parts of a speech follow one another.

You will need: the printed transcript of part of a speech, scissors, at least one other person.

Take part of a simple speech that has a clear logic. Print out between five and seven paragraphs and then cut them up so that each paragraph is on a separate piece of paper. Shuffle the pieces of paper and spread them out on the table. Now ask someone who hasn't seen the original speech to arrange them in the correct order.

This exercise will force you to think about how the different parts of a speech fit together and why.

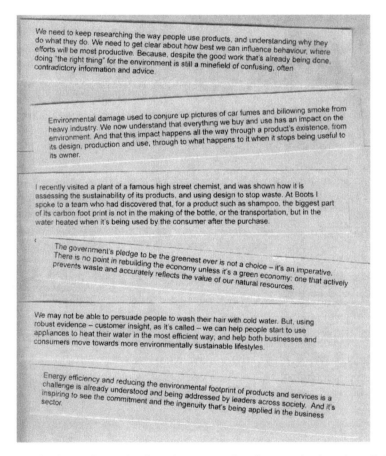

We need to keep researching the way people use products, and understanding why they do what they do. We need to get clear about how best we can influence behaviour, where efforts will be most productive. Because, despite the good work that's already being done, doing "the right thing" for the environment is still a minefield of confusing, often contradictory information and advice.

Environmental damage used to conjure up pictures of car fumes and billowing smoke from heavy industry. We now understand that everything we buy and use has an impact on the environment. And that this impact happens all the way through a product's existence, from its design, production and use, through to what happens to it when it stops being useful to its owner.

I recently visited a plant of a famous high street chemist, and was shown how it is assessing the sustainability of its products, and using design to stop waste. At Boots I spoke to a team who had discovered that, for a product such as shampoo, the biggest part of its carbon foot print is not in the making of the bottle, or the transportation, but in the water heated when it's being used by the consumer after the purchase.

The government's pledge to be the greenest ever is not a choice – it's an imperative. There is no point in rebuilding the economy unless it's a green economy: one that actively prevents waste and accurately reflects the value of our natural resources.

We may not be able to persuade people to wash their hair with cold water. But, using robust evidence – customer insight, as it's called – we can help people start to use appliances to heat their water in the most efficient way; and help both businesses and consumers move towards more environmentally sustainable lifestyles.

Energy efficiency and reducing the environmental footprint of products and services is a challenge is already understood and being addressed by leaders across society. And it's inspiring to see the commitment and the ingenuity that's being applied in the business sector.

The example above shows the first six paragraphs of a speech given by a British Minister, Lord Henley, at the Green Alliance conference in November 2010. http://ww2.defra.gov.uk/news/2010/11/11/henley-keynote-eco-design/

C.41 Spoken jigsaw puzzle

Aim: to to get you thinking about how and why different parts of a speech follow one another.
You will need: the transcript of part of a speech, scissors, at least four other people.

Take part of a simple speech that has a clear logic. Print out between five and seven paragraphs and then cut them up so that each paragraph is on a separate piece of paper. Shuffle the pieces of paper and give one to each person.

Each person reads and memorizes (more or less) what is on their piece of paper. Now put the pieces of paper away and in turn each person speaks the text they've just memorized. When everyone has recited their text, try to put the pieces of the speech, and the people, in the right order. You can each recite your texts as many times as is necessary. At the end the group should be lined up so as to be able to recite the speech in the correct order.

This exercise will force you to think about how the different parts of a speech fit together and why.

C.42 Identify the skeleton of meaning

Aim: to identify what is more, and what less, important in a speech.
You will need: a speech transcript, a highlighter pen.

Read the transcript of a speech. For each paragraph (or section) of the speech, highlight elements to make a sentence that sums up the whole paragraph or gives the essential of what is being said. The elements you underline don't have to follow one another directly in the text.

Example

> It is also true today, and will be for the foreseeable future, that Britain pays its way in the world by exporting manufactured goods. Around 60 per cent of our exports are manufactures. And whilst it is true that the balance of payments doesn't constrain economic policy in the immediate way it did 30 or 40 years ago, nonetheless ultimately a country must pay its way or face severe financial consequences. For Britain that means our manufacturing industry must be competitive.
>
> Patricia Hewitt, Secretary of State for Trade & Industry, UK
> at Merrill Lynch, London, January 2002

Even if you read only the highlighted text above, you get the most important part of the message.

In a variation on this exercise (Kalina 2000: 178) you can cover up the text and try to recreate the speech from memory. Or try to translate the hidden text into an active language.

C.43 Redaction

Aim: to prioritise information in a speech.
You will need: a speech transcript.

Take the transcript of a speech. Go through it as quickly as you can and with a marker pen black out what immediately appears to you to be redundant. Look at the text that is still visible afterwards. Does it still get the main message across? If not, you have mistakenly blacked out something important. Now go through the speech again and try to black out yet more redundancies. Leave only the essential parts of the message. Does it still get the main message across? Compare with another student's version. Can you do the same a third time with the same speech?

This exercise will help you to practise distinguishing the essentials from the decoration in a speech. This is important not only for understanding the speech as a whole and giving the right weight to the right parts of the speech when you interpret, but this skill will also come in handy when you have very fast speakers and it becomes necessary to compress the original in order to keep up.

Example

> Original:
> It is also true today, and will be for the foreseeable future, that Britain pays its way in the world by exporting manufactured goods. Around 60 per cent of our exports are manufactures. And whilst it is true that the balance of payments doesn't constrain economic policy in the immediate way it did 30 or 40 years ago, nonetheless ultimately a country must pay its way or face severe financial consequences. For Britain that means our manufacturing industry must be competitive.
>
> 1. ███████████████████████████████████ Britain pays its way in the world by exporting manufactured goods. ███ 60 per cent of our exports are manufactures. And whilst it is true that the balance of payments doesn't constrain economic policy ███████████████ ████████████ nonetheless ████████ a country must pay its way ████ ██████████████████. For Britain that means our manufacturing industry must be competitive.
>
> 2. ███████████████████████████████████ Britain pays its way in the world by exporting manufactured goods. ████████████ ██ ██ ██ ██████████████████████ ████ that means our manufacturing industry must be competitive.
>
> Patricia Hewitt, Secretary of State for Trade & Industry, UK
> at Merrill Lynch, London, January 2002

Even if you read only the highlighted text above, you get the most important part of the message.

C.44 Introduction to structure maps

Aim: to identify the function of each part of a speech, and recognize how parts of speech fit together.
You will need: a speech transcript, word-processing software, a pair of scissors.

Initially this exercise is probably best organized by a teacher. As you get better at it, students can create their own. In word-processing software the person organising the exercise creates a table of two columns and pastes the text of speech into the left-hand column. In the right-hand column they make a note of what they think is going on in each section of the speech.

Cut out each of the sections from the right-hand column and shuffle them up. Then give each pair of students doing the exercise one copy of the speech transcript (the left-hand column only) and one set of cut-out sections, in random order. Each pair of students has to arrange the cut-out sections next to the part of the speech they relate to. For instance, they might arrive at the example below.

Example

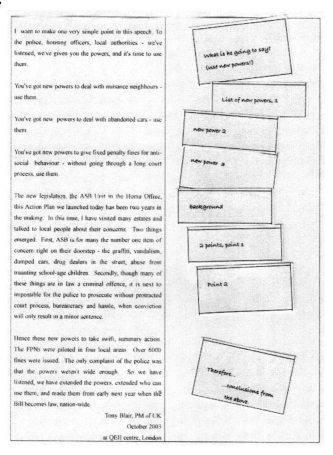

C.45 Create structure maps

Aim: to identify the function of each part of a speech.
You will need: a speech transcript, word-processing software.

Create a table of two columns and paste the text of the speech into the left-hand column. In the right-hand column make a note of what you think is going on in each section of the speech. Don't worry about the details of the content, this exercise is all about the structure. You should end up with something like the following.

Example

I want to make one very simple point in this speech. To the police, housing officers, local authorities – we've listened, we've given you the powers, and it's time to use them.	**What is he going to say? (Use new powers!)**
You've got new powers to deal with nuisance neighbours – use them.	**List of new powers, 1**
You've got new powers to deal with abandoned cars – use them.	**new power 2**
You've got new powers to give fixed penalty fines for anti-social behaviour – without going through a long court process, use them.	**new power 3**

The new legislation, the ASB Unit in the Home Office, this Action Plan we launched today has been two years in the making. In this time, I have visited many estates and talked to local people about their concerns. Two things emerged. First, ASB is for many the number one item of concern right on their doorstep – the graffiti, vandalism, dumped cars, drug dealers in the street, abuse from truanting school-age children. Secondly, though many of these things are in law a criminal offence, it is next to impossible for the police to prosecute without protracted court process, bureaucracy and hassle, when conviction will only result in a minor sentence.	**background** **2 points, 1** **2**
Hence these new powers to take swift, summary action. The FPNs were piloted in four local areas. Over 6000 fines were issued. The only complaint of the police was that the powers weren't wide enough. So we have listened, we have extended the powers, extended who can use them, and made them from early next year when the Bill becomes law, nation-wide. Tony Blair, PM of UK October 2003	**Therefore...** **...conclusions from the above.**

You can also do this exercise with spoken speeches, in which case the spoken word replaces what's in the left-hand column, which remains blank, and you note the structure map in the right-hand column again. You can also note the structure map directly onto a blank piece of paper.

Source: Gillies 2005: 23

C.46 Mind Maps

Aim: to practise organizing points in your mind by organizing them on paper first.
You will need: a piece of paper, a mind.

Create a mind map of a speech. Try this first from transcripts of speeches and later from the spoken word. Can you recreate the speech from a mind map? Does mind mapping improve the way you analyze a speech? What is mind mapping? Time to find out!

Write the title of the subject in the centre of the page, and draw a circle around it. For each major part of the speech draw lines out from this circle. Label these lines with any additional information or subheadings. Can you recreate the speech in the same language? Or interpret it into another using this mind map? Compare your mind map with the other students in the group.

For more information see http://www.mindtools.com/pages/article/newISS_01. htm

Example

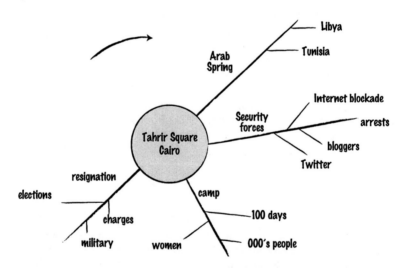

This example is just one type of mind map. There are many more you can find out about for yourselves online.

Source: Szabó 2003: 134; Nolan 2005: 298

C.47 Notes on a single page

Aim: to practise organizing points in your mind and on the page.
You will need: a piece of paper.

When listening to a speech that you are going to interpret consecutively, set yourself the task of taking all your notes on a single piece of paper (no bigger than A4!). This limitation will force you to think more about what you are hearing, what you are noting and how the relationships between parts of the speech can be expressed on the page. You should see the structure of the speech start to appear more clearly on the page.

Source: Walker, D.

C.48 Le fil rouge

Aim: to identify the main message of a speech.
You will need: a speech.

This is the favoured technique of, among others, the Parisian interpreting schools. It is based upon the fact that if you understand the whole speech and its message, you can then use logic to remember what you have to say. The technique is an extended exercise in analysis.

As you are listening, ask yourself the following questions about not only the speeches with which you are practising interpreting, but also the interviews, radio and internet programs that you listen to. Take no notes, but use the answers to these questions to try to recreate the speech/interview etc afterwards.

Practise several times with the first lot of questions below, and when you feel comfortable with that, for subsequent speeches ask yourself the next batch of questions as well. And so on.

Whenever you haven't been given the information needed to answer one of the questions below, make a mental note of this. That gap, in itself, may help you to recreate the speech.

- ask yourself **who**, **what**, **to whom**, whenever you listen to something.
- what are the **causes** and **consequences** being described?
- **why** is this information given? (What is the speaker getting at?)
- **what** is the speaker **not saying** and why?
- **what** is the speaker likely to say **next**?

Source: also Borg, Interpreters and Conference Interpreting Forum

C.49 Identify ideas*

Aim: to identify the smallest meaningful units of a speech.
You will need: a speech transcript, word-processing software.

Using word-processing software remove the line divisions from the text of a speech. (Even better, get another student to do it for you, and you for them, so that neither of you have seen the original layout of the speeches you'll be working with.) Read through the unbroken text and hit the Return key twice every time you can identify a subject, its verb, and, often but not always, its object. Do this in such a way that each separate part of the text created in this way makes sense on its own. These small bits of speech are 'ideas*' (and will each become a unit on your notepad page.)

Speeches may sound like uninterrupted streams of words at first, but you will see that actually they are always made up of smaller, deliberately separate sections. And those sections are split again into smaller units – ideas. Ideas, in this sense of the word, are the smallest meaningful parts of the speech. These sometimes equate to sentences in a written text, but not always.

Example

This is the original text without the original paragraph breaks in it. Below is the version where I have hit 'return' each time I saw the end of a Subject Verb Object group.

In the areas for which I have some responsibility, there were also, as the Prime Minister has mentioned, some important developments at Feira. We took stock of the European Union's relations with Russia and the situation there, including in Chechnya, in the light of the recent EU-Russia Summit, which I think was regarded as fairly successful. It is too early to judge President Putin's economic programme; however, our basic message is that a sound programme will be vital to boost investor confidence. On Chechnya, there have, it is true, been some recent *moderately* positive developments in response to international and European Union pressure: for example the recent ECHO mission was able to take place and western humanitarian agencies have greater access to the area. The conflict nevertheless continues and we still have considerable concerns. In particular, we want to see much greater access for humanitarian aid agencies. We want to see genuinely independent investigation into reports of human rights abuses, and we want to see a real dialogue between the Russian government and the Chechens.

EU Commissioner Chris Patten
European Parliament on July 3rd 2000

In the areas for which I have some responsibility, there were also, as the Prime Minister has mentioned, some important developments at Feira.

We took stock of the European Union's relations with Russia and the situation there, including in Chechnya, in the light of the recent EU-Russia Summit, which I think was regarded as fairly successful.

It is too early to judge President Putin's economic programme;

however, our basic message is that a sound programme will be vital to boost investor confidence.

On Chechnya, there have, it is true, been some recent *moderately* positive developments in response to international and European Union pressure:

for example the recent ECHO mission was able to take place and western humanitarian agencies have greater access to the area.

The conflict nevertheless continues

and we still have considerable concerns.

In particular, we want to see much greater access for humanitarian aid agencies.

We want to see genuinely independent investigation into reports of human rights abuses,

and we want to see a real dialogue between the Russian government and the Chechens.

Notice how short some of the ideas are and how long others are. But the long ones couldn't be made any shorter without some part of them no longer making sense on its own.

Source: Gillies 2005: 38

C.50 Highlight the links*

Aim: to identify and show links on the page.
You will need: a speech transcript.

Practise finding links in the transcripts of speeches by highlighting them in the text as you read. This exercise can be done on paper or digital versions of the transcript as long as you have a way of highlighting.

Example

In the areas for which I have some responsibility, there were also, as the Prime Minister has mentioned, some important developments at Feira.

We took stock of the European Union's relations with Russia and the situation there, including in Chechnya, in the light of the recent EU-Russia Summit, which I think was regarded as fairly successful. It is too early to judge President Putin's economic programme; however, our basic message is that a sound programme will be vital to boost investor confidence.

On Chechnya, there have, it is true, been some recent *moderately* positive developments in response to international and European Union pressure: for example the recent ECHO mission was able to take place and western humanitarian agencies have greater access to the area. The conflict nevertheless continues and we still have considerable concerns. In particular, we want to see much greater access for humanitarian aid agencies. We want to see genuinely independent investigation into reports of human rights abuses, and we want to see a real dialogue between the Russian government and the Chechens.

EU Commissioner Chris Patten
European Parliament on July 3rd 2000

C.51 Ideas* and Links* – introduction to note structure

Aim: to identify, and show on the page, ideas and links.
You will need: a speech transcript, word-processing software.

This exercise shows how ideas and links between them can become notes on the consecutive notepad. It's also an exercise in breaking down and analyzing the speech.

Using word-processing software remove the line divisions from the text of a speech. (Even better, get another student to do it for you, and you for them, so neither of you have seen the original layout of the speeches you'll be working with.) Read through the unbroken text and hit the Return key twice every time you can identify a subject, its verb and, often but not always, its object. Do this in such a way that each separate part of the text created in this way makes sense on its own. These small parts of the speech are 'ideas*' (and will each become a unit on your notepad page).

Speeches may sound like uninterrupted streams of words at first, but you will see that actually they are always made up of smaller, deliberately separate sections. Ideas, in this sense of the word, are the smallest meaningful parts of the speech. These sometimes, but not always, equate to sentences in a written text.

When you've done that, find and highlight the links in the text!

Example

This is the original text without the original paragraph breaks in it. Below is the version where I have hit 'return' each time I saw the end of a Subject Verb Object group, and links have been highlighted and underlined.

In the areas for which I have some responsibility, there were also, as the Prime Minister has mentioned, some important developments at Feira. We took stock of the European Union's relations with Russia and the situation there, including in Chechnya, in the light of the recent EU-Russia Summit, which I think was regarded as fairly successful. It is too early to judge President Putin's economic programme; however, our basic message is that a sound programme will be vital to boost investor confidence. On Chechnya, there have, it is true, been some recent *moderately* positive developments in response to international and European Union pressure: for example the recent ECHO mission was able to take place and western humanitarian agencies have greater access to the area. The conflict nevertheless continues and we still have considerable concerns. In particular, we want to see much greater access for humanitarian aid agencies. We want to see genuinely independent investigation into reports of human rights abuses, and we want to see a real dialogue between the Russian government and the Chechens.

EU Commissioner Chris Patten
European Parliament, July 3rd 2000

After:

In the areas for which I have some responsibility, there were also, as the Prime Minister has mentioned, some important developments at Feira.

We took stock of the European Union's relations with Russia and the situation there, including in Chechnya, in the light of the recent EU-Russia Summit, which I think was regarded as fairly successful.

It is too early to judge President Putin's economic programme;

however, our basic message is that a sound programme will be vital to boost investor confidence.

On Chechnya, there have, it is true, been some recent *moderately* positive developments in response to international and European Union pressure:

for example the recent ECHO mission was able to take place and western humanitarian agencies have greater access to the area.

The conflict nevertheless continues

and we still have considerable concerns.

In particular, we want to see much greater access for humanitarian aid agencies.

In doing this exercise you are creating a representation of the division between ideas and the links that join those same ideas together. This exercise is also a good introduction to note-taking.

C.52 Note only the links*

Aim: to identify links and see if they work as memory prompts for you.
You will need: a speech transcript, word-processing software.

Practise note-taking from the texts of speeches, noting only the link words in the margin (or only link words plus one word per paragraph). Try to reproduce the speech from your notes.

It is worth consulting with other students and teachers to see whether they agree with your choice of link words. Not all words that can be used as links are necessarily being used as links. This will help to develop your analytical skills as you are forced to justify your choices to others and they offer you their viewpoint.

(The breaks between sections are noted with the symbol **ll**, the lack of a link being as important as the presence of one.)

Example

In the areas for which I have some responsibility, there were **also**, as the Prime Minister has mentioned, some important developments at Feira.	**also**
We took stock of the European Union's relations with Russia and the situation there, including in Chechnya, in the light of the recent EU-Russia Summit, which I think was regarded as fairly successful. It is too early to judge President Putin's economic programme; **however**, our basic message is that a sound programme will be vital to boost investor confidence.	**ll** **but**

On   Chechnya,   there   **||**
have, it is true, been some
recent *moderately* positive
developments in response to
international and European
Union pressure: **for example**   **eg.**
the recent ECHO mission was
able to take place and western
humanitarian agencies have
greater access to the area. The
conflict **nevertheless** continues   **but**
and we still have considerable   **and**
concerns. **In particular**, we want   **eg.**
to see much greater access
for humanitarian aid agencies.
We want to see genuinely
independent investigation into
reports of human rights abuses,
and we want to see a real
dialogue between the Russian   EU Commissioner Chris Patten
government and the Chechens.   European Parliament on July 3rd
2000

C.53 Hands up if your hear a link

Aim: to identify links.
You will need: a speech.

One person gives a speech and raises their hand (or stamps their foot) whenever
they speak a logical link during their speech. To make the exercise more
challenging, make it the listeners, and not the speaker, who have to raise their
hands when they hear a link.

Initially those listening will only be listening. Later you can do the same
exercise while the listeners are also taking notes (and later expected to give the
speech back).

C.54 Give note-taking structure to a text

Aim: to depict the structure of the speech on the page, and practise breaking speeches down.

You will need: a speech transcript, word-processing software.

You have probably been introduced to note-taking techniques aimed at creating a certain structure on the page, a structure that makes it easier to read the notes back. These might include separating ideas* from one another on the page; starting on the left and noting diagonally across the page (perhaps Subject, Verb, Object); noting links* on the left; noting lists vertically on the page; and noting qualifying information directly underneath that which it qualifies.

In the example below, all of these techniques have been applied to a speech transcript using only the Return and Tab keys.

There is no one right or wrong way to do this exercise, but regular practice will get you into the habit of recognizing the structures within a speech.

Example: before

> Environmental damage used to conjure up pictures of car fumes and billowing smoke from heavy industry. We now understand that everything we buy and use has an impact on the environment. And that this impact happens all the way through a product's existence, from its design, production and use, through to what happens to it when it stops being useful to its owner.
>
> The government's pledge to be the greenest ever is not a choice – it's an imperative. There is no point in rebuilding the economy unless it's a green economy: one that actively prevents waste and accurately reflects the value of our natural resources.
>
> Lord Henley, at Green Alliance conference
> November 2010
> http://ww2.defra.gov.uk/news/2010/11/11/henley-keynote-eco-design/

Example: after

> Environmental damage
>
>   used to conjure up pictures of
>
>   car fumes and
>   billowing smoke from heavy industry.

We now
          understand
that

everything we buy and
          use

          has an impact

                    on the environment.
And
that

this impact
          happens
                    all the way through a product's existence,
                    (from its design,
                              production and use,
                              through to what happens to it when it
                              stops being useful to its owner)

The government's pledge to be the greenest ever

                    is not

                              a choice –
                              it's an imperative.

There is no point in rebuilding the economy

unless it's

                    a green economy:
                    one that

                              actively prevents waste and
                              accurately reflects the value
                              of our natural resources.

C.55 Create information hierarchies

Aim: to rank information by order of importance.
You will need: one other person, news articles.

One person compiles several pieces of information, in no particular order, and presents them to the others in the group. Rather than interpret or memorize the information, they have to organize it in order of importance. This exercise helps not only to develop your ability to discriminate between more and less important information, but it also offers you an opportunity to work with information relating to topical events and thus improve your general knowledge.

Example

> Great Britain. The discovery, on Monday, of secret plans to prevent terrorist attacks at Heathrow has reignited fears of a terrorist attack in the UK. Scotland Yard has begun an investigation into the loss of the plans, found on the roadside by a motorist. The plans included a schedule of security patrols, the position of marksmen on roofs, road closures and escape routes that terrorists might use.
>
> (Taken from a news item 2004)

Let's look at what you might do with the elements above. First, you establish the subject area (the fight against terrorism) and then describe the broader context (September 11, the Iraq war, US-UK coalition). Then establish the specific subject of the text (the threat of terrorist attacks in the UK). Next, establish a ranking of the pieces of information in descending order of importance: the existence of plans relating to terror attacks (with sub-list of schedules, marksmen, road closure, escape routes); the loss/theft of these plans; the immediacy of the threat.

- the fight against terrorism (September 11, the Iraq war, US-UK coalition)
- the threat of terrorist attacks in the UK
- the existence of plans relating to terror attacks (schedules, marksmen, road closure, escape routes)
- the loss/theft of these plans
- the immediacy of the threat
- documents found on the roadside, Heathrow airport, Monday, Scotland Yard investigation, motorist.

Source: Kremer 2005: 787

C.56 Connective exercises

Aim: to anticipate the relationships between pieces of information.
You will need: two other people.

One person creates and reads out, or notes on a whiteboard, a series of unlinked phrases. Someone else then has to give a short speech joining the same phrases back together, using links*, to arrive at a plausible end result. It might be an idea to work in pairs the first few times you do this exercise, to get the hang of it, and then later to try it alone.

In the example below the links are underlined.

Example 1

Cold War over
Japan claims control over Kuriles
Gorbachev's visit to Japan unsuccessful.

The Cold war is long since over <u>but</u> tensions still exist between Japan and Russia as a result of Japan's territorial claim to the Kuriles islands. It was this issue <u>that led to</u> Gorbachev's visit to Japan ending in failure.

Example 2

Abortion in Britain may be performed up to the 28th week
The termination of pregnancy after the 20th week involves considerable risk
Long waiting lists at the NHS leave women no choice.

Abortion in Britain may be performed up to the 28th week <u>even though</u> the termination of pregnancy after the 20th week involves considerable risk for the pregnant woman. Unfortunately, <u>because</u> waiting lists are so long in the NHS women are often left with no choice but to have abortions after week 20.

This type of exercise is very useful because it trains you to give shape to points to be made, convey them more clearly and, finally, learn to build a text.

Source: Ballester and Jimenez 1992: 241

C.57 Re-introducing context

Aim: to practise analyzing what is implicit in what is explicitly mentioned.
You will need: at least one other person, a series of newspaper headlines (preferably current).

One person presents a newspaper headline. The others must then expand on the headline by adding in as much historical and contextual information as they can think of and by making explicit anything that is implicit. At first this can take the form of a group brainstorming session. But later each person should be able to do this immediately in the form of a presentation or speech. Prompt each other with questions if necessary.

Example 1

Having turned a blind eye over many years the US is now pursuing doping in sport seriously

Despite the use of performance enhancing drugs in athletics particularly, but also in other sports like cycling, being an open secret, in the past the US authorities have not dealt with the issue as a criminal matter. This has now changed with a number of high profile police raids and a statement from the police outlining their current (new) approach. The IOC has long been accused of ignoring the issue, but the establishment of WADA, the Anti-Doping Agency, with American support seems to herald a new approach.

Example 2

You can also ask yourself, or each other, questions to prompt more information.

Bhopal victims will be paid compensation

Q: What happened in Bhopal? (Where is Bhopal?)
A: In 1984, in Bhopal in India, there was a chemical disaster, the Union Carbide chemical plant explosion, which killed thousands immediately and tens of thousands in the years that followed.

Q: Why is compensation an issue so long afterwards?
A: Because the owners refused to accept responsibility for the accident. Victims will now receive compensation for their injuries and the loss of loved ones. It is a major step forward for campaigners who see this not only as a victory against Union Carbide, which has long refused to pay compensation, but also as a precedent in similar campaigns against large multi-nationals who are rarely held to account for acts of environmental pollution.

Source: Kremer 2005: 787

C.58 Uncover the implicit

Aim: to learn from a professional commentator how to read what is left implicit in political speeches.
You will need: access to the internet.

Sometimes set-piece political speeches are printed in full in newspapers or online and then analyzed by expert commentators. Don't miss the opportunity to read and learn from these. Speeches are always made in a political and historical context and well-informed journalists are excellent at explaining that context to us. When you've seen a few examples like the one below – in which the actual speech is reprinted centre page and the journalist's analysis either side – see if you can do the same with contemporary speeches. It's best to take contemporary speeches because it is very difficult to recreate the context of a speech given in the past.

C.59 Semantic Network Activation* 1

Aim: to improve the process of choosing what to note.
You will need: at least one other person, a notepad, some ideas.

One person describes a context and a word or phrase that describes a significant participant in that context. The other person has to build as many semantic networks (that is, describe as many relations as possible) between the two.

Example

Context : the environment
Participant: CO_2

Possible semantic networks
- One of the major problems our environment faces is the build up of CO_2 in the atmosphere.
- CO_2 is one of a series of gases that causes global warming, a major environmental issue at present.
- etc. etc.

Source: Alexieva 1994: 203

C.60 Semantic Network Activation* 2

Aim: to improve the process of choosing what to note.
You will need: at least one other person, a notepad, some ideas.

One person creates a short set of notes (see below) and shows them to the other person. They also then describe the context in which the notes function. The other person has to build as many semantic networks (that is, describe as many relations as possible) between the notes and the context.

Example

Context: pollution prevention can be profitable in German steel industry
Notes:

> *recycle*
> > *90% water*
> > > *solid wastes*

Possible semantic network:
- 'The German Steel Industry has developed no-waste technologies. It recycles 90% of its industrial water and converts 90% of the solid wastes into useful materials.'

Source: Alexieva 1994: 203

C.61 Note-taking from lectures

Aim: to learn listening and analysis techniques from the non-interpreting world.
You will need: an open mind.

It is a fact that is sometimes overlooked in the interpreting world, but note-taking was not invented by, or for, conference interpreters. Nor are they the only people who take notes from spoken presentations and speeches. For centuries people have taken, and they continue to take, notes in lecture halls and at conferences all over the world. It's worth having a look at the strategies that are employed in this type of note-taking, as they are heavily reliant on analysis of the structure and function of the incoming speech to create clear and useful notes. The strategies will not all be directly applicable to consecutive note-taking, but many of them are.

Source: Kesselman-Turkel and Peterson 1982

C.62 Note-taking with time lag

Aim: to listen to longer parts of a speech before noting and so promote analysis.
You will need: a spoken speech, a notepad.

When note-taking, try to maximize the time-lag between hearing the original and noting anything. What are the one or two words that you could note that will sum up a whole section of the speech for you? Can you note less because you've listened to more (before noting anything down)?

This exercise will require a more thorough analysis and understanding of the incoming speech. If we simply write what we hear when we hear it, we are not analyzing what we hear. Remember though, a big time-lag is not a goal in itself, it merely facilitates analysis of the original speech, by stealth if you like.

C.63 Semantic dictation

Aim: to listen to, and understand, a whole speech.
You will need: at least one other person.

One person reads out, or preferably speaks, a passage of text a couple of minutes long in the B language* of the listeners. Ideally the speaker is using their A language*. The passage might be a short description of an individual or, later, a longer chronological narrative. The others listen, and when the speaker has finished they write down a version of what they have heard in the same B language*. The end result should be somewhere between a half and a full page of A4.

This exercise can be used as an introductory exercise for consecutive interpreting because you will have much more time to think about what you've heard and how to reproduce it in writing than you would if you were interpreting consecutively.

Source: Tryuk 2002: 56

C.64 Take notes after the speech

Aim: to analyze the speech as a whole before deciding how to note it.
You will need: a speaker.

Listen to a speech without taking notes. When the speech has been completed, make some notes that will help you to reproduce the speech. Give a consecutive rendering of the speech.

By hearing the whole speech first and only then making notes we have a picture of the entire speech that we must analyze in order to make the most useful notes possible. Our notes are therefore much more likely to reflect the structure and the underlying meaning of the speech rather than getting hung up on the individual words.

Source: Weber 1989: 166

C.65 Take notes but don't use them

Aim: to demonstrate (in order to later avoid) that note-taking detracts from listening.
You will need: a speaker, a notepad.

While listening to a speech, take consecutive notes as per usual. At the end of the speech put your notes to one side and try to reproduce the speech from memory.

The fact that this is difficult will demonstrate very clearly how much attention we devote to our notes when in fact we should be listening to the speaker more carefully. Repeat the exercise, this time listening more carefully to the speaker.

Source: Seleskovitch and Lederer 1989: 59

C.66 Analyze how speeches are written

Aim: to learn how speeches are written in order to facilitate analysis of other speeches.
You will need: speech-writing guides.

You'll find lots of guides on how to write speeches on-line or in your university library. It's worth reading them and concentrating on those types of speeches that you are most likely to be asked to interpret (see A.16). From these guides make a list of the main recommendations for someone wishing to write a given type of speech, for example, a speech when making an award to someone.

Example

In his book *Writing Great Speeches*, Alan Perlman (1998: 69–80) suggests the following guidelines for public speakers introducing other speakers.

Speeches of introduction should...

1 give a sense of what is to come
2 familiarize the audience with the speaker's achievements
3 create a sense of anticipation
4 add finesse to the obvious.
5 be maximum 7 minutes in length
6 be positive always
7 build suspense
8 include quotes
9 link to theme of today's conference
10 be characteristic of speaker to follow plus illustration of same
11 give applause markers e.g. 'please join me in welcoming...'

(These are numbers assigned for the purposes of this exercise, not by Perlman.)

Then find examples of that type of speech on-line and compare them with the list of recommendations. Have the recommendations been put into practice? Most likely you'll see that some or most of them have, even though the speaker may not have read the same guidelines as you. That's because they, or their speech-writer, will have learnt to write speeches somewhere, and because the conventions of how to write speeches are limited in number.

Start with the texts of the speeches and later do the same with recordings of the spoken word. The numbers in superscript in the text below correspond to recommendations in the list above.

It's my great pleasure to welcome you to our 39th annual conference on bank structure and competition. This year's focus on corporate governance[1][9] is especially relevant.

We've seen too many once-revered companies end up severely damaged, in some cases beyond repair, by failures in corporate governance, Arthur Andersen, Enron...[9].

Those of you in financial firms are affected through your credit exposure to firms that followed questionable accounting practices, and through your own corporate governance practices. This has led to greater investor skepticism and increased uncertainty in the equity and credit markets...[3].

During the conference you'll be discussing these issues in greater detail[1].

The role of boards of directors. Changes in financial regulation, accounting standards and disclosure rules. The impact on financial firms and financial markets[1].

In this effort, we have enlisted some of the most prominent members of the financial industry to speak with you this week[9]. They include banking executives, regulatory authorities, administration officials and financial and legal scholars[1].

Perhaps the most eagerly awaited speaker in this stellar line-up[7], however, is the person I'm about to introduce[7] – a man, really, who needs no introduction[3][4]. We have the privilege of hearing from someone whose accomplishments and stature have made him a respected name throughout the world[9]. Someone[7] whose words are analyzed by everyone from Wall Street to Main Street[2]. And someone whose unquestioned integrity[4] stands out even more brightly today, at a time when negative behavior seems to be darkening the news[3][4][9].

He is Alan Greenspan, chairman of the board of governors of the Federal Reserve System[2]. Alan, we wish you could be here in person, as you have been every year since the conference began. But we know you've been advised, after minor surgery, to stay put for a while[6]. Alan Greenspan is serving his fourth four-year term as chairman[2], having been designated to this position by Presidents Reagan, Bush Senior and Clinton. It was in August 1987 when he originally took office as chairman and to fill an unexpired term on the Board[2]. He also serves as chairman of the Federal Open Market Committee[2], the System's principal monetary policymaking body.

Most important, as I'm sure you're all aware[9], the current President Bush thinks 'Alan Greenspan should get another term,' and the chairman has said he'll serve if nominated. I think we'd all agree this is great news for our country and for the economy.

The details of Alan's background and his tremendous achievements are well documented[4]. His bachelors, masters and doctorate degrees in economics from New York University[2]. His 30-year career as head of Townsend-Greenspan, an economic consulting firm in New York City[2]. And his service as chairman of the President's Council of Economic Advisers under President Ford[2], as well as on many other public and private boards[2].

He's received numerous awards and honors for his work, and his outstanding reputation and extraordinary talents are widely known[2]. Over the course of more than a decade, his adept handling of his complex responsibilities at the Fed have made him a hero – not only to people in business and government, but to millions of average citizens from all walks of life. It's truly a great honor to have the chairman as our keynote speaker[7].

Please join me in welcoming Alan Greenspan[11].[5]

Michael H. Moskow
Conference on Bank Structure
May 2003

Be aware that recommendations may differ from one language and culture to another, so be sure to compare, for example, English speeches with English recommendations and Japanese speeches with Japanese recommendations.

Source: Gillies 2005: 18

C.67 Learn to write speeches

Aim: to internalize speech-writing techniques.
You will need: an audience to assess your speeches, speech-writing guides.

From speech-writing guides that you find on-line or in your university library, make a list of the main recommendations for someone wishing to write a given type of speech, for example, a speech when making an award to someone. Now use the recommendations to write speeches that other students can interpret during practice sessions. Being able to build up (create) a speech will be helpful when you need to break other speeches back down again (analysis). You'll also find it easier to anticipate what a speaker is going to say next if you've done this exercise regularly.

Source: Gillies 2005: 18

C.68 Recreate real meetings

Aim: to use context to help analyze a speech.
You will need: an agenda or programme from a real meeting.

Initially you should do this exercise with a teacher/interpreter who can use their experience to help make things realistic. Once you've got the basics you can do it in practice groups.

You will be able to find agendas and programmes on the internet for events that took place in real life. Choose one on a subject that is not too esoteric and assign one of the named speakers from the agenda to each person in the group. Each person should then prepare a speech as though they were the named speaker assigned to them. The speeches will be interpreted as part of the simulation of a meeting (mock conference).

Each speaker should find out the following in relation to the speaker whose role they are playing. It's fairly easy to find out all this information online.

- Has the speaker written anything on the topic before?
- Does the location have anything to do with promoting literature on the topic?
- Is the speaker linked to any special causes, events, etc.?
- Where does the speaker generally voice his/her opinion?
- Is the speaker in any way related to the place housing the event?
- Will the location influence the speaker's words in any way?
- Why has this person been chosen for this occasion?
- Is the occasion incidental or of relevance to the location?

Before the speaker speaks, allow the 'interpreter' to ask the speaker these same questions. When you are comfortable with this exercise the interpreter will have to find out the answers for themselves as part of their meeting preparation and without help from the speaker.

Much of what a speaker may say can be anticipated if we know enough about their background. And if you want to analyse why a speaker is saying something, and which parts of what they say are most important for them, then you must be familiar with that background.

Source: Monacelli 1999: 17

C.69 Work with real documents

Aim: to make a rapid analysis of important points in a text.
You will need: real meeting documents.

Ask your teacher to supply copies of a set of meeting documents (which they have permission to distribute in this way). Some groups in some institutions, like the EU and UN, and many national parliaments, publish meeting documents online and you'll be able to access them directly, but it's often helpful to have documents from a teacher who can give you the background information to a given meeting. You may also find annotating paper documents easier than annotating digital ones, but of course annotating .pdf documents will save you a lot of printer-ink and paper!

What you'll notice is that the document, report etc. on a given subject may stretch to tens or hundreds of pages. So you won't be able to read it all. Ask your teacher for tips on how to skim-read documents like this. For example, you might read the contents page first to get an overview of each document. Or you might flick through looking at only the titles on each page.

Give yourselves a fixed time-limit (for example, no more than 15 minutes) to go through a large document or pile of several documents. You won't just be reading for terminology, but also to get an idea of what the document is trying to say, and to whom. Highlight the phrases that sum up whole sections of the text, illustrations and terms. Compare with colleagues. Why did you highlight what you did?

Source: Makarova 1994: 201

Memory and recall

You will often hear people say, 'I have a terrible memory' or 'I wish I had as good a memory as he does'. But it's wrong to believe that your memory is good or bad and that nothing can be done about it. It's more likely that you aren't using your memory effectively. If you think to yourself, 'Oh dear, what a lot of information to remember!', you will most likely have trouble remembering much of it later. Indeed, if you are just trying to 'memorize' what you hear, you probably won't be able to. But if you can identify the type of information that you are hearing and the format in which it's being presented to you, then the interpreter has a number of tools at their disposal to back up their memory. Try, for example, to listen to a speech and break it down into one of the following types of memory prompts:

- Narrative: the speech tells a story in which one part follows another chronologically or by cause and effect.
- Structural: the speech is made up of clearly distinct parts, for example, beginning/middle/end or Point 1/Point 2/Point 3.
- Visual: the speech lends itself to visualization in the mind's eye.
- Logical: each part of the speech leads logically to the next, for example by cause and effect.
- Notes: in this part of the book we'll be working without notes, but notes are, of course, one of the important memory prompts an interpreter can use. Deciding what to note is an important part of the memorization process.

There are also countless 'Improve your memory!' books and courses that prove that what's important is how you use your memory. With just a few weeks of work anyone can achieve extraordinary feats of memory. (See Lorayne (1958), Lorayne and Lucas (1974), and Daniels in the Bibliography). Not all these techniques may be suited to interpreter training but the principles on which they are based can be used by interpreters in certain situations. For example, most people remember better the concepts they understand, the things they can visualize, things they are genuinely interested in, or things that are very unusual. All of these can be exploited by the interpreter. There is not space here to describe memory techniques in any detail, but you should find out something about how memory works, what techniques exist to harness its potential and what specifically works for you.

This section on Memory and Recall comes after Active Listening/Analysis because the first step to remembering for the interpreter is always listening and understanding. If you weren't listening and understanding (cognitively *and* linguistically), then it is almost impossible to remember anything. The first step towards improving how much you can remember, then, is to listen and understand. It is perhaps misleading that so many interpreting curricula include weeks of 'memory' work, or interpreting from 'memory'. If we called this part of our courses 'understanding a speech as a whole' or 'consecutive without notes' instead, it would be a little less daunting and closer to the reality of the exercise.

In this part of the book you'll find a few ideas to demonstrate how powerful your memory already is and to help you use it more effectively. This section is split into two parts: first memorizing things you hear or see; and second, recalling from memory knowledge you already have (activation*). The exercises aimed at memorizing don't deal with memorizing vocabulary, which we've already looked at above in Part B on Language, but rather with memorizing the narrative information of a speech.

Be careful not to stop using your memorization and recall skills once you start taking notes in consecutive interpreting. Regular practice of memorization skills, their integration into your consecutive technique, and exercises like those in this section can help avoid over-reliance on notes and compensate for the simple fact that the consecutive interpreter never has time to note everything. It is perhaps useful not to see memorization, recall and notes as competing skills, but part of the same skill. Note-taking is a tool to help you recall the original speech; it is a memory technique. But we often overlook this because of the intricacy of note-taking techniques, sometimes getting led astray by the search for symbols for everything under the sun, rather than trying to develop a technique that requires fewer symbols, but ones that help our memory work more effectively.

Practise memory skills alone to start with, then try to combine interpreting speeches, or parts of speeches, from memory with delivery skills, by trying not only to recall the content correctly but also to observe the principles of good delivery.

Everybody can learn to use memory techniques and their own memory more effectively, though it does require regular practice.

C.70 Remembering sentences

Aim: to practise memorization, and be introduced to consecutive.
You will need: someone (probably a teacher) who can prepare simple sentences.

This is an exercise that's useful at an early stage in the study of consecutive.

One person reads out a single simple sentence. Another repeats, or paraphrases, the sentence in the same language without having taken any notes (see no. 1 in the example below). This should be relatively simple. So the next step is take a longer sentence, with more information, but one which still expresses a single idea* (see no. 2 in the example below and the glossary for the definition of 'idea' used in this book). Again, the other person repeats or paraphrases the sentence in the same language without having taken any notes.

Next, one person reads out two simple sentences (two ideas*) joined by a logical link (no. 3 in the example below). The other person interprets. Initially it will probably be easier for your teacher to prepare the sentences rather than you, but as you get the hang of it you can also do this exercise on your own.

Example

1.   The Prime Ministers of France and Spain met last week at a summit meeting.

2.   The Prime Ministers of France and Spain met in private last week in the margins of a summit meeting of EU leaders to discuss the Euro crisis.

3.   The Prime Ministers of France and Spain met in private last week in the margins of a summit meeting of EU leaders to discuss the Euro crisis. However, they were unable to reach agreement on how Spanish and French banks could be best protected from the crisis.

Once you're happy doing that, move on to the next stage – try rendering the sentences in another language.

Source: Van Hoof 1962: 107

C.71 Rucksack packing exercise 1

Aim: to practise basic memorization.
You will need: a simple speech text, at least two other people.

One person takes the role of 'reader' and reads out a sentence taken from a speech transcript (initially in the source language). One of the others repeats, or paraphrases, the sentence in the same language. The reader then reads out the same sentence plus a second sentence. The next person in the group repeats, or paraphrases, both sentences in the same language. Next the reader reads out the same two sentences plus a third. The next person in the group repeats, or paraphrases, all three sentences in the same language etc., etc.

The repetition of the sentences already read out eases the burden on memory and makes the final part of the task, the memorization of up to 10 sentences, considerably less daunting that it might otherwise have been.

Source: Heine 2000: 218 and Szabó 2003: 76

C.72 Rucksack packing exercise 2

Aim: to practise basic memorization.
You will need: a simple speech text, at least two other people.

This is a more difficult version of the previous exercise.

One person takes the role of 'reader' and reads out a sentence taken from a speech transcript (initially in the source language). One of the others repeats, or paraphrases, the sentence in the same language. The reader then reads out only a second sentence (without repeating the first sentence as in the previous exercise). The next person in the group repeats, or paraphrases, both sentences in the same language. Next the reader reads out a third sentence and the next person in the group repeats, or paraphrases, all three sentences in the same language etc., etc.

The repetition of the sentences already read out eases the burden on memory and makes the final part of the task, the memorization of up to 10 sentences, considerably less daunting that it might otherwise have been.

Source: Heine 2000: 218

C.73 Info-Chain

Aim: to practise memorizing short spoken narratives.
You will need: at least four other people, a room with a door.

Divide up into two groups. At least two people stay in the room, at least two go out. One of the people in the room tells a story to one of the others in the room. (If you have enough people it's not a bad idea to have a couple of people just listening so that they can follow how the story changes.) Now call in one person from outside and have the person who's just heard the story retell it. And so on until all the people outside have come in, heard the story and retold it.

Where and why did changes in the story's message occur?

Source: Szabó 2003: 108

C.74 Liaison interpreting

Aim: to practice memorizing short spoken exchanges in a real interpreting situation.
You will need: at least two other people, an outline script for a conversation between two people.

Create the outline of a conversation between two people on some practical issue. For example, a business person asking his opposite number how something works and getting an explanation in reply. A third person then interprets between the two without taking notes.

Source: Van Hoof 1962: 108

C.75 Recreate the news

Aim: to memorize short chunks of related information.
You will need: a video or audio recording of several news items.

Watch, or listen to, a short news item. Stop the recording. Reproduce it from memory (paraphrasing rather than trying to repeat word for word).

Alternatively, listen to several news items, noting just one word per news item, and try to recall them all at the end. News items are usually such that if you can recall the subject at all, much of the other information will come back to you. That's because either there is a causal relationship between the things in each news item ('widespread flooding' – 'thousands of people left homeless'); or because news items describe singular but significant changes to something we are familiar with already; or because they recount unusual and therefore memorable events.

Source: Heine 2000: 218

C.76 Interpret from a picture

Aim: to practise using visual memory prompts.
You will need: a speech based on a picture, means of making that picture visible to a group, at least two other people.

Each student prepares a speech based on an image, in any format that can later be seen by everyone in the group (large poster, an OHP slide or a large computer screen). For example, you could use a picture of some type of building or machinery and then describe how it works or why it was built as it was; alternatively, use a picture of a landscape, city or painting that the speaker will be comfortable talking about. Each part of the speech given by the person speaking should relate specifically to something in the picture, though the speaker can expand far beyond what is visible in the picture.

Without taking notes, the others listen and then reproduce the speech using only the picture, which is still visible, as a memory prompt. You will notice that the visual back-up offered by the image makes remembering the speech very easy. This exercise is closely linked to the deverbalization* technique mentioned elsewhere.

Example

Describe the church in the picture below in your own words, but include the information in the inlay. Another student then tries to recreate your speech from memory, using only the picture to help.

- built in 14th century.
- left spire 80m, right 60m.
- legend has it that two different town authorities were paying for the building of the spires and one ran out of money before the other.
- its gothic style, as can be seen from the long thin shape of the windows.
- unusual because Gothic buildings are usually stone, and this is built in brick. No stone in Poland, so they used brick.
- gold crown added to right-hand spire in 1666.
- porch, bottom right, added in 19th century so that bourgeois ladies didn't get wet waiting in the rain outside the church.
- every day at 12 from the windows atop the left-hand spire a trumpeter plays and interrupts a trumpet signal.
- this celebrates the trumpeter who warned the city of the approach of the Mongol hordes in the 13th century and who died, shot by an arrow, in the middle of his warning. This is why the signal is interrupted each day.

A variation on this exercise is as follows. Do the same as above, but when the interpreter comes to interpret, have them sit or stand in such a way that they can no longer see the picture. The others in the group, who can see the image, can prompt the interpreter if they have difficulties.

C.77 Interpret from a picture you can't see

Aim: to practise using visual memory prompts to aid memorization.
You will need: a speech based on a picture, means of making that picture visible to a group, at least two other people.

Each student prepares a speech based on a picture. For example, you could use a picture of a building or machinery and then describe how it works or why it was built as it was. Alternatively, use a picture of a landscape, city or painting that the speaker will be comfortable talking about. Each part of the speech given by the person speaking should relate specifically to something in the picture.

Without taking notes the others listen and try to visualize in their mind's eye what they are hearing. One person must then reproduce the speech using only the mental image they have created as a memory prompt.

Try doing this first in the same language and then from one language into another.

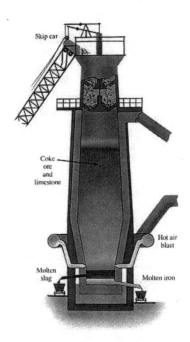

C.78 Interpret film plots

Aim: to demonstrate that understanding is the key to remembering.
You will need: at least one other person who has relatively detailed knowledge of a film plot.

One person relates the story of a film or book which the interpreter at least has not seen. It should take about 10 minutes and be in the speaker's A language*. The interpreter interprets into their A language*.

Source: Lederer 2001: 169

C.79 Tell a story

Aim: to use your understanding of a whole speech as a memory prompt.
You will need: a speaker.

This is one of the exercises that is mentioned in the introduction to this section as being less daunting if you consider it not as a 'memory' exercise but as an exercise in listening in order to understand a whole speech.

Prepare speeches for one another. One person gives a speech. Someone else gives the speech back from memory. Do this first in the same language as the original and later in a different target language.

For this exercise speeches should be simple but interesting narratives. The more unusual or interesting these speeches are, the easier they will be to understand and recall from memory. You can use progressively more difficult speeches over a period of four to eight weeks. To see how you might gradually increase the difficulty of the speeches you use, see A.17. If you give each other speeches that are too difficult to recall from memory you quickly lose motivation and wrongly convince yourself that you can't interpret from memory. Stick to simple speeches and make them more difficult slowly and gradually!

Once you can manage to recall a speech three minutes long, you don't need to extend the length of the speeches. Recalling a two-minute narrative is within everybody's grasp and more than three minutes is arguably not useful.

Source: Mikkelson 2000: 81

C.80 Interpret fairy tales

Aim: to use understanding of a whole speech as a memory prompt.
You will need: a speaker, preferably from a different culture.

One person retells a fairy tale that the listener *does not* already know. (This works best if you are lucky enough to be in a very multinational group with different traditional fairy tales.) The 'interpreter' listens and then retells the story.

Fairy tales are a great way of boosting confidence in your memory because they generally only have one main point, the conclusion to which everything else inevitably leads. Understanding the ending is usually enough to reconstruct the rest of the story.

C.81 Visualization

Aim: to practice visualization and using visual memory prompts.
You will need: a few short speeches or extracts on practical, non-abstract subjects.

Try to visualize a given sentence such as 'At the start of the century Italian families saw many of their children emigrate to all sorts of countries in search of a better future.' Create a very clear mental image of the sentence and its meaning, for example, picture a map of Italy and then families climbing aboard boats to leave.

Start with speeches containing simple, tangible items, like 'a blue shirt' and then move on to more abstract notions such as 'business'. Try to find an image even for these abstract notions ; it could be a glass-fronted skyscraper representing a company's HQ, for instance. You could even go further in trying to visualize very abstract concepts like 'generosity' (imagine a person handing out food to the needy), or 'illness' (imagine a patient in their hospital bed). The bigger and more absurd the image you visualize, the easier it will be to recall it later.

Source: Kremer 2005: 787; Sherwood-Gabrielson *et al* 2008: 60

C.82 Memory linking

Aim: to demonstrate and practise the visual linking technique.
You will need: a list of objects.

Look at the following list of 20 words for one minute. Then close the book and try to recall them all, in order.

> carpet, paper, bottle, bed, fish, chair, window, telephone, cigarette, nail, typewriter, shoe, microphone, pen, television, plate, doughnut, car, coffee pot, brick.

Most of you will have got between 12–18 items right, but not necessarily in the right order. Now read the following and try again.

The first thing you have to do is get a picture of the first item, 'carpet', in your mind.

To remember the second item, 'paper', you must associate or link it with carpet. The association must be as ridiculous as possible. For example you could picture yourself writing on a piece of carpet. A piece of paper lying on a carpet, though, Is not ridiculous enough and you will not remember it. See the one you think is most ridiculous.

The next step then is to link paper to the next item, 'bottle'. You can stop thinking about carpet entirely now. Make an entirely new ridiculous link between bottle and paper. See yourself reading an enormous bottle.

We have linked carpet to paper, and then paper to bottle. We now come to the next item, which is 'bed'. Picture yourself sleeping in a large bottle instead of a bed, or perhaps taking a drink from a bed instead of a bottle.

Next see a giant fish sleeping in your bed, or a bed made out of a giant fish. Now link 'fish' and 'chair'. See a gigantic fish sitting on a chair. Next see yourself throwing chairs through a closed window.

See your window as a large telephone dial.

See yourself picking up the phone and cigarettes flying out of the ear-piece.

You're hammering a lit cigarette into the wall instead of a nail.

Your typewriter keys are all nails, pricking your fingers as you type.

See yourself wearing typewriters instead of shoes or see a large shoe with keys on that you're typing on.

You're broadcasting into a large shoe.

You're writing with a microphone or you're talking into a giant pen.

See a million pens gushing out of the TV.

You're watching a TV show on your plate as you eat.

See yourself biting into a doughnut, but it cracks in your mouth because it's a plate.

See a large doughnut driving a car or you are driving a doughnut instead of a car.

Picture a car on your sideboard with coffee percolating in it.

See bricks pouring out of the spout of the coffee pot.

That's it. If you have actually 'seen' these mental pictures in your mind's eye then you will have no trouble remembering the twenty items in sequence, from 'carpet' to 'brick'.

edited quote from Lorayne, 1958

Now try to recall the list of twenty objects. Many people will now find it almost impossible to forget the list in its entirety and in the right order.

Although in theory this technique could be used to remember entire speeches, it is probably best used as a complementary tool with other memory tools, like your notes. Some parts of some speeches will lend themselves to this sort of visual linking better than others.

Source: Lorayne 1958: 32–36

C.83 Visual memory linking

Aim: to demonstrate the power of visual linking.
You will need: a bit of imagination, an open mind.

This exercise is based on a memory technique called visual linking. Each element of the speech will be associated with a visual image in the mind's eye. And each image will be linked to the next, creating an unbroken chain of images through the speech. For more about memorization techniques see Lorayne (1958), Lorayne and Lucas (1974), and Daniels in the bibliography.

In the example below, first follow the instructions for creating a series of visual links. Then ask somebody to read out, or paraphrase aloud, the speech that follows. Can you recall the speech on the basis of the visual images? Try to give back the speech, initially in the same language as the original. To do this effectively, and quickly enough to make use of it in consecutive interpreting, you'll need to practise it a fair bit. If it works well for you, move on to doing the same from one language into another.

Example

One person visualizes the following in their mind's eye.

Imagine a map of France and the UK, and on that map a person is bouncing around like on a trampoline between France and the UK. (Cultural differences)

As they are bouncing up and down on the UK you see the picture turn to a side-view and that the UK is actually the flat top of a huge number 5, part of a larger number, 1995.

You look at the person bouncing on top of the number 5 and you see that it is in fact Tony Blair, who then takes a huge leap forwards and flies through the nought of a huge representation of the figures 2005.

When he lands he is outside a very English house, looking in through the windows. As he peers in through the window inside he can see someone sitting in an armchair in their own private living room. (Private information)

At that moment a series of artillery shells crash through the windows. (National security)

The person gets up from their armchair and wanders over to the shattered windows. He looks out into the distance and has an expansive view of the horizon. (All govt bodies)

In the middle of the view is a field of huge potato plants that you can see growing as you watch. (Potato Council)

One of the plants is a little different, however, and you see a huge red and white lighthouse push out of the soil and up into the sky. (Lighthouse Commission)

Next imagine a huge hand sweeping down to grasp the lighthouse and whisk it up and away. Your view pans backwards and you see that the hand belongs to a journalist. See a stereotypical journalist in your mind's eye.

They are busily taking notes with a pen that looks a lot like a red and white lighthouse and watching intently as a person is strapped into a chair and tortured by men in army uniforms. (PoW camps and torture programme)

See the journalist then take their pen and stick it into the arm of the person in the chair, as though it were a syringe. See the syringe. (Sterilization programme)

Now see the journalist turn around and watch a clichéd Frenchman walk across the scene. Perhaps wearing a beret, perhaps with a sweater on his shoulders, the sleeves tied in front – whatever your most exaggerated image of a Frenchman might be. (Guy Mollet)

See this Frenchman walk across a huge map of Europe from France to the UK, then turn around and try to pull France towards the UK, closing the Channel. (Union)

Then see him give up, turn to one side and shrug to Churchill who has appeared next to him.

The Frenchman then wanders back across the map. The centre of France becomes a huge hole into which he empties all the money from his pockets. (Economic crisis)

He then continues his walk across the map; his first step lands in Algeria, the second in Egypt.

He looks back across the map to see an Englishman, imagine a parody of an Englishman, sitting gently sipping wine on top of the UK on the map. (Drinking in moderation)

Around his table are lots of road signs in French, and he is nodding knowingly as he reads them.

Then a train races by, just a few metres away from him. The train is decorated in the Union Jack. (Arriving on time)

Now ask the person to go through the list of images and check they have them all. Now tell the interpreter that the speech to follow will be about freedom of access to government information for citizens in the UK and then read, or paraphrase aloud, the speech below. Tell the interpreter to go through their list of images as they listen to the speech. They should be able to relate what is said to the images they have in their mind's eye.

Freedom of information

It won't be a surprise if I tell you that there are differences in the culture of government between the UK and France. Today I'd like to talk you about one of those differences: public access to government documentation, as enshrined in the Freedom of Information Act (FoI).

The FoI was one of Tony Blair's manifesto promises in the election campaign of 1997 and came into force in 2005. The aim, as the name suggests, was to allow the public access to government documentation and thus improve transparency in government. The Act entitled citizens to request information and documentation from public authorities.

The authorities were entitled to withhold only two types of information: private individual information and matters of national security. The Act covers all government documentation and bodies, including some you may not even have known about. For example, you can request the minutes of the British Potato Council, or correspondence from the Commissioners of the Northern Lighthouses.

The people who make use of the FoI most frequently are not ordinary citizens, but journalists who regularly turn up unusual stories. For example that the UK ran a torture program in its prisoner of war camps after the second World War or that in the 1960s the NHS sterilized certain 13 and 14 year old girls against their will. But my personal favourite is one that appeared in the UK press in 2011.

UK government documents dating from September 1956 and released last year following a FoI request show that in 1956 Guy Mollet, French Prime Minister and former resistance fighter, came to London to propose a union between France and the UK. The British Prime Minister rejected the idea, but suggested France join the Commonwealth instead. But nothing came of it.

You might be surprised to hear this, but it's worth remembering the political context of the time. Churchill had actually made the same suggestion in 1940. France had just been through 2 World Wars and was in the depths of an economic crisis. It was also fighting a war in Algeria and the Suez crisis was raging.

It never happened of course. But I can't help wondering what might have been! We might have had the best of both worlds. The British might drink in moderation and French road signs might be a little easier to follow. British trains might arrive on time and French people might arrive on time!

(training speech)

Now you've seen that the technique works, you can do the same with other speeches. Listen, and as you listen create the visual images and the links between them. To do this effectively, and quickly enough to make use of it in consecutive interpreting, you'll need to practise.

This technique shouldn't necessarily be used for whole speeches as it has been here, although there is no reason why it can't be. However, it is very useful to be able to apply this technique as a complement to other techniques, like note-taking, when the need arises or when part of a speech lends itself to the use of this technique.

C.84 Location linking technique

Aim: to practise visualization and using visual memory prompts.
You will need: a few short speeches, or extracts, on practical, non-abstract subjects.

Pick a room or a building you know very well, for example your home. In your mind's eye walk into the building or look around the room and remind yourself of the order of the main objects there. Always follow the same order. Now visualize each of the items you want to recall in turn – they could be from a vocabulary list or the successive points of a speech to be interpreted – and link each of them in your mind's eye to an object in your room or building. Link them by creating a hybrid object that is the combination of what's in your real room and the thing you want to remember. For example, if the speaker talks about the economic crisis, you could see your lampshade as a large Euro sign slowly melting away.

Going back round the room in your mind, you can recreate the chain of points because you know, and will never forget, what order the objects are in in your room.

C.85 Structured speeches 2

Aim: to practise using structure as a memory prompt.
You will need: a speech based on a simple structure, at least two other people.

Each member of the group writes a short speech with a simple structure. For example, for/against/conclusion or past/present/future. One person announces the structure of their speech in advance and then gives the speech. Another person interprets from memory afterwards. Notice how knowing the structure in advance helps you to remember the speech.

Start by doing this exercise in a single language, your A language* (for example, English into English).

Variations on this exercise include interpreting between two languages rather than one as above, and giving the speech without announcing the structure in advance.

C.86 Counting on your fingers

Aim: to memorize a speech using the number of logical links* as a prompt.
You will need: at least one other person.

One person gives a relatively straightforward speech. The others count the logical links in the speech on their fingers. Then one person gives a brief summary of the speech, counting off each part on their fingers as they go.

The fact of having identified sections of the speech and associated them with one finger each should help to anchor the information in your memory.

Source: Lederer 2001: 169

C.87 Deliberately don't note something

Aim: to use the decision not to note as a memory prompt.
You will need: a speech, a notepad.

While you are listening to a speech to be interpreted consecutively (and taking notes as usual), take a deliberate decision not to note a certain item, idea* or section. Note instead something that indicates that there is a 'gap' in your notes, for example, an empty pair of brackets if it was a bit of secondary information or an exclamation mark for a funny remark. You will find that the fact of *deliberately* deciding not to note something anchors it in your memory very effectively. The opposite of course is also true: if you haven't noted something because you didn't have time, then you will have far more trouble recalling it.

Source: Gillies 2005: 114

C.88 Note left-handed

(Unless of course you are left-handed, in which case, note right-handed!)

Aim: to practise choosing what to note.
You will need: speech transcripts and/or spoken speeches.

Once in a while take notes writing with your 'other' hand. Because you write so much more slowly with your 'other' hand, you will have to think much more carefully about what you note down. That careful 'choosing' should also anchor the information associated with each thing you note in your memory and mean that you are less likely to forget it, regardless of whether or not you look again at your notes later.

C.89 Highlight and hide

Aim: to use analysis as a memory prompt.
You will need: a speech transcript, a highlighter pen.

Read the transcript of a short speech once through. Highlight the most important ideas* (and only these) with a marker pen. Now cover the entire text and try to recreate it from memory.

This exercise offers a very interesting combination of analysis and memory skills. Identifying and highlighting the main ideas should anchor them in your memory and make recalling them much easier.

Source: Kalina 2000: 179

C.90 Brainstorm without a pen

Aim: to recall and speak terms and expressions in advance of the need to do so while interpreting.
You will need: a subject, at least two other people.

While brainstorming with colleagues, try not writing anything down. At the end of the brainstorming session try to write down as many of the terms, expressions and information items that came up as possible.

In this exercise the aim of the brainstorming session is not to create a list of words or phrases on a piece of paper, but to activate* them in the interpreter's mind so that they can be recalled and used more quickly when interpreting. Trying to recall them at the end of the brainstorming session mimics the recall powers you will have to apply in the booth, and repeats, in a shorter time period, the brainstorming session itself. Recalling and writing them down, and even the mechanical mouthing of the words to yourself, will help activate* them.

C.91 News round-up presentation without notes

Aim: to practise recalling previously prepared terms and expressions without using your notes.
You will need: to have read, and prepared a presentation on the week's news, at least two other people.

Once or twice a week one person prepares and presents a summary of the main news of the past few days. Tasks can be divided up within the group. For example, one person could present the news from each country, or alternatively one person could present national news, one Asian news, another European news etc.

In this exercise the presenters may take all the time they need to prepare, but when they come to present they may not look at the notes they have prepared at all. It's very easy to become over-reliant on written notes, but if you've read the news in question, understood it and taken notes on it, you should be able to remember most of it without notes. Learning your presentation by heart is not allowed, and not useful here!

C.92 Improvize from prepared information

Aim: to activate* the terminology and concepts and actively speculate on what the speaker might say.
You will need: a well-prepared subject.

Take a topic that has been prepared by everyone and on which you have read a good deal of material. Before the speaker starts giving the speech (or you start looking at a text for sight-translation), ask the interpreter(s) to pretend to be the speaker and improvize for a few minutes on the topic.

Source: Béziat

C.93 Take notes after the speech

Aim: to promote recall, isolate skills.
You will need: a speech, a notepad.

Listen to a speech without taking notes. When the speech has been completed, make some notes that will help you to reproduce the speech. Then give a consecutive rendering of the speech.

This exercise isolates the two skills of note-taking and listening from one another, and also the two skills of recalling and speaking. So when you're listening, you're only listening; when you're creating your notes, you're only recalling, but not listening as well. When you come to speak you have been through recalling the whole speech once already (in creating the notes), so the recall effort will be considerably less as you deliver your version of the speech.

Source: Weber 1989: 166

C.94 Take notes but don't use them

Aim: to demonstrate that notes detract from listening; promote better listening and memorization and thus better recall.
You will need: a speech, a notepad, a healthy dose of courage.

While listening to a speech take notes as per usual. At the end of the speech put your notes to one side and try to reproduce the speech from memory.

Some teachers use this exercise, which is very difficult, to demonstrate how much attention students devote to note-taking when in fact they should be listening to the speaker more carefully. A more positive angle on the same exercise would be to see how the choice of what we note anchors those elements noted more clearly in our memories. If you choose the right thing to note, the act of noting it means, paradoxically, that you are less likely to forget it and actually less likely to need to see it in your notepad in order to remember it.

Source: Seleskovitch and Lederer 1989: 59

C.95 Word association

Aim: to recall and activate* known facts.
You will need: at least one other person.

In a group of two or more, try to recall groups of associated words. For example, rivers, capital cities, world leaders. You can either go round the group in turn or each person might have to come up with a series of associated words in one go.

Source: Heine 2000: 218; Szabó 2003: 126

C.96 Acronym testing

Aim: to activate* recall of known facts.
You will need: at least one other person.

In groups of two or more, one student gives an acronym, or initialization (for example, UNESCO or OSCE) and the next must immediately give the full title in the same language (or, to make it a bit more difficult, in a different language). This can be done into, or out of, your native language. What you don't know, you will learn from your partners.

Source: Zalka 1989: 186

C.97 Numbers and names speeches

Aim: to vary the memory prompts that promote better recall.
You will need: a speech with lots of numbers.

One person prepares and delivers a speech with lots of numbers in it. The others note only the numbers and proper names. Can you recreate the speech from these?

Source: Szabó 2003: 78

C.98   Mnemonic activation 1

Aim: to activate* recall of generic terms.
You will need: at least one other person, several lists of similar items.

One person offers a list of items, and the others must offer a generic term for the end of the list.

Example 1

Lecturer: eagles, hawks, falcons, kites, ospreys, buzzards…

Students: eagles, hawks **and other birds of prey.**

Example 2

Lecturer: prescriptions, dental treatment, sight tests, vouchers for glasses…

Students: dental treatment and **other free Social Security benefits.**

Source: Ballester and Jimenez 1992: 240; Gran 1995:157

C.99 Mnemonic activation 2

Aim: to activate* recall of synonymous terms.
You will need: at least one other person, several lists of similar items.

One person says a word, the others must offer synonyms.

Example 1

> Trainer: environment
>
> Students: ecology, atmosphere, the air we breathe, our natural surroundings, our medium...

Example 2

> Trainer: Mrs. Thatcher
>
> Students: the former British Prime Minister, the former British Premier, The Iron Lady, Mr. Major's predecessor, Mr. Gonzalez' former counterpart, Britain's longest-governing Prime Minister.

This exercise aims to activate linguistic reflexes (synonyms, antonyms, lexical structures) and basic strategies for interpreting – defining or describing when the exact word escapes us.

Source: Ballester and Jimenez 1992: 240; Ilg 1978: 79

Note-taking

What, and how, to note will be part of any interpreting course and what you're told will differ somewhat from one place to the next. However, the majority of techniques are widely used, including those for which practice exercises are suggested below. The basics can be found in books by Rozan (1956), Jones (1998), and Gillies (2005).

By taking notes from speech transcripts note-taking can be practised in isolation from the other skills that go to make up consecutive interpreting. In this way we remove the time pressure associated with note-taking from a speaker, as well as the simultaneity of taking notes and listening at the same time.

We all know that in the heat of a real consecutive our notes are a bit messier than we'd like. By practising techniques regularly, and in isolation, you will create automatisms so that even under pressure your notes don't turn into an unstructured mess.

Listening and understanding the original speech are more important than note-taking. But if you have a sound note-taking system, ingrained through a lot of practice, then you *won't need* to put so much mental effort into taking the notes, they'll be better notes and you'll have more mental capacity free for listening and understanding the speech. You also won't have to put so much effort into reading your notes in the second phase of consecutive, so your presentation will be better.

C.100 Ideas* and links* – introduction to note structure

Aim: to identify ideas and links, and show them on the page.
You will need: a speech transcript, word-processing software.

Using word-processing software, remove the line divisions from the text of a speech. (Even better, get another student to do it for you, and you for them, so that neither of you have seen the original layout of the speeches you'll be working with). Read through the unbroken text and hit the Return key twice every time you can identify a subject, its verb and, often but not always, its object. Do this in such a way that each separate part of the resulting text makes sense on its own. These small bits of speech are 'ideas*' (and will each become a unit on your notepad page).

Speeches may sound like uninterrupted streams of words at first, but you will see that actually they are always made up of smaller, deliberately separate sections. Ideas, in this sense of the word, are the smallest meaningful parts of the speech. These sometimes equate to sentences in a written text, but not always.

When you've done that, find and highlight the links in the text!

Example: before

This is the original text without the original paragraph breaks in it. Below is the version where I have hit 'Return' each time I see the end of a Subject Verb Object group, and links have been highlighted and underlined.

In the areas for which I have some responsibility, there were also, as the Prime Minister has mentioned, some important developments at Feira. We took stock of the European Union's relations with Russia and the situation there, including in Chechnya, in the light of the recent EU-Russia Summit, which I think was regarded as fairly successful. It is too early to judge President Putin's economic programme; however, our basic message is that a sound programme will be vital to boost investor confidence. On Chechnya, there have, it is true, been some recent *moderately* positive developments in response to international and European Union pressure: for example the recent ECHO mission was able to take place and western humanitarian agencies have greater access to the area. The conflict nevertheless continues and we still have considerable concerns. In particular, we want to see much greater access for humanitarian aid agencies. We want to see genuinely independent investigation into reports of human rights abuses, and we want to see a real dialogue between the Russian government and the Chechens.

EU Commissioner Chris Patten
European Parliament on July 3rd 2000

Example: after

In the areas for which I have some responsibility, there were also, as the Prime Minister has mentioned, some important developments at Feira.

We took stock of the European Union's relations with Russia and the situation there, including in Chechnya, in the light of the recent EU-Russia Summit, which I think was regarded as fairly successful.

It is too early to judge President Putin's economic programme;

however, our basic message is that a sound programme will be vital to boost investor confidence.

On Chechnya, there have, it is true, been some recent *moderately* positive developments in response to international and European Union pressure:

for example the recent ECHO mission was able to take place and western humanitarian agencies have greater access to the area.

The conflict nevertheless continues

and we still have considerable concerns.

In particular, we want to see much greater access for humanitarian aid agencies.

In doing this exercise you are creating a representation of the divisions and links between ideas that is very similar to consecutive notes. Consequently this exercise is a good introduction to note-taking.

C.101 Give note-taking structure to a text

Aim: to depict the structure of the speech on the page; practise breaking speeches down.
You will need: a speech transcript, word-processing software.

You have probably been introduced to note-taking techniques aimed at creating a certain structure on the page, a structure that makes reading the notes back easier. These might include separating ideas* from one another on the page; starting on the left and noting diagonally across the page (perhaps Subject, Verb, Object); noting links* on the left; noting lists vertically on the page; and noting qualifying information directly underneath that which it qualifies.

In the example below all of these techniques have been applied to a speech transcript using only the Return and Tab keys.

There is no one right or wrong way to do this exercise, but regular practice will get you into the habit of recognizing the structures within a speech.

Example: before

> Environmental damage used to conjure up pictures of car fumes and billowing smoke from heavy industry. We now understand that everything we buy and use has an impact on the environment. And that this impact happens all the way through a product's existence, from its design, production and use, through to what happens to it when it stops being useful to its owner.
>
> The government's pledge to be the greenest ever is not a choice – it's an imperative. There is no point in rebuilding the economy unless it's a green economy: one that actively prevents waste and accurately reflects the value of our natural resources.
>
> Lord Henley
> at Green Alliance conference
> November 2010

Example: after

> Environmental damage
>
> used to conjure up pictures of
>
> car fumes and
> billowing smoke from heavy industry.

We now
             understand
that

everything we buy and
                 use

                              has an impact

                                          on the environment.
And
that

this impact
             happens
                        all the way through a product's existence,
                        (from its design,
                                     production and use,
                                     through to what happens to it when it
                                     stops being useful to its owner)

The government's pledge to be the greenest ever

                              is not

                                          a choice –
                                          it's an imperative.

There is no point in rebuilding the economy

unless it's

                              a green economy:
                              one that

                                          actively prevents waste and
                                          accurately reflects the value
                                          of our natural resources.

C.102 Monolingual interpreting

Aim: to practise the note-taking techniques in isolation from the comprehension skill.
You will need: a speech transcript and/or a speaker able to give a relatively slow speech.

Interpret not from one language into another but from and into the same language (for example English into English). In doing this you have removed the element of linguistic comprehension of the original speech and thus left more mental capacity available for deciding what should be noted and how to usefully note it. Doing this exercise repeatedly should allow you to internalize* the note-taking techniques you have learned. When you've done that, go back to interpreting between languages.

C.103 One word per paragraph

Aim: to practise choosing what to note.
You will need: speech transcripts and/or spoken speeches.

Read speech transcripts and note only one word per section of the speech. Then try to recreate the speech orally from these notes afterwards. Why did you choose the word you did? Did it help you remember?

Choosing the right things to note, and differentiating between those and the things you will remember without notes, are fundamental parts of your note-taking technique. The 'right' things to note are the ones that bring back most information from your memory (and also things that are difficult to remember at all, like figures and dates).

C.104 Note left-handed

(Unless of course you are left-handed, in which case, note right-handed!)

Aim: to practise choosing what to note.
You will need: speech transcripts and/or spoken speeches.

Take notes writing with your 'other' hand. Because you write so much more slowly with your 'other' hand you will have to think much more carefully about what you note down. You will have to make everything you note count.

Choosing what to note is a fundamental part of your note-taking technique and this exercise will force you to choose very carefully. The 'choosing' itself should also anchor information in your memory.

C.105 Five-point speeches

Aim: to practise choosing what to note.
You will need: at least one other person, prepared five-point speeches.

One person prepares a short speech containing, say, five clear points – the listeners agree to note only five words while listening to the speech and interpret on the basis of those notes.

Those listening must listen and analyze the speech in order to decide which five words best represent the core points of the speech and will therefore help recall the whole speech afterwards.

C.106 Semantic network activation 1

Aim: to improve the process of choosing what to note.
You will need: at least one other person, a notepad, some ideas.

One person describes a context and a word or phrase that describes a significant participant in that context. The other person has to build as many semantic networks (that is, describe as many relations) as possible between the two. This exercise will show you which pairs of expressions work to prompt information recall about given subjects, and what information they prompt. Later, when taking notes on the same subjects, you will be better able to choose which minimal elements to note in order to recall as much information as possible.

Example

Context : the environment
Participant: CO_2

Possible semantic networks

- One of the major problems our environment faces is the build up of CO_2 in the atmosphere.
- CO_2 is one of a series of gases that causes global warming, a major environmental issue at present.
- etc. etc.

Source: Alexieva 1994: 203

C.107 Semantic network activation 2

Aim: to improve the process of choosing what to note.
You will need: at least one other person, a notepad, some ideas.

One person creates a short set of notes (see below) and shows them to the other person. They also then describe the context in which the notes function. The other person has to build as many semantic networks (that is to say, describe as many relations as possible) between the notes and the context.

Example

Context : pollution prevention can be profitable in Germany steel industry
Notes:

>   *recycle*
> *90% water*
> *solid wastes*

Possible semantic network:
*   'The German Steel Industry has developed no-waste technologies. It recycles 90% of its industrial water and converts 90% of the solid wastes into useful materials.'

Source: Alexieva 1994: 203

C.108 Take notes after the speech

Aim: to note the broad outline of a whole speech, rather than detail.
You will need: speech recordings and /or one other person.

Listen to a short speech (3–4 minutes) without taking notes. When the speech has been completed, make some notes that will help you to reproduce the speech. Give a consecutive rendering of the speech from your notes.

By hearing the whole speech first and only then making notes we have a picture of the entire speech which we must analyze in order to make the most useful notes possible. Our notes are therefore much more likely to reflect structure and ideas than the individual words, on which we often get hung up.

Source: Weber 1989: 166

C.109 Keep on keeping on

Aim: to reduce your dependence on notes in order to arrive at better notes.
You will need: Exercises C.54–C.88.

It may seem strange to mention them here, but all of the active listening and memory exercises above will have an indirect influence on your notes. The better your analysis, and the better you know what your memory can and can't do, the fewer notes you'll need to take, and the less often you'll need to refer to your notes to recall the original.

C.110 Take notes from transcripts and slow speeches

Aim: to practise the mechanics of note-taking techniques with reduced time-pressure.
You will need: a speech transcript and/or a speaker able to give a relatively slow speech.

Take notes from speech transcripts and then from slow speeches. Make a deliberate effort to apply the note-taking techniques that you have learnt.

When you start learning note-taking techniques, you will understand the techniques, but you won't automatically be able to apply them under time pressure. Practising from transcripts or slow speeches will help you to internalize* (make automatic) the note-taking mechanisms that you have learnt. In that way, when you are working for real and under greater time pressure, they can be used instantly without your having to think to yourself, 'How should I note that?'

Source: Van Hoof 1962: 117

C.111 Prepare speeches in consecutive note form

Aim: to make preparation time more efficient.
You will need: speech transcripts, a notepad.

Prepare speeches for lessons and practice sessions in consecutive note-taking style and use those notes to give your speeches. These notes will not correspond exactly to what might have been noted from a spoken speech (the role of memory will be different if we prepare hours/days in advance, for example), however, it can still be a very useful exercise. You can use either speech transcripts as a starting point, or prepare a speech of your own from material you've researched.

In preparing speeches this way you will be practising note-taking techniques (i.e. the brevity and clarity of your notes, the use of diagonal notes or margins) but without the time pressure associated with note-taking from live speeches.

Example

Ladies and Gentlemen. Let me warmly welcome our distinguished Chinese guests to Austrade's Business Club Australia, a hub for business meetings throughout the Olympics. Let me also congratulate China on the terrific start to the Beijing Olympics – the events have been sensational, the facilities are fantastic, and China's friendliness and warm hospitality will ensure that these will be a great Olympic Games…

Australian Minister for Trade, Simon Crean
11th August 2008 Beijing

I

hi

ZH °
(to Austrade Bus. Club)
(Olympic hub)

_____

+   I

congrat

ZH/
(Olymp start)

_____

events
facilities

✓

_____

ZH friend ⁿˢ
Hosp

→

✓ games

_____

C.112 Practise diagonal notes

Aim: to make note-taking automatic (and reduce the mental effort it requires).
You will need: a speech transcript, a notepad.

Take notes from speech transcripts and try to apply the diagonal and vertical note-taking techniques you have learnt about in class or from your reading. Then try to read back the speech from your notes. Without the time pressure associated with noting from a live speech you'll have the chance to deliberately apply the techniques you've learnt and in this way gradually make them more automatic.

Example: before

Climate change is one of the greatest economic, social, and environmental challenges of our time. Expert scientific evidence confirms that human activity is altering the climate. This is changing rainfall patterns, reducing water availability in Australia and increasing the frequency of severe weather events such as bushfires and storms.

The Australian Government takes the challenge of climate change seriously. The first action of the new Australian Government in December last year was to ratify the Kyoto Protocol.

Australian Minister for Trade
Simon Crean
11th August 2008 Beijing

Example: after

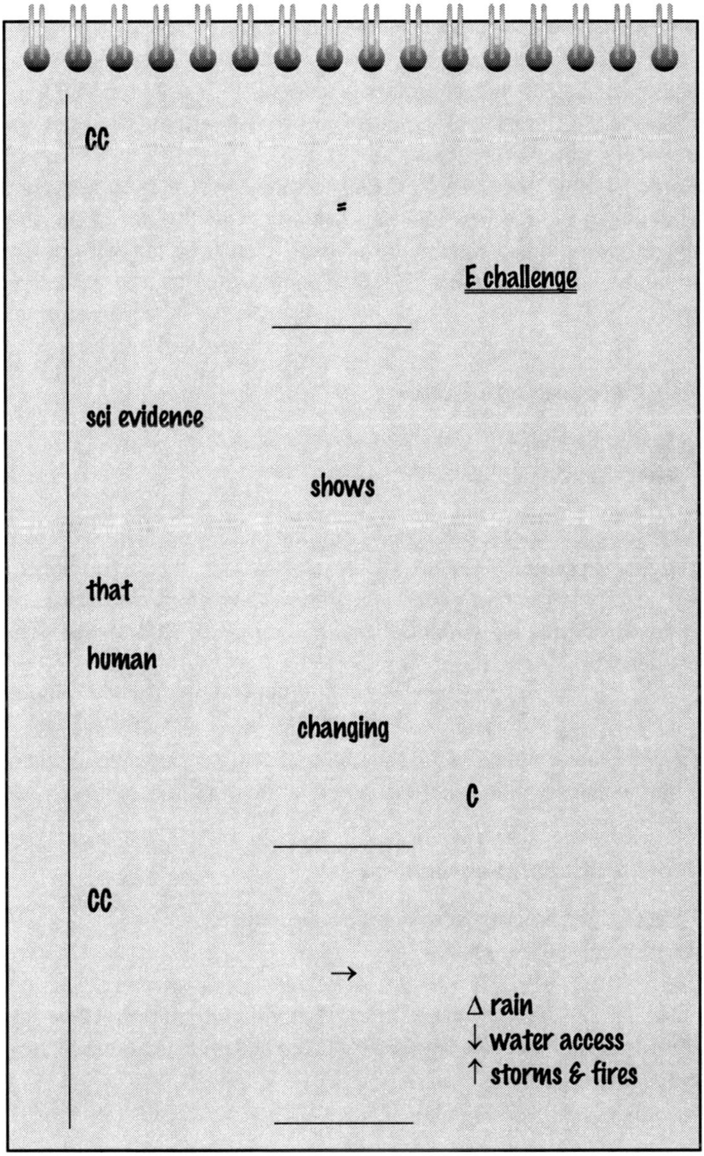

CC

=

<u>E challenge</u>

_____

sci evidence

shows

that

human

changing

C

_____

CC

→

△ rain
↓ water access
↑ storms & fires

_____

C.113 Divide the page in two

Aim: to practice noting vertically rather than horizontally.
You will need: a notepad, a speech and/or transcript.

To force yourself to use the technique of 'verticality', use a large but narrow pad, or divide the page of your notepad in two, down the middle. You now no longer have the space to note horizontally.

Remember, though, that this is a means to an end and once you are comfortable with verticality in your notes you can dispense with the line down the middle of your page and go back to using a full page. You'll be left with notes that are vertically aligned, but with plenty of space on the page.

Source: Rozan 1956: 21

C.114 Highlight margin items

Aim: to get into the habit of identifying links*, structural pointers etc.
You will need: a speech transcript.

Many interpreters swear by the use of margins at the left-hand side of the page – to highlight important elements of the speech like links, structural pointers (numbering and paragraph markers) and whose point of view is being expressed. And even those interpreters who don't use a margin still tend to note these things on the left-hand side of the page.

Read speech transcripts and circle, or highlight, links that you would note in the margin if it were a speech you had to interpret consecutively. Discuss what you noted with your colleagues; did you note the same things? Now do the same for the other elements you might have noted in the margin.

C.115 Note link and one word only

Aim: to practise choosing what to note; noting links*.
You will need: speech transcripts.

Practise note-taking from speech transcripts, noting only one word per paragraph plus the link, or lack thereof, between the paragraphs (note the latter in the margin). Try to reproduce as speech.

When you're comfortable with this, move on to do the same with spoken speeches.

Example: before

Environmental damage used to conjure up pictures of car fumes and billowing smoke from heavy industry. We now understand that everything we buy and use has an impact on the environment. And that this impact happens all the way through a product's existence, from its design, production and use, through to what happens to it when it stops being useful to its owner.

The government's pledge to be the greenest ever is not a choice – it's an imperative. There is no point in rebuilding the economy unless it's a green economy: one that actively prevents waste and accurately reflects the value of our natural resources.

Lord Henley
at Green Alliance conference November 2010

Example: after

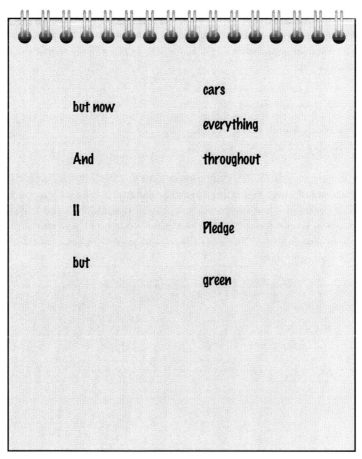

cars

but now

everything

And

throughout

‖

Pledge

but

green

‖ denotes 'no link'

C.116 Noting less

Aim: to practice clear but very concise notes.
You will need: a speech transcript and/or a speech.

Deliberately note as little as possible from a speech transcript, or later, a spoken speech. See how far you can go in noting less and less without losing the main points of the speech in your interpreted version. Discover your own limits in practice time so that you don't go beyond them when you are working for real!

C.117 Try different equipment

Aim: to find out what works for you.
You will need: a variety of pens and pads.

Try taking notes on a variety of different size notepads – A4, reporter's pad, passport-sized pad, tall thin pad etc – with a variety of different types of writing implement: thin felt tip, fat felt tip, rollerball, biro, pencil etc. Find out which you are most comfortable writing with, on what size pad, and which combination is easiest to use when reading back your notes. Although most teachers recommend a reporter's notepad and a biro – and this works best for most people – it may not be the case for you.

C.118 Rewrite your notes

Aim: to automatize note-taking techniques.
You will need: a set of your own notes.

After taking consecutive notes from a speech, rewrite your notes, correcting them into an ideal set of notes that reflects the note-taking techniques you are learning. Under time pressure when interpreting, you will probably not have used all the techniques you would have liked. 'Correcting' your notes like this will help to ingrain these techniques so that next time, even under pressure, you will use the techniques you want to use.

Source: Rozan 2003: 68

C.119 Telescoping

Aim: to identify surplus notes taken in order to reduce notes taken next time.
You will need: a set of your own notes.

Take a set of consecutive notes you have just produced while listening to a speech. Go through them and try to create a shorter set of notes from which you would still be able to reproduce the original speech.

Under pressure we often note things that afterwards we realize were of no help to us at all. Revising your notes after the speech, without that time pressure, you will find there are many 'improvements' and shortcuts that you can make in your notes. Doing this exercise regularly will help you to note more succinctly while listening in the future.

Source: Rozan 1956: 58

C.120 Compare notes

Aim: to justify your note-taking choices in order to fine tune them, picking up tips from others.
You will need: at least one other person.

Compare your notes with those of other students, and if possible with your teacher's notes. Can you explain to yourself, and the others, why you noted something as you did? After the discussion ask yourself if you would now change anything in your notes. You can compare your notes in your notepad; or, for variety, try taking notes on a whiteboard to show everyone.

Letting other people see your work, and/or having to explain it to them, will help you to step back from what you have done and assess it with greater objectivity. If you find yourself saying, 'I don't know why I noted it like that' or worse, 'I don't know what that is supposed to be', then it's a chance to correct your note-taking technique before it makes you make a serious mistake.

C.121 Practise your structure and symbols

Aim: to create automatisms in your note-taking and note-reading.
You will need: short extracts from speech transcripts.

Take notes from very short extracts of a speech text and separate these notes clearly on the page into distinct units. Use speeches that address typical issues for which you regularly use symbols. Go back and see if you can read your notes.

This exercise may be considered controversial by some as it removes note-reading entirely from any logical understanding of a whole speech or point made. However, Van Hoof's own example (overleaf), and several others in his book, are almost all clear to us now because of the obvious structure and symbols used. If Van Hoof's notes are legible 50 years later, then why shouldn't yours be 5 minutes later?

2. Faire *traduire oralement*, en insistant tout spécialement sur la valeur à donner aux symboles:

if no OK I ⊙" ? ["] ┗ " reason ["] as spkrs " again B " prelim rept OK ↗ 1° mat' : d skilled w ✓ prix ~ gvt # d ✓ WE needs ↗" WE needs ↗' chom ← imigr > defl" Ms → ⊙ B rept	Sw : WP not → early ⊙ GB " object" GB " OK ┗ ask Ms ⊙ prelim rept w method/WP stat'cs tjs < faits ✓ child mort welfar ship-bldg : ↗ cap' hay OK but corn (hoped A 1) deçu ← climat 57 slower ↗ ind' prod" ✓ [prod" cap']	US " OK B : de+ ──── " need + coop" ┗ " [w C] concl ns ← ;' so far " agri prod" ↗ + in 57/58 yet dairy sales (butter) ╲ ✓ ← ⊖ prix ╲ so gvt → aid (↗ expts) ↗ prix ← only [supply ↛ dem"] also acts # inflat"

116

Source: Van Hoof 1962: 116

C.122 Reading your notes days later

Aim: to assess and improve the clarity of structure, handwriting and symbols in notes taken in consecutive.
You will need: a speech.

Take notes from a fairly straightforward speech. Put the notes to one side and come back to them a day or a week later. Can you still use those notes to produce a useable consecutive?

In the real world you are unlikely to ever need to do this. But the exercise is still a useful way of making yourself aware of any lack of clarity in your notes. If Van Hoof's notes above are legible 50 years later, then why shouldn't yours be a couple of days later?

Source: Van Hoof 1962: 116

C.123 Practise noting names

Aim: to demonstrate that there is not only one way to do something, and that notes must be unambiguous.
You will need: a list of names, or a series of photos, of famous people from a variety of countries, and at least one other person.

Read out a list or show a series of photos of famous people from different countries. Make sure that at least two of the people on the list have the same initials (e.g.

Tony Benn, Tony Blair). The listener must note down their names in as short a form as possible while ensuring that they will be able to reproduce the full list, with both first and surnames for each person mentioned.

How short the notes are will depend on how well the listener knows the people listed. For some, the initials will suffice; for others a first name or a last name will be enough; others may choose to note the person's function, e.g. PM for Prime Minister. In the example below you'll see how the names might have been noted by American, Japanese and Polish interpreters.

The rule to remember is that whatever you note must be flawlessly unambiguous to you!

Example

	US	JP	PL
Barack Obama	Pres	Obama	Obama
Donald Tusk	Donald Tusk	Donald Tusk	DT
Yoshihiko Noda	Yoshihiko Noda	PM	Yoshihiko Noda
Julia Gillard	Julia Gillard	Gillard	Julia Gillard
Manuel Barroso	Barroso	Barroso	MB
Newt Gingrich	NG	Gingrich	Newt

C.124 Take notes standing

Aim: to test note-taking techniques in different postures.
You will need: a speaker.

Practise taking notes in different positions; for example, while sitting at a desk or table with the pad on your lap; while sitting without a table; and while standing.

Depending on the market where you end up working, or the meetings you attend, you may have to be proficient at note-taking in all three positions. However, it is quite likely that you take notes more quickly and clearly in your 'favourite' position. So practising all three is important.

Reformulation

Most of the exercises you might use to practise reformulation skills apply to both consecutive and simultaneous interpreting and you will find them in the 'Simultaneous Interpreting' section of the book. There are a few exercises that apply only to consecutive, and they are listed here.

C.125 Note only in target language

Aim: to eliminate source language interference* from notes.
You will need: a speech, a notepad.

From time to time force yourself to take notes only in the target language.

In doing this you will avoid source language interference* in the second phase of consecutive, your interpreting, and make yourself think a bit more about what you are listening to. This is, however, only an exercise and should be used as such occasionally, and not as a rule for how to take notes. When interpreting for real you should take notes in whatever language, or combination of languages, works best for you.

Source: Seleskovitch and Lederer 2002: 54

C.126 Do the same speech twice

Aim: to identify technique problems.
You will need: a speaker, or a recorded speech, a voice recorder.

Listen to, and interpret, the same speech twice. Record your interpreted versions. Compare the difference in the two interpreted versions. Why is the second speech an improvement? The answer to this question should show you which elements of technique you need to work on.

For example, if a complicated grammatical structure threw you in the first round but not in the second (because you then knew it was coming), you might need to work on anticipating and coping with these sorts of structures.

Source: Van Dam 1989: 169

C.127 Record your interpreting

Aim: to objectively assess your own language production, and gauge progress over time.
You will need: video camera or voice recorder.

Make a video, or audio, recording of yourself interpreting in consecutive. Is the language you are producing as good as you would like? As good as your teacher would like? Why not? Keep the recordings and have another look at them a few months later. Are you improving?

C.128 Consec from consec

Aim: to practise communicating when interpreting.
You will need: at least two other people, one speech.

One person leaves the room while the source speech is given, but returns to listen to, and then interpret consecutively, the consecutive interpretation of that speech.

This is an excellent, if sometimes rather harsh, way of seeing just how clear and meaningful the first bit of interpreting was. It works because the second interpreter, unlike everyone else, hasn't heard the source speech and needs the first interpreter to say something that makes real sense all on its own. It's particularly effective if the second interpreter doesn't understand the language of the original speech. They won't then naturally correct language interference* in the first interpreted version, as they might if they understood the language of the first speech.

Source: Seleskovitch and Lederer 2002: 107

Self-monitoring

Self-monitoring exercises are equally valid for consecutive and simultaneous interpreting, and are covered below in the section on simultaneous. There are a few exercises that apply only to consecutive, and they are listed here.

C.129 Film or record yourself

Aim: to isolate the self-monitoring skill.
You will need: a video camera.

There is nothing like seeing yourself on film. The camera never lies! Memory, on the other hand, is not always reliable. After class or practice we might 'forget' things we don't so much like to hear about our interpreting and remember only things we like to hear. In this way your subconscious might stop you dealing with a technique problem for quite some time. If you are to self-monitor effectively, this is a useful exercise to make yourself aware of what you're really doing when you're interpreting, and therefore what to look out for when self-monitoring.

It's a good idea to keep some of the very first films you make so that you can look at them a few months later, compare them with newer films, and see that you really have made some progress.

Source: Schweda-Nicholson 1985: 149

C.130 Referee each other's work

Aim: to remind yourself of the elements you wish to self-monitor.
You will need: at least one other student interpreter.

Before you interpret a speech tell the other students which technique issues you want to work on and that they should look out for. For example, 'I want to finish all my sentences' or 'I want to give sentences a natural intonation pattern'.

Every time you do one of the things you are not supposed to, the others hold up their hands or call out 'Stop!' and you have to go back and start that part of the speech again, this time without the technique flaw.

Split attention

It's easy to think that simultaneous is the only mode of interpreting that requires us to do several things at the same time. The very name 'simultaneous' is a big clue. But you would be wrong to think that. Consecutive interpreting involves just as much 'simultancity', it's just that the interpreter will not be speaking and listening at the same time, as in simultaneous, but rather writing their notes and listening at the same time.

In both modes of interpreting the interpreter is doing several things at the same time. For example, when listening to a speech to be interpreted consecutively we are listening, analyzing and taking notes at the same time, and at the moment when we note something down we are already listening to the next part of the speech.

One of the skills that an interpreter working in consecutive has to master, along with the others listed in this section, is that of managing their mental capacity. We all have a finite mental capacity and we divide that capacity up between the various tasks that we carry out when interpreting. However, the amount of capacity required for each task varies continually and the interpreter must focus more or less attention on each of the tasks without diverting too much effort from any of the tasks. If we manage things badly, we simply don't have any capacity left for one of the tasks. You will have experienced this when interpreting. If you have to think too hard about something there will be part of the speech that you just don't hear. Your brain has no spare capacity to process sounds heard and you become functionally deaf for a second or two.

Any of the exercises in this book that require actual interpreting involve, of course, a degree of multi-tasking. But in this section I've listed only those exercises in which the split of attention between two or more tasks is clearest to the person doing the exercise. Being aware of, 'seeing', yourself doing two different tasks at the same time is a useful way of understanding and practising this capacity management.

C.131 Improvisation exercise 1

Aim: to learn to think about one thing while saying another.
You will need: an audience of at least one other person.

Improvise a speech of two minutes on a subject volunteered by a colleague. As you improvise you should be thinking ahead to your next sentence/paragraph or the rest of the speech so that the speech remains fluent. This mirrors the split attention that the interpreter needs when reading back their notes in consecutive.

You can make this exercise easier by defining the structure of your speech in advance. For example, say that you are going to argue 'For, against, and then conclude' or that you will talk about the 'Past situation, the present, and how you see the future' of this particular issue.

The other members of the group referee and stop you if you hesitate, repeat yourself or stop making sense.

C.132 Improvisation exercise 2

Aim: to learn to think about one thing while saying another.
You will need: an audience of at least one other person.

Improvise a speech of two minutes on a subject volunteered by a colleague. As you improvise you should be thinking ahead to your next sentence, paragraph or the rest of the speech so that the speech remains fluent.

As you speak, every 30–60 seconds the other person shows a card with a keyword on it. The person speaking must think ahead in order to incorporate the word/idea coherently into the improvised speech. This mirrors the split attention that the interpreter achieves when reading back their notes in consecutive.

The other members of the group referee and stop you if you hesitate, repeat yourself or stop making sense.

C.133 Improvisation exercise 3

Aim: to learn to think about one thing while saying another.
You will need: an audience of at least one other person, a speech transcript, cards prepared as below.

Skim read the transcript of a speech and jot down the speaker's name or function, the subject matter and a few key words (in the order they appear in the speech). Note these vertically on a card or piece of paper about a quarter the size of a page of A4. Give the card to your practice partner and ask them to improvise a speech, speaking as though they were the person named and using all the key words described.

Example

Environment Minister New Zealand

Climate Change

severe weather events

agriculture

sheep

economic importance of

farmers

a good thing

warmer winters

increased rainfall

detrimental effects

C.134 Interpret from a picture you can't see

Aim: to recall and speak at the same time.
You will need: a speech based on a picture, means of making that picture visible to a group, at least two other people.

Each student prepares a speech based on a picture. For example, you could use a picture of a building or machinery and then describe how it works or why it was built as it was. Alternatively use a picture of a landscape, city or painting that the speaker will be comfortable talking about. Each part of the speech given by the person speaking should relate specifically to something in the picture. The listeners can't see the picture.

Without taking notes the others listen and try to visualize in their mind's eye what they are hearing. One person must then reproduce the speech using only the mental image they have created as a memory prompt. As they recreate the speech they will be visualizing the image in their mind's eye, recalling the information linked to it and speaking at the same time.

Try doing this first in the same language and then from one language into another.

C.135 Shadow and write

Aim: to listen and do something else without missing any of what you're listening to.
You will need: a speech, a notepad.

Shadow or paraphrase a speech (in the same language) while at the same time writing something completely unrelated on a piece of paper – for example, multiplication tables. Gradually increase the speed and complexity of the speeches you are using.

Source: Mikkelson 2000: 82

C.136 One word per paragraph

Aim: to practise choosing what to note without stopping listening.
You will need: spoken speeches.

Listen to a speech and note only one word per section of the speech. As you try to decide what to note for each section, pay particular attention to the listening task. Don't forget to keep listening! Then try to recreate the speech orally from these notes afterwards. Why did you choose the word you did? Did it help you remember? Did you not hear any of the original speech because you were thinking too hard about what to note?

C.137 Take notes from slow speeches

Aim: to practise note-taking and listening at the same time.
You will need: a speech transcript and/or a speaker able to give a relatively slow speech.

Whenever you take consecutive notes from a speech, you are doing several things at once: at least listening, analyzing and taking notes. Start by taking notes of slow speeches. Make a deliberate effort to listen to and hear all of the speech whilst also thinking about what it means and how to note it down. You'll see that as you think about how to note something, your attention on the listening task wanders. Don't let it!

Source: Van Hoof 1962: 117

C.138 Note-taking with time lag

Aim: to highlight and practise the simultaneity of note-taking and listening.
You will need: a spoken speech, a notepad.

When note-taking, try to maximize the time-lag between hearing the original and noting anything. You will be forced to think more about analyzing the original and what you note down while still listening to the speech. The simultaneity of note-taking and listening will become very clear during this exercise, as will your own capacity limits. Learning where those limits are will help you manage your capacity better.

C.139 Note-reading according to Jones

Aim: to practise reading ahead in your notes without interrupting your interpreting.
You will need: a speech transcript, a notepad.

Take notes from the transcript of a speech. Do it relatively quickly, without going back over the speech time and time again. When you've finished, read back the speech from your notes. Try to apply the technique described by Roderick Jones below and you'll immediately see how your attention is divided between the tasks of talking, reading ahead and recalling what you've read.

> There is a specific technique that interpreters can try to develop, and which can be compared to a pianist reading music while playing but not sight-reading. The pianist who has practised a piece is in a similar situation to the consecutive interpreter: essentially they know what they want to play but the sheet-music is there to remind them. The pianist looks at the opening bars and then starts playing, and continues reading ahead of the notes they are playing, their eyes on the music always being a little ahead of their fingers on the keyboard. Similarly the interpreter should look at the first page of their notes then start speaking while looking up at their audience. As the interpreter moves towards the end of the passage they have looked at, they glance down at their notes again to read the next passage. In other words they do not wait until they finish one passage to look again at their notes, which would mean that the interpretation would become jerky, reading then speaking, reading then speaking. Rather, the interpreter, while still talking, is already reading ahead, preparing the next passage, thus providing for a smooth, uninterrupted and efficient interpretation.
>
> *Source:* Jones 1998: 64

Source: Jones 1998: 64 © St. Jerome Publishing

C.140 Double note-taking

Aim: to listen to and understand two source texts.
You will need: two recordings and two devices to play both at the same time, a notepad.

Take a piece of paper and divide it into two columns. Listen to two tapes at the same time (in your two languages) and take notes on both at the same time, dividing your notes into the appropriate column. This helps you to cultivate split attention.

Source: Sherwood-Gabrielson *et al.* 2008: 224

Part D

Simultaneous interpreting

Simultaneous interpreting is quite a shock to the system, mostly because we are doing so many difficult things at once, and we need to concentrate on all of them. Many of the exercises in this section serve to ease you into full simultaneous by slowing down or breaking up the process of listening, analyzing, reformulating and speaking at the same time. As such they are well suited to the early stages of the course if you are learning consecutive and simultaneous at the same time, and they are an ideal transition from consecutive to simultaneous interpreting if your interpreting school has taught consecutive interpreting exclusively for a period before moving on to simultaneous.

It is less easy to isolate the component skills in simultaneous than in consecutive, not least because there is only one phase to simultaneous, where there are two distinct phases for consecutive. However, there are skills that can be practised in isolation. Just going into a booth and interpreting simultaneously is not always the best, and never the only, way of practising the skills required for simultaneous interpreting.

The goal of these exercises is to practise and activate those component skills that, when performed together, go to make up simultaneous interpreting. It is possible, therefore, to practise successfully without interpreting particularly accurately, as will be the case in some of the exercises below.

The exercises below cover the following skills:

- Delivery
- Split attention
- Time lag/Décalage
- Anticipation
- Reformulation
- Self-monitoring
- Stress management

Delivery

The delivery skills required in simultaneous interpreting and the exercises that might usefully be undertaken to improve them are in large measure the same as for consecutive interpreting and are outlined above in Part C on consecutive interpreting. Others, specific to simultaneous, are noted below.

D.1 Do consecutive from simultaneous

Aim: to demonstrate that simultaneous is also a communicative act.
You will need: at least three people, prepared speeches.

When practising simultaneous, ask a colleague not only to listen to your work but to use your simultaneous interpreting as the source for a consecutive interpretation.

Source: Seleskovitch and Lederer 1989: 175

D.2 Inverted conference

Aim: to demonstrate that simultaneous is also a communicative act.
You will need: at least four people, prepared speeches.

A group of at least four people prepares a number of speeches on the same subject in such a way that each person will be able not only to give a speech but also to react to the others' speeches and have a debate. (A little like a mock-conference.) For each part of the exercise, half of the group will be 'speakers' and half will be 'interpreters' and you will swap roles later. Ideally the language the interpreters work into should be understood by everyone.

Now, instead of the interpreters going off to the booths and the speakers staying in the room, have the 'speakers' go into the booths to give their speeches and engage in debate with one another. The 'interpreters', still in the room, will listen to the speeches via headphones and interpret directly to one another in the room (and to the speakers in the booths via the microphone). The speakers should be able to hear the interpreting if the microphones are switched on. The fact that the 'interpreters' are sitting normally at a table in a room, perhaps even with a few normal listeners around them, rather than behind a glass screen in a booth, will demonstrate very quickly if you have forgotten that simultaneous interpreting is also an exercise in communication. Scrunching up your face, hunching over the microphone, inappropriately varying the volume of your speech, and staccato or mumbled delivery are not acceptable in a normal conversation, nor should they be in the booth. The interpreters' job is to try to talk to one another as normally as possible while interpreting.

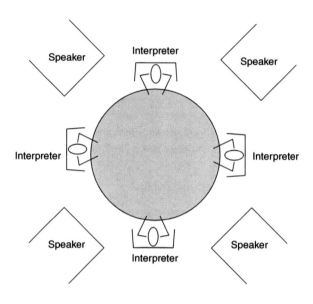

D.3 Whispering

Aim: to demonstrate that simultaneous is also a communicative act.
You will need: at least 3 people, prepared speeches.

Instead of interpreting from a booth for the person who will be listening to you, stay in the room and do whispered interpreting for them. The effect is much the same as above, in the 'Inverted conference'. Being face-to-face with your listener makes you really talk to them, really communicate. This works well enough with one listener, but if you can do it for three or four huddled around the interpreter the effect is even better.

Source: Getan-Bornn

D.4 Do it again

Aim: to isolate presentation skills for simultaneous interpreting.
You will need: a speech recording.

Repeatedly interpret the same speech until you arrive at a satisfactory version.

The artificial nature of the task is outweighed by the value of the exercise. By hearing the speech a second or third time you reduce the intellectual effort of interpreting, thus allowing yourself to concentrate on presentation skills. Also, the improved solutions arrived at in the second and third attempts can be reused later in other speeches.

Source: Van Dam 1989: 169

D.5 Shadow a bad speaker*

Aim: to familiarize yourself with possible delivery problems and practise correcting them.
You will need: a speech recording of a poor speaker.

Shadow a speech which has a large number of delivery problems (i.e. frequent restarts, umming and erring, self-correction etc.). Eliminate these shortcomings in your version.

Source: Kalina 2000: 180

D.6 Turn the volume down

Aim: to practise managing your speaking volume.
You will need: a recorded speech.

Speaking too loudly can annoy listeners and your colleagues. It can also be bad for your hearing and voice. It's also unnecessary and usually the result of turning the headphone volume up as we get worried about not understanding the speaker.

Practise interpreting with the headphone volume turned down low, and speak more quietly as well.

Source: Taylor-Bouladon 2001: 115

Split attention

Speaking and listening at the same time is not all that difficult, as the first exercise here, used as an introduction to simultaneous, shows; but *thinking* and listening at the same time is. And because we are not used to doing it we stop doing one of the two very well – we stop listening or we start talking rubbish, for example.[1] It is therefore worth practising dividing our attention before we get to try full-blown simultaneous. As such, many of these exercises will be a useful introduction to simultaneous.

Many of the exercises below can be done either in or outside the booths, depending on the facilities available.

Any of the exercises in this book that involve actual interpreting also involve, of course, a degree of split attention. But in this section I've listed only those exercises in which the split of attention between two or more tasks is clearest to the person doing the exercise. Being aware of, 'seeing', yourself doing two different tasks at the same time is a useful way of understanding and practising split attention.

Some of the exercises below involve shadowing*. This is quite a controversial issue amongst interpreter trainers. Many feel that it is not useful, since parroting words rather than thinking about their meaning goes against one of the fundamental principles of interpreting. If in doubt, consult with your teachers about the usefulness of an exercise.

D.7 Improvisation exercise 1

Aim: to learn to think about one thing while saying another.
You will need: an audience of at least one other person.

Improvise a speech of two minutes on a subject volunteered by a colleague. As you improvise you should be thinking ahead to your next sentence, paragraph, or the rest of the speech so that the speech remains fluent. This mirrors the split attention that the interpreter achieves when working.

You can make this exercise easier by defining the structure of your speech in advance. For example, say that you are going to argue 'For, against, and then conclude' or that you will talk about the 'Past situation, the present, and how you see the future' of this particular issue.

The other members of the group referee and stop you if you hesitate, repeat yourself or stop making sense.

D.8 Improvisation exercise 2

Aim: to learn to think about one thing while saying another.
You will need: an audience of at least one other person.

Improvise a speech of two minutes on a subject volunteered by a colleague. As you improvise you should be thinking ahead to your next sentence, paragraph, or the rest of the speech so that the speech remains fluent.

As you speak, every 30–60 seconds the other person shows a card with a keyword on it. The person speaking must think ahead in order to incorporate the word/idea coherently into the improvised speech. This mirrors the split attention that the interpreter achieves when working. Also this activity accurately recreates the lack of control we have on content when in the booth, and trains you to think on your feet.

The other members of the group referee and stop you if you hesitate, repeat yourself or stop making sense.

D.9 Two words at a time

Aim: to listen and do something else without missing any of what you're listening to.
You will need: a list of simple questions.

One person prepares a list of terms or expressions on a single subject. They then read out one of the items in the list in the source language. One person must give a target language version at the same time as a second word is read out. The target language version of that is given as a third word is read out, etc. To increase the level of difficulty, use whole phrases rather than single words.

Example

Student 1	Powerstation†	Powercut	Power supply	National grid	Generating capacity
Student 2		Powerstation	Powercut	Power supply	National grid

† Students 1 and 2 would be speaking in two different languages, but for the purposes of this demonstration both are in English.

The next step in this exercise is to do the same thing with entire sentences.

Source: Szabó 2003: 76

D.10 Two questions at a time 1

Aim: to listen and do something else without missing any of what you're listening to.
You will need: a list of simple questions.

Designate two people, one to ask and one to answer questions. The Asker prepares a list of 5–10 questions. These can be general or personal to start with; later you can create a list of questions on a single technical area, for example one that you're preparing for class.

Once the questions have been prepared the Asker asks a question. The Answerer must answer it. While they are answering the first question a second question is asked, to which the Answerer will answer while a third is asked etc. Initially the question and answer can be in the same language, later in a different language.

D.11 Two questions at a time 2

Aim: to listen and do something else without missing any of what you're listening to.
You will need: a list of simple questions.

A question is asked and the person answering must answer 'Yes' or 'No' and repeat the question while listening to the next question.

Example

Student 1	Is consecutive interpreting fun?	Are links an important part of a speech?	Is listening more important than taking notes?	Does visualising the speech help remember it?
Student 2		No, consecutive interpreting is not fun.	Yes, links are an important part of a speech.	Yes, listening is more important than taking notes

This can be made more difficult by moving up from Yes/No questions to Why? questions requiring a longer, more considered response – this most resembles real simultaneous interpreting.

The exercises above are arguably more useful than shadowing exercises because not only do you have to speak and listen at the same time but also understand and think. This is therefore more like the tasks interpreters complete in the booth.

Source: Kurz 1992: 249; Kalina 1992: 254; Szabó 2003: 76

D.12 Listen and count

Aim: to listen and do something else without missing any of what you're listening to.
You will need: to be able to count.

Listen to a colleague making a simple narrative speech while you count backwards aloud. Start counting from a different number for each speech i.e. 357, 173 etc. Afterwards summarize to the others what you heard and remember from the original speech.

Source: Visson 1999: 126; Lederer 2001: 172;
Seleskovitch and Lederer 1989: 170

D.13 Listen and do sums

Aim: to listen and do something else without missing any of what you're listening to.
You will need: a list of mathematical exercises.

One person reads out a simple mathematical task. A second person must solve the task and answer while listening to the next task. This can be done monolingually or from a source language into a target language.

Source: Szabó 2003: 76; Lederer 2001: 172; Kalina 1992: 254

D.14 Sight translation* – one sentence at a time

Aim: to learn to (read and) think about one thing while saying another.
You will need: an audience of at least one other person.

Take a text that is suitable for sight translation (see A.19). All sight translation is in effect a division of your attention as you read ahead in the text while still speaking your translation. As such this is a useful preparatory exercise for simultaneous.

   Read one sentence of the text. Stop. Think about how you would say that in the target language*. Speak your version as you read the next sentence of the text. Stop. Think about how you would say that second sentence in the target language. Speak your version as you read the next sentence of the text etc...

D.15 Sight translation*

Aim: to learn to (read and) think about one thing while saying another.
You will need: an audience of at least one other person.

All sight translation is in effect a division of your attention as you read ahead in the text while still speaking your translation. As such this is a useful preparatory exercise for simultaneous.

   Give yourself a minute or two to quickly look over the text before you start, as would normally happen in a professional situation.

The technique for this is very similar to the technique we use for note-reading, which was described by Roderick Jones elsewhere (C.24). The interpreter should look at the first part of the text and then start speaking while looking up at their audience. As you get towards the end of the sentence you have looked at (or clause in the case of longer sentences), look again at the text and read the next sentence (or clause). In other words, don't wait until you have finished speaking one sentence (or clause) before looking at the text again. It will feel a little unnatural and you'll have to experiment and practise, but it does work!

D.16 Interpret in slow motion

Aim: to gradually familiarize yourself with the simultaneity of speaking, listening and thinking (translating) at the same time.
You will need: a voice recorder.

This is a good exercise for the very early stages of simultaneous.

Play a sentence from a recording, listen, stop the recording, think about how to interpret it, speak the interpretation. Repeat.

To increase the level of difficulty: listen to a sentence, stop the recording, think about how to interpret it, speak the interpretation while listening to the next sentence, stop the recording, think about how to interpret it etc. Little by little the thinking pause can be reduced.

Source: Van Hoof 1962: 134; Van Dam 1989: 170;
Nadstoga 1989: 112; Szabó 2003: 154

D.17 Interpret silently

Aim: to accustom yourself to thinking (translating) and listening at the same time, but without the additional interference from your own audible voice.
You will need: a speech recording.

Interpret a speech silently in your head. Then interpret the same speech aloud.

Speaking can interfere with our hearing, or listening to, the original speech. In this exercise that problem is eliminated.

Begin by doing this from your A language* into your A language, them move on to C into A and finally, if applicable, A into B.

Source: Van Hoof 1962: 134

D.18 Listen first, interpret second time

Aim: to reduce the difficulty of the split attention element of interpreting.
You will need: a speaker, or a speech recording.

One person gives a speech and the interpreter listens. The speaker then gives the speech a second time, but this time the interpreter interprets. Knowing where the speaker is going and what the speech is about takes some of the difficulty out of simultaneous. But not all of it! Initially this will still be a difficult enough exercise to be challenging, but not so difficult as to be discouraging, as full-on simultaneous can often be early in the course.

The speech should not be read out, but spoken from notes. In that way the two versions spoken will be slightly different, but the main messages will be the same.

D.19 Consecutive first

Aim: to reduce the difficulty of the split attention element of interpreting.
You will need: a speaker, or a speech recording.

Interpret a speech first in consecutive mode. Analyze and discuss your performance. Now go into the booth and interpret the same speech simultaneously. A second step might be for the speaker to add a little bit to the end of the speech that wasn't heard in the version done consecutively.

The speech should not be read out, but spoken from notes. In that way the two versions spoken will be slightly different, but the main messages will be the same.

Source: Déjean le Féal 1997: 619

D.20 Reported interpreting

Aim: to introduce you to simultaneity.
You will need: a speech to interpret, preferably a listener.

A person in the booth listens to a speech given in the room and speaks at the same time as the speaker, but rather than interpreting they give a report in their own words of what the speaker is saying, much like a sports commentator would do when commentating on a match. The interpreter may not use cognates* or direct translations in their version. After the speech the interpreter leaves the booth and recounts to the others what was said in the booth.

Source: Lederer 2001: 173

D.21 Number plates

Aim: to mentally multi-task.
You will need: a street with some cars on it.

Go along any street, trying to repeat all the numbers and letters of the car number plates (going either in the same or the opposite direction). To make things more challenging, do the same and simultaneously translate or convert the number plates from one language into another. As a further level of difficulty, repeat the above and also count the number of cars in each colour in one of your active languages (e.g. 5 reds, 7 whites, 4 cherry, etc.)

Final level of difficulty: do the same, simultaneously translating the plates into a target language and counting the number of cars in each colour in both languages.

Source: Kornakov 2000: 242; Sherwood-Gabrielson *et al* 2008: 224

D.22 Read and listen

Aim: to split attention.
You will need: a speech recording and an unrelated text.

Read a text while listening to a recording of a speech on an unrelated subject. Afterwards try to recall the main points of both the text and the speech.

Source: Mikkelson 2000: 82

Time lag/Décalage

The interpreter's time lag, also known as décalage* or Ear Voice Span* is the time differential between the speaker's saying something and the interpreter's speaking that same part of the message.

There have been a number of attempts to establish when an interpreter should best begin speaking once the speaker has started. Well-known strategies include: 'when you have a unit of meaning*' (Lederer); 'when you can finish a sentence, any sentence' (Jones, this technique is also known as the salami technique); 'as soon as you can'; 'as late as you can'; and 'it depends' – to name but a few. In reality interpreters do not work with a single standard time lag, but rather their time lag to the original speech – whether measured in seconds or semantic units – varies depending on a number of factors, including the speed and density of the speech. It is worth familiarizing yourself with, and practising the different methods since it can offer new ideas or help understand problems. At the same time, remember that a time lag is not a goal in itself. It is a tool that makes simultaneous interpreting possible. Anticipation, another of the interpreter's tools, is just as useful in winning time for the interpreter to think in.

Like most interpreters you will end up varying your time lag depending on what's going on at any given moment of a speech. The exercises below will help you to vary your time lag when you want to, and so help your interpreting.

D.23 Spotting meaningful chunks

Aim: to identify meaningful chunks and avoid word-for-word interpreting.
You will need: a recorded speech.

Play a recording of a speech. Listen. Stop the recording when you think you have heard either (a) a unit of meaning or (b) enough information to complete a sentence. At this moment speak your interpretation, then start the recording again. Repeat this process to the end of the speech.

Learning to identify these chunks more and more quickly will leave you more time for other processing during simultaneous.

Source: Moser-Mercer

D.24 Maximise your time lag* 1

Aim: to vary your approach and thus create flexibility; to make you aware of your limits.
You will need: a speech.

When interpreting a speech, practise staying as far behind the speaker as possible ('behind' meaning you give your version of what the speaker says as long after they have said it as possible, not 'behind' in its geo-spatial sense of the word!).

By stretching your time lag limits, you will also extend the range of what you consider your 'normal' time lag. This in turn gives you more flexibility to analyze and think about what you're interpreting, if necessary.

Example

> *'The closeness of the UK's relationship with the US is no secret.'*
>
> If a speaker begins part of their speech by saying the above and the interpreter tries to start interpreting immediately after the word *'closeness'* then the interpreter is potentially creating problems for themselves later. Firstly, until you here the word *'relationship'* you don't know what *'closeness'* refers to and it's a word that may be translated differently into other languages depending on context. Also your options as to how to construct the rest of your sentence are severely limited if you begin immediately with a translation of *'The closeness...'*.
>
> According to the unit of meaning approach the interpreter would begin interpreting after, *'The closeness of the UK's relationship'* and according to the salami technique after *'The closeness of the UK's relationship with the US'*.
>
> Practise waiting longer and see what new reformulation options it allows you, but also where the limits of your short-term memory are.
>
> *'The closeness of the UK's relationship with the US is no secret. But Britain's relationship with our European neighbours...'*.
>
> Try waiting until the speaker has begun their next sentence, for example, and you'll see that many more options open up to you. For example, if you start interpreting when you hear *'But Britain...'* you might interpret something like...
>
> *'It's no secret that the UK has a very close relationship with the US. But...'*.
>
> British Ambassador to Spain, Giles Paxman
> British-Hispanic Foundation's XV Annual Forum 18th November 2011

Source: Van Hoof 1962: 134; Visson 1999: 125

D.25 Minimize your time lag* 2

Aim: to vary your approach and thus create flexibility; to make you aware of your limits.
You will need: a speech.

Try to stay as close to the speaker as possible when interpreting ('close' meaning you say what the speaker says as soon after they have said it as possible, not 'close' in its geo-spatial meaning!). Notice how the burden on your short-term memory is eased, but also how your reformulation and analysis capacities are limited by doing this.

By stretching your time lag limits, you will also extend the range of what you consider your 'normal' time lag. There will be times when you need to stick closely to a speaker, for example if they are going very quickly. Practising this in advance, and finding out your limitations, will be useful when you have to do it for real.

Source: Van Hoof 1962: 144

D.26 Vary your time lag*

Aim: to vary your approach and thus create flexibility; to make you aware of your limits.
You will need: a speaker.

Once you have more or less mastered at least one time lag technique (unit of meaning, salami, etc.), try this exercise. Agree with your speaker that they will start a speech speaking slowly and then gradually speed up. When you start interpreting, try to lag behind as much as possible. The speaker will then gradually speed up their delivery of the speech, during which time the interpreter must gradually reduce the lag in order to continue to work comfortably.

A variation on this same exercise is to have the speaker vary the speed of their delivery: quick, slow, quick, normal, slow etc. In reality interpreters constantly vary their time lag throughout every speech, so this exercise is a good simulation of the real world.

Source: Van Hoof 1962: 134

D.27 Make salami

Aim: to discover the shortest time lag that ensures you can always create a meaningful sentence.

You will need: a speech.

When interpreting, practise creating the shortest possible (meaningful) sentences, for example by chopping up one long sentence with two clauses into two separate sentences (hence the name 'salami').

When interpreting, you should only begin speaking when you are sure that, with the information you've heard, you can complete a sentence (the shortest one possible). However, you don't have to complete the sentence you started (you can change as you go along and complete a different one) and you don't have to complete the same sentences as the speaker (you can break long sentences into shorter ones). You do, of course, have to get the same message across as the speaker!

If you use this technique correctly you should never find yourself leaving a sentence unfinished, for example if the speaker stops mid-sentence.

A speaker says, '*The closeness of the UK's relationship with the US is no secret.*'

The interpreter can start the sentence, '*The UK has a close relationship with the US.*' as soon as the speaker says the word '*US*'. At this stage the interpreter doesn't know where the speaker will take that sentence, so creating a shorter sentence avoids trouble.

Example: before

The closeness of the UK's relationship with the US is no secret. But Britain's relationship with our European neighbours is now so interlinked, be it in trade, in security, or in foreign policy, that the reality, unsurprisingly, is that the British government and our civil servants spend much more time thinking about European issues than about transatlantic ones – and that was before the Euro crisis! Moreover, I am convinced that our closeness to Europe and influence in decision taking bodies in Europe, is one of the key reasons why the US regards the UK as more than just another middling power.

British Ambassador to Spain, Giles Paxman
British-Hispanic Foundation's XV Annual Forum
18 November 2011

Example: after

> The UK has a close relationship with the US. That is no secret. But Britain's relationship with our European neighbours is now very interlinked. This goes for trade, security, and foreign policy. As a result the British government and our civil servants spend much more time thinking about European issues than about transatlantic ones. They did so even before the Euro crisis! What is my opinion? The UK is close to Europe. And it influences decision taking bodies in Europe. This is one of the key reasons why the US regards the UK as more than just another middling power.

Source: Jones 1998: 91; Szabó 2003: 150

D.28 Shuffle the sentence

Aim: to practise extending time lag only with certain parts of the speech.
You will need: a speech.

Practise changing the order of elements in the clause or sentence, i.e. practise holding individual words or parts of the clause/sentence and working them back in much later (e.g. a date can very easily be switched from first to last in a sentence).

Example

> **In the past few days** the UK has been portrayed in the German press as a difficult partner in Europe. But there is much which binds the UK and its European neighbours, especially Germany.
>
> The UK has been portrayed in the German press as a difficult partner in Europe **in the past few days**. But there is much which binds the UK and its European neighbours, especially Germany.
>
> Simon McDonald, British Ambassador to Germany
> December 2011

D.29 Shuffle the clauses

Aim: to practise extending time lag only with certain parts of the speech.
You will need: a speech.

Practise changing the order of the clauses in a sentence without changing its meaning.

Example

> **Owing to the growing importance of the Internet in young people's lives,** governments and society more widely need to strike a balance between safety and freedoms on the web.
>
> Governments and society more widely need to strike a balance between safety and freedoms on the web **given the growing importance of the Internet in young people's lives.**
>
> Simon McDonald, British Ambassador to Germany,
> 10th December 2010

D.30 Time lag* with numbers only

Aim: to stretch the limits of your time lag.
You will need: a list of numbers, a speaker.

Have someone make a recording of a long series of random numbers. Interpret from that recording. Start by interpreting just one number behind the original and then progressively try to stay further behind until you are three, four or even five numbers behind the original.

Start by doing this exercise from your A language into your A language and then later work from other languages into your A language.

Anticipation

Student interpreter: Do you find that with experience your time lag behind the speaker is longer and longer?

Experienced interpreter: Actually no, I find though that I can anticipate what's coming next much better.

Anticipation can relieve some of the intellectual strain involved in interpreting. By anticipating what is coming next the interpreter is eliminating the element of surprise in the speech they are listening to. Doing this not only frees up mental capacity for other tasks but also reduces stress levels. Not knowing what's coming next can be a source of anxiety, particularly for young interpreters. Of course the interpreter has to check their anticipated version with what is actually said before producing their version, but this is quicker than processing the information from scratch. If we anticipate wrongly, then that too is helpful, and is a signal to devote more attention to source speech.

D.31 Analyze how speeches are written

Aim: to familiarize yourself with speech types in order to better anticipate content.
You will need: speech-writing guides in each of your languages.

You'll find lots of guides on how to write speeches on-line or in your university library. It's worth reading them and concentrating on those types of speeches that you are most likely to be asked to interpret (see A.16). From those guides make a list of the main recommendations for someone wishing to write a given type of speech, for example a speech when making an award to someone.

Example

In his book *Writing Great Speeches*, Alan Perlman (1998: 69–80) suggests the following guidelines for public speakers introducing other speakers.

Speeches of introduction should:

1   give a sense of what is to come
2   familiarize the audience with the speaker's achievements
3   create a sense of anticipation
4   add finesse to the obvious
5   be maximum 7 minutes in length
6   be positive always
7   build suspense
8   include quotes
9   link to theme of today's conference
10   be characteristic of speaker to follow plus illustration of same
11   give applause markers e.g. 'please join me in welcoming...'

(The numbers assigned for the purposes of this exercise are not by Perlman.)

Find examples of that type of speech on-line and compare them with the list of recommendations. Have the recommendations been put into practice? Most likely you'll see that some or most of them have, even though that speaker may not have read the same guidelines as you. That's because they, or their speech-writer, will have learnt to write speeches somewhere, and because the conventions of how to write speeches are limited in number.

Start with the texts of the speeches and later do the same with recordings of the spoken word. The numbers in superscript in the text below correspond to recommendations in the list above.

It's my great pleasure to welcome you to our 39th annual conference on bank structure and competition. This year's focus on corporate governance[1,9] is especially relevant.

We've seen too many once-revered companies end up severely damaged, in some cases beyond repair, by failures in corporate governance, Arthur Andersen, Enron....[8].

Those of you in financial firms are affected through your credit exposure to firms that followed questionable accounting practices, and through your own corporate governance practices. This has led to greater investor skepticism and increased uncertainty in the equity and credit markets...[3].

During the conference you'll be discussing these issues in greater detail[1].

The role of boards of directors. Changes in financial regulation, accounting standards and disclosure rules. The impact on financial firms and financial markets[1].

In this effort, we have enlisted some of the most prominent members of the financial industry to speak with you this week[9]. They include banking executives, regulatory authorities, administration officials and financial and legal scholars[1].

Perhaps the most eagerly awaited speaker in this stellar line-up[7], however, is the person I'm about to introduce[7] – a man, really, who needs no introduction[3,4]. We have the privilege of hearing from someone whose accomplishments and stature have made him a respected name throughout the world[3]. Someone[7] whose words are analyzed by everyone from Wall Street to Main Street[2]. And someone whose unquestioned integrity[4] stands out even more brightly today, at a time when negative behavior seems to be darkening the news[3,4,9].

He is Alan Greenspan, chairman of the board of governors of the Federal Reserve System[2]. Alan, we wish you could be here in person, as you have been every year since the conference began. But we know you've been advised, after minor surgery, to stay put for a while[6]...

Alan Greenspan is serving his fourth four-year term as chairman[2], having been designated to this position by Presidents Reagan, Bush Senior and Clinton. It was in August 1987 when he originally took office as chairman and to fill an unexpired term on the Board[2]. He also serves as chairman of the Federal Open Market Committee[2], the System's principal monetary policymaking body.

Most important, as I'm sure you're all aware[9], the current President Bush thinks 'Alan Greenspan should get another term,' and the chairman has said he'll serve if nominated. I think we'd all agree this is great news for our country and for the economy.

The details of Alan's background and his tremendous achievements are well documented[4]. His bachelors, masters and doctorate degrees in economics from New York University[2]. His 30-year career as head of Townsend-Greenspan, an economic consulting firm in New York City[2]. And his service as chairman of the President's Council of Economic Advisers under President Ford[2], as well as on many other public and private boards[2].

He's received numerous awards and honors for his work, and his outstanding reputation and extraordinary talents are widely known[2]. Over the course of more than a decade, his adept handling of his complex responsibilities at the Fed have made him a hero – not only to people in business and government, but to millions of average citizens from all walks of life. It's truly a great honor to have the chairman as our keynote speaker[7].

Please join me in welcoming Alan Greenspan[11,5]

Michael H. Moskow
Conference on Bank Structure
May 2003

D.32 Learn to write speeches

Aim: to familiarize yourself with speech types in order to better anticipate content.
You will need: speech-writing guides in each of your active languages, a small audience.

Once you're comfortable with the exercise above, 'D.31 Analyze how speeches are written', go on to the next step and use the same recommendations to write speeches for one another to interpret during practice sessions. Knowing how to build up (create) a speech yourself will mean you'll find it easier to anticipate what a speaker is going to say.

Source: Gillies 2005: 18

D.33 Give structured speeches 1

Aim: to recognize structure in speeches.
You will need: at least one other person, several speeches.

Each member of the group writes a short speech with a simple structure. For example, for/against/conclusion or past/present/future. One person gives the speech and the listeners have to guess the structure of the speech as they listen. Start with simple structures and move on to more complicated speeches. For example, a more complicated structure might be: 3 points in favour, the last divided into 2 sub-points/2 points against, both divided into 2 examples/3 points in conclusion and so on.

D.34 What comes next 1

Aim: to anticipate plausibly.
You will need: a speech transcript, over-head projector or large screen.

Take a speech transcript, either on a sheet of paper or projected onto a screen, and cover all but the first sentence. Try to guess what comes next. Uncover further sections of the text (initially whole sentences, then ever smaller segments). The others in the group must anticipate what follows. In this exercise you don't necessarily need to get it right; it is useful to be able to anticipate a range of plausible possibilities.

Source: Kalina, 2000: 180; Mikkelson 2000: 82

D.35 What comes next 2

Aim: to anticipate plausibly.
You will need: a recorded speech.

Play a recorded speech and press pause every few seconds. Try to anticipate what comes next, focussing both on what is grammatically possible and what is semantically possible (does what follows make logical sense?).

   In this exercise you don't necessarily need to get it right; it is useful to be able to anticipate a range of plausible possibilities.

Source: Mikkelson 2000: 82

D.36 What comes next 3

Aim: to anticipate plausibly
You will need: a speech transcript

Read a few sentences from the middle of a speech transcript. Reproduce and anticipate as much information as possible. Not only what comes next, but what might have preceded the text and what might have also been said but wasn't. You can do this with or without topic related preparation.

Source: Walker, K.

D.37 Cloze* exercise

Aim: to anticipate plausibly.
You will need: a speech transcript.

One person reads aloud and then pauses mid-sentence. The others try to arrive at the largest number of plausible alternative versions of the rest of the sentence. This will test your ability to anticipate speakers. It will also be useful later in the booth, where making it to the end of a sentence, whatever is going on around you, will be an imperative.

> [The relationship between China and Australia] is broad-based, strong and valued by both countries. Both countries see tremendous potential for...
>
> F. Adamson, Australian Ambassador to China
> 27th October 2011

> [The relationship between China and Australia] is broad-based, strong and valued by both countries. Both countries see tremendous potential for...
>
> ... further exchanges.
> ... further cooperation on environmental issues.
> ... an acceleration of trade cooperation over the next few years.
> ... further engagement, particularly in the services sector.

Source: also Kalina 2000: 180; Nolan 2005: 24

D.38 Highlight and anticipate

Aim: to anticipate plausibly.
You will need: a speech transcript.

Read a text through once. Highlight the most important ideas (and only these) with a marker pen. Reread the highlighted ideas and now try to anticipate a further, as yet unread, part of the text.

Source: Kalina, 2000: 180

D.39 Torn newspapers

Aim: to practise using logic and/or lexical probability to reconstruct missing parts of the original.
You will need: a newspaper, a pair of scissors, perhaps a felt-tip pen.

Cut or tear up newspaper articles. Alternatively, black out parts of the text with a felt tip. Try to guess what the missing content might be. In your own language you'll quickly see that there's a high degree of linguistic probability as to what comes next.

Source: Makarova 1994: 209

D.40 Fill in the blanks

Aim: to practise using logic to reconstruct missing parts of the original.
You will need: a speaker.

Using speeches you have used in practice, have the speaker mumble a few words incomprehensibly at certain stages in the speech. On the basis of logical analysis the listeners must fill in the gaps and offer plausible versions. This can be done with both consecutive and simultaneous speeches. Do this exercise first as a monolingual exercise, so from English to English, and then later from one language to another.

In one version of this exercise the speaker deliberately mumbles or coughs instead of saying one half of a collocation relating to general cultural knowledge from the language being spoken. For example, 'cheddar cheese' would be halved to 'cheddar *cough*' and the interpreters would be required to complete the gap. Other British examples of the type of collocation with which English speeches could be liberally sprinkled are: Amnesty International, Buckingham Palace, Hereditary Peers, London Eye, Scotland Yard.

Source: Visson 1999: 127; Szabó 2003: 87

D.41 Shadow and eliminate interference

Aim: to practise avoiding typical examples of interference between language pairs.
You will need: at least one other person, a prepared speech.

Practise shadowing speeches in your own language which have been deliberately sprinkled with constructions taken from another language that you interpret from, but which are inappropriate in the language you are using. Correct the structural and syntactic errors while shadowing.

This is an excellent way of tackling the reformulation challenges that all languages offer, without the added difficulty of the comprehension task. Later, when faced with a source language, you will already be familiar with the techniques and strategies that will allow a sound rendering in the target language.

Finding someone to give this sort of speech may be difficult. You need someone who can emulate language spoken with heavy language interference. Alternatively it could be a fellow student who has a passive language that isn't good enough to be active (because of the language interference) but which they don't mind giving speeches in for this exercise.

Source: Kalina 2000: 181

D.42 Do it again

Aim: to demonstrate how good anticipation relieves strain on mental capacity.
You will need: a speech recording.

Interpret the same speech twice, record both versions and compare the difference. Having heard the speech once already, your 'anticipation' of what's coming next the second time you hear it should be almost perfect.

Also, ask yourself why the second speech is an improvement on the first. Are there any particular grammatical constructions, or logical points, that you failed to anticipate? And what are the signals that you missed this time but want to notice next time?

Source: Van Dam 1989: 169

Reformulation

Reformulation can mean changing the words (or not using words that are similar in both of your languages, cognates*) but it also means changing whole expressions, the word order, clause order and sentence structure. The goal is to arrive at a version that is grammatically and syntactically correct, sounds natural in the target language and communicates the same message as the original.

D.43 Written translation

Aim: to arrive at translation solutions without the time pressure associated with interpreting.
You will need: transcript of a speech.

Translating texts in writing, including the transcripts of speeches, can be a useful tool for students of simultaneous interpreting. When translating we have more time to consider different language versions of given expressions and ideas and we have more time to take in the structure and conventions of political speeches. When translating in writing you can solve the translation problems without any time pressure, so the solutions should be good ones. Make a note of those solutions somewhere close to hand and review them from time to time. That way they will come to mind later when you are interpreting on the same subject.

Source: Visson 1999: 127

D.44 Read translations

Aim: to borrow solutions from experienced professionals.
You will need: the video (or audio) version of a speech and its official translation.

Ask the speaker to give an oral version (not a reading) of a speech. After interpreting it, consult the official translation of the speech and see how the translator, who had more time and experience to work with, dealt with the problem passages.

Multilingual international institutions like the UN and the EU, and bilingual national parliaments (Canada, Belgium etc.), are good places to find speeches that have been recorded and then also translated.

D.45 Group translation

Aim: to arrive at, and explain, translation solutions without the time pressure associated with interpreting.
You will need: transcript of a speech, at least one other person.

Two or more students translate (in writing) a speech transcript and then compare their versions before agreeing on a final 'best' combined version. Defending and explaining your version to another student is an excellent way of exploring the meaning and nuances of words and expressions. What you thought you knew may be challenged and your knowledge fine-tuned as a result. Also, pooling your intellectual resources like this will mean everyone benefits from each other's best suggestions.

Source: Zanier Visintin 2008: 464

D.46 Keep a logbook 1

Aim: to collect ready-made solutions for recurring expressions.
You will need: a small notebook.

While reading and listening to your foreign languages you will notice that some expressions come up very frequently but are quite difficult to put into your active language. Record these expressions and try to come up with usable versions in your active language(s).

Make a distinction between new terminology and recurring expressions. Items of terminology tend to come up very rarely and are therefore less useful per item. One suggestion would be to note recurring expressions from the front and vocab from the back of the same book. Alternatively you could keep a book for each.

You don't have to come up with a new interpreting solution for everything you hear. Having some frequently occurring expressions translated in advance is a perfectly legitimate strategy and will save you time and effort. Examples of such phrases might be 'Standort Deutschland', 'la démocratization du haut debit' etc.

It is probably a good idea to come up with different translations depending on the context in which an expression appears. You'll be unlikely to find a version in your language of the expressions above that works every time. Share and borrow these expressions with your co-students. Plagiarism is the highest form of flattery!

Source: also Sainz 1993: 139; Gillies 2001: 68; Nolan 2005: 61

D.47 Parallel texts

Aim: to see how the same information is expressed and addressed differently in different languages.

You will need: texts about the same events in two different languages – major news events are the easiest examples.

Read and compare articles on the same topic but written independently in both languages. Find examples of the same thing being described in both texts. Make a note of the two versions. In this way you avoid literal, or dictionary, translations because you can see how similar ideas are expressed independently in two languages without interference from the source language, something that the interpreter must always seek to avoid.

When doing this exercise you should choose two texts from people or organizations with comparable political point of views, bias, or lack of bias. If you compare a left-wing text with a right-wing text the corresponding terms and expressions are likely to be politically different and therefore dangerous for an interpreter.

Example

These two articles appeared on the same day in July 2012. In the text below the expressions which correspond to one another, as independently drafted descriptions of the same phenomena, are numbered and underlined.

French automaker Peugeot to shed 8,000 jobs[1]	**La suppression de 8.000 emplois[1] chez PSA crée un choc san précédent**
French automaker PSA Peugeot Citroen has announced to **slash 8,000 jobs[1]** and close a major **plant[2]** outside Paris as it struggles with mounting losses, in a move that could spark more **restructuring[3]** and political tension in austerity-strapped Europe.	Le groupe Peugeot-Citroën a annoncé hier l'arrêt de la production à Aulnay-sous-Bois, première fermeture **d'usine[2]** en France depuis vingt ans. Les politiques et les **syndicats montent au créneau[6]**.

The Aulnay plant near Paris, which employs more than 3,000 workers, **will stop making cars**[4] in 2014 as Peugeot reorganises its under-used domestic production capacity, the company said on Thursday.

Aulnay, which builds the Citroen C3 subcompact, will become the first French car plant to close in more than two decades, challenging new Socialist President Francois Hollande's pledge to revive industrial production.

"I know how serious these measures are for the people concerned, and for our entire company," Chief Executive Philippe Varin told reporters. "But a company can't preserve jobs when it is burning 200 million euros ($245m) a month in cash."

...Jean-Marc Ayrault, the French prime minister, said the government was studying the closure plan, which he called a "great shock", but stopped short of condemning it, which incurred the wrath of the CGT, France's biggest industrial union.

Peugeot said another plant in the western city of Rennes will shed 1,400 workers as it shrinks in step with demand for larger cars such as the Peugeot 508 and Citroen C5.

Some **3,600 non-assembly jobs**[5] will also **be scrapped**[1] across the country.

Unions decry[6] **decision**

Comme pour tenter de préparer les esprits, Arnaud Montebourg avait déclaré mercredi qu'il redoutait « *un choc pour la nation* ». La formule n'était pas excessive. L'annonce, hier, par PSA de la suppression de 8.000 postes en France a provoqué un véritable séisme, suscitant la colère des syndicats et de la classe politique. Le groupe Peugeot-Citroën ne s'est pas contenté de dévoiler un énième plan de départs volontaires. Il a fait part de sa décision **d'arrêter la production automobile**[4] dans l'usine d'Aulnay-sous-Bois et de réduire la voilure à Rennes. Corollaire de la baisse des effectifs dans la production, **les fonctions administratives seront également touchées, à hauteur de 3.600 postes**[5]. Ces départs pourront se faire sur la base du volontariat, mais jusqu'à mi-2013 seulement...

...Les précautions verbales du président de PSA, Philippe Varin, n'ont pas suffi à éteindre l'incendie. « *Personne ne sera laissé au bord du chemin* », a-t-il garanti, tout en précisant que la moitié des 3.000 salariés d'Aulnay pourraient être reclassés à Poissy. Ce dernier a également promis de « *revitaliser* » Aulnay. Pour apaiser les inquiétudes grandissantes sur l'usine de Rennes, le dirigeant s'est engagé à lui affecter un nouveau véhicule.

Combined with France's share of 6,000 European job cuts announced last year, the latest measures **will reduce Peugeot's 100,000-strong domestic workforce**[1] by close to 10 per cent, excluding subcontractors and service providers.

Workers at Aulnay downed tools after the announcement, halting production. Hundreds gathered under protest banners at the main entrance to the plant, the biggest industrial employer in the depressed, multiethnic Seine-Saint Denis district northeast of Paris.

...Peugeot's global **sales fell**[7] 13 per cent to 1.62 million light vehicles in the first six months - contrasting with a more modest 3.3 per cent decline reported by Renault and a 10 per cent gain for the Volkswagen brand...

Renault and Fiat are also **reducing headcount**[1], while GM's Opel division plans to close its Bochum plant in Germany by 2017.

Al Jazeera
http://www.aljazeera.com/
news/europe/2012/07/
20127121546390440.html

PSA justifie ces décisions par la dépression du marché automobile européen, où **les volumes ont chuté**[7] de près de 25 % depuis 2007. Dans ce contexte, la situation financière du groupe s'est brutalement dégradée depuis un an. Philippe Varin a évoqué un « *rythme de pertes intenable* », écartant toutefois le risque de faillite grâce à une « *sécurité financière de 9,5 milliards d'euros* ». « *Mais cette réserve n'est pas infinie* », a-t-il prévenu. Malgré ces difficultés, une aide financière de l'Etat semble écartée. « *Ce n'est pas à l'ordre du jour*, a-t-il déclaré. *Notre préoccupation est de remplir les usines du groupe. Injecter de l'argent n'est pas ce qui permettrait de les faire tourner.* »

...Le ministre a été chargé de présenter le 25 juillet un « *plan de soutien* » à l'industrie automobile. C'est à cette date que PSA doit annoncer les deux autres volets de son **projet de redressement**[3] – investissements et baisse des prix des véhicules -ainsi que ses résultats financiers pour le premier semestre 2012...

Les Echos 13th July 2012
http://www.lesechos.fr/
entreprises-secteurs/
auto-transport/
dossier/0202171808246/
0202171808457-la-suppression-
de-8-000-emplois-chez-psa-
cree-un-choc-sans-precedent-
343994.php

D.48 Parallel texts for political standpoint

Aim: to identify the language elements that are characteristic of a given political viewpoint.
You will need: at least two articles or speeches representing opposite views on the same subject.

If you're preparing for a class or a meeting in which two sides of an argument are likely to be aired, and which you will have to interpret, it's useful to have a look at publications that represent both sides of that argument, or different ends of the political spectrum, in order to get an idea of how some of the same things are expressed differently by people representing the two sides. Read and compare the articles. Find examples of the same thing being described in both texts. Make a note of the two versions. How does the language they use to describe the same events differ?

In the example below two newspapers, one with a predominantly left-of-centre readership and another with a predominantly right-of-centre readership, report on the same welfare reforms. In bold, and numbered 1–6, are expressions describing the same thing slightly differently.

In addition to corresponding expressions you'll also find expressions that set the tone for the article in one or other, or both, texts. These can also be useful as you prepare. Below, the negative expressions related to claiming social security benefits in the *Mail on Sunday* text (on the right) are underlined.

Housing benefit for under-25s could be[1] scrapped, PM to announce

...

The government wants to cut as much as £10bn from the **welfare budget[2]** by 2016, and is looking at setting regional benefit levels and cutting benefits from striking workers. Cameron and the Treasury set the £10bn target for new welfare **cuts[3]** in last year's autumn statement and the PM will go into detail in a speech on Monday.

... he will propose that 380,000 **people under 25 are stripped of housing benefit[4]** and forced to join the growing number of young adults who still

---

Cameron to axe[1] housing benefits for feckless under 25s as he declares war on welfare culture

Radical new welfare cuts targeting feckless couples who have children and expect to live **on state handouts[2]** will be proposed by David Cameron tomorrow.

His bold **reforms[3]** could also lead to 380,000 people under 25 being stripped of housing benefits and forced to join the growing number of young adults who still live with their parents.

In a keynote speech likely to inflame tensions with his deputy Nick Clegg, the Prime

live with their parents. He will make exemptions for those that have been victims of domestic violence. The savings – which will mean an **average loss per person of around £90 per week**[5] – are likely to be in the order of £1.8bn.

Labour accepts that the housing benefit budget is out of control and last week the party welcomed proposals of cuts from the left-of-centre thinktank the IPPR, but in the contest of a massive housebuilding programme.

...Cameron also wants more done to cut jobseeker's allowance for those refusing to seek work actively. The government has already tightened up requirements in this area, but the PM wants to go further. 'We aren't even asking them, "Have you got a CV ready to go?",' Cameron said.

He is also looking at restricting child benefit to those who have more than three children and **forcing a small minority of unemployed people**[6] – an estimated 5,000 to 10,000 – to take part in community work if they fail or refuse to find work or training after two years.

The *Guardian*, 24th June 2012 Copyright Guardian News & Media Ltd 2012. http://www.guardian.co.uk/ society/2012/jun/24/ housing-benefit-under- 25s-welfare

Minister will call for a debate on the welfare state, focusing on reforms to 'working-age benefits'.

Among the ideas being considered by Mr Cameron are:

– **Scrapping most of the £1.8 billion in housing benefits**[4] paid to 380,000 under-25s, **worth an average £90 a week**[5], forcing them to support themselves or live with their parents.

– Stopping the £70-a-week dole money for the unemployed who refuse to try hard to find work or produce a CV.

– Forcing a hardcore of workshy claimants to do community work after two years on the dole – or lose all their benefits.

...

He also favours new curbs on the Jobseeker's Allowance, demanding the unemployed do more to find work. He said: 'We aren't even asking them, "Have you got a CV ready to go?".' A **small minority of hardcore workshy**[6], an estimated 5,000 to 10,000, could be forced to take part in community work if they fail or refuse to find work or training after two years.

Mail on Sunday, 23rd June 2012 © Associated Newspapers Ltd http://www.dailymail.co.uk/news/ article-2163773/David-Cameron- axe-housing-benefits-feckless- 25s-declares-war-welfare- culture.html

1. In the *Mail on Sunday*'s text this is definite, thus reinforcing a positive impression
4. The *Guardian* relates this to people – 'people ... stripped of', whereas the *Mail on Sunday* dehumanizes the process by relating it to the payments 'scrapping ... benefits'.
5. As in 4. The *Guardian* seeks to talk about the people's 'loss to...' and the *Mail on Sunday* about the money involved (abstract) 'benefits...worth'.

D.49 Multiple paraphrasing

Aim: to train flexibility of expression.
You will need: a few sentences taken from speeches, possibly three other people.

Take any sentence in your active language(s), preferably from a speech that might be interpreted, and paraphrase it into as many versions as you can. Ten different versions should be your target in a B language, twelve would be excellent. In your own language more than fifteen versions is a minimum.

If you like a bit of pressure or competition you could do this as a group, with each person taking turns to give the next version.

Example

> The strength of our institutions has maintained Britain's reputation as a world leader in science, engineering and design.
> Giles Paxman, British Ambassador to Spain,
> 5th June 2012
>
> 1. The robustness of our institutions has kept Britain's reputation as a global leader in science, engineering and design.
>
> 2. It's thanks to the strength of our universities that Britain has kept its reputation as a world leader in science, engineering and design.
>
> 3. Britain continues to be known as a pioneer in science, engineering and design because it has such sound universities.
>
> 4. Britain's continuing reputation as a world leader in science, engineering and design is based on the excellence of our institutions.
>
> 5. etc.

Source: Van Hoof 1962: 114; Guichot de Fortis 2009: 4

D.50 Paraphrase (in same language)

Aim: to practise reformulating.
You will need: speech extracts, possibly one other person.

Take short extracts of authentic speeches and try to reformulate them. That is, to say the same thing in the same language, but in your own words. Being able to say the same thing in a number of different ways will be an essential part of your interpreting repertoire.

There are three variations of this exercise, in order of difficulty: you can do this using a transcript and write your own version; or using a transcript and 'sight-translating' to arrive at your version; or get someone to read (or better, give a spoken version of) the speech and paraphrase that. Each time reformulate in the same language as the original, which should be one of your active languages.

Example

> Ladies and Gentlemen, a very warm welcome to the British Embassy this evening. Many thanks to you all for coming. And many thanks to the Deutsch-Britische Gesellschaft for organising this evening.
>
> The Gesellschaft hardly needs an introduction. Only four years after the war, in 1949, a group of Düsseldorf citizens decided that they needed to help reconstruct the relationship between Germany and Britain. They started a series of conferences in Königswinter to bring together German and British parliamentarians, academics and opinion-formers...
>
> British Ambassador's speech for Deutsch-Britische Gesellschaft
> 9th September 2003

> Dear Friends, I am very pleased to see you here at the UK consulate tonight. Well done for coming. And well done as well to the Deutsch-Britische Gesellschaft for arranging the festivities.
>
> I don't need to tell you about the Gesellschaft. Not half a decade after the hostilities of 39–45 ended a small band of Rheinlanders determined that they should do their bit to rebuild the UK's ties with Germany. They began with a set of colloquia near Bonn aimed at uniting influential German and British MPs, intellectuals and media players.

Source: also Gran 1995: 157; Kalina 2000: 180

D.51 Deverbalization 1

Aim: to avoid language interference from the source language.
You will need: speech extracts, possibly one other person.

This technique has been the foundation of interpreting teaching, particularly in Paris, for over 30 years. The interpreter tries, while listening to (initially a short extract of) a speech, to visualize what they are hearing rather than translate it. They then describe the picture they see in their mind's eye in the target language.

This is best done with practical, slow speeches in simultaneous, rather than abstract speeches.

Source: Seleskovitch and Lederer 1989: 257; Nolan 2005: 39

D.52 Deverbalization 2

Aim: to avoid language interference from the source language.
You will need: a newspaper article.

Choose an interesting newspaper article and read it carefully. Try to create a mental picture of the events, people and chronology described in the article. Put the original article text away and try to recreate, in spoken form, the content of the article, using only the mental picture you created.

Source: Nolan 2005: 39

D.53 Reverbalization

Aim: to interpret meaning not words.
You will need: a speech.

One person finds a relatively straightforward, short speech and makes copies for everyone in the group. Everyone reads through the text quickly to get an overall idea of the speech. One person (and this may be easier for a teacher to do than a student) then gives the speech, without reading it, and deliberately uses synonyms for as many of the major words in the speech as possible, without changing the meaning of the speech. The other(s) interpret.

This exercise can be done for consecutive or simultaneous practice.

Source: Szabó 2003: 138

D.54 Dubbing 1

Aim: to deverbalize; avoid language interference from the source language; finish sentences.
You will need: a video recording of part of a soap opera that all students are familiar with, or where the plot-line is obvious.

This is an excellent exercise early on in an interpreting course.

Play a short extract of the recording to the group. Everyone listens. Now assign a character to each member of the group and play the recording again, this time with the sound muted. Each member of the group must now recreate and speak their part of the dialogue as faithfully as possible.

In a variation of this exercise, skip the first stage and don't watch the extract with the sound audible.

Source: Szabó 2003: 90; Nolan 2005: 39

D.55 Improvization exercise

Aim: to avoid unfinished sentences, always having something to say.
You will need: an audience of at least one other person.

Improvise a speech of two minutes on a subject volunteered by a colleague. As you improvise you should be thinking ahead to your next sentence, paragraph or the rest of the speech so that the speech remains fluent. But whatever you do, don't stop!

The other members of the group referee and stop you if you hesitate, repeat yourself or stop making sense. By doing this exercise you will be practising finding grammatical and idiomatic solutions under pressure – essential for an interpreter.

D.56 Interpret from a picture

Aim: to deverbalize, avoiding language interference from the source language.
You will need: a speech based on a picture, means of making that picture visible to a group, at least two other people.

Each student prepares a speech based on a picture. For example, you could use a picture of some type of building or machinery and then describe how it works or why it was built as it was. Alternatively, use a picture of a landscape, city or painting that the speaker will be comfortable talking about. Each part of the speech given by the person speaking should relate specifically to something in the picture.

The others listen, with or without taking notes, looking at the picture as the speech is given. One person must then reproduce the speech, basing their version primarily on the picture rather than the words they have heard or noted down.

Try doing this first in the same language and then from one language into another.

Example

Describe the Cracow church in the picture below in your own words, but include the information below. Another student then tries to recreate your speech, using only the picture to help.

- built in 14th century
- left spire 80m, right 60m
- legend has it that two different town authorities were paying for the building of the spires and one ran out of money before the other
- its Gothic style, as can be seen from the long thin shape of the windows
- unusual because Gothic buildings are usually stone, and this is built in brick. No stone in Poland, so they used brick
- gold crown added to right-hand spire in 1666
- porch, bottom right, added in 19th century so that bourgeois ladies didn't get wet waiting in the rain outside the church
- every day at 12 from the windows atop the left-hand spire a trumpeter plays an interrupted trumpet signal
- this celebrates the trumpeter who warned the city of the approach of the Mongol hordes in the 13th century and who died, shot by an arrow, in the middle of his warning. This is why the signal is interrupted each day

D.57 Interpret from a picture you can't see

Aim: to deverbalize.
You will need: a speech based on a picture, at least two other people.

Each student prepares a speech based on a picture. For example, you could use a picture of some type of building or machinery and then describe how it works or why it was built as it was. Alternatively, use a picture of a landscape, city or painting that the speaker will be comfortable talking about. Each part of the speech given by the person speaking should relate specifically to something in the picture.

The others listen, with or without taking notes, and try to visualize in their mind's eye what they are hearing. One person must then reproduce the speech.

Try doing this first in the same language and then from one language into another.

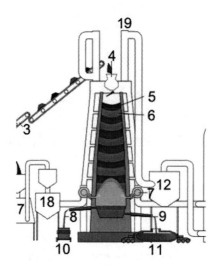

D.58 Describe a photo

Aim: to deverbalize, avoiding language interference from the source language.
You will need: several photographs of people talking.

Choose a photograph of yours that depicts people talking together. Try to remember what they actually did say on that occasion. Write out a brief narrative, with dialogue, for each photo. A variation of this exercise is to do the same in another active language.

Source: Nolan 2005: 39

D.59 Sight paraphrasing

Aim: to practise reformulation, create simple speeches for early simultaneous.
You will need: a speech transcript, at least one other person.

One student is asked to sight paraphrase (as opposed to sight translate) the text of a speech from their A language into their A language. A second student interprets the paraphrased version simultaneously into another language.

The student paraphrasing is practising reformulation, while this exercise also offers a very good way of making the transition from easy to difficult texts in simultaneous – the paraphrased version will be simpler than the text but more complex than you might have produced as a speech yourselves.

Source: Carsten

D.60 Monolingual interpreting

Aim: to practise reformulating in isolation from language comprehension.
You will need: a speaker with the same A language as you.

Interpret not from one language into another, but from and into the same language (for example English into English). In practice this means paraphrasing the original, not parroting it. In doing this you have removed the element of language comprehension of the original speech. This frees up mental capacity for better reformulation.

D.61 Say the opposite

Aim: to practise reformulating.
You will need: speech extracts.

Invert the meaning of a text, in the same language. There are several variations of this exercise, in order of difficulty: you can do this using a transcript and write your own version; or use a transcript and 'sight-translate' to arrive at your version; or get someone to read (or better, give a spoken version of) the speech and paraphrase that. Each time reformulate in the same language as the original, which should be one of your active languages.

A further variation might be to interpret between languages and invert the meaning, but since this would be more difficult than actually interpreting itself, it's not very useful for students learning to interpret.

Example: before

> Ladies and Gentlemen, a very warm welcome to the British Embassy this evening. Many thanks to you all for coming. And many thanks to the Deutsch-Britische Gesellschaft for organising this evening.
>
> The Gesellschaft hardly needs an introduction. Only four years after the war, in 1949, a group of Düsseldorf citizens decided that they needed to help reconstruct the relationship between Germany and Britain. They started a series of conferences in Königswinter to bring together German and British parliamentarians, academics and opinion-formers...
>
> British Ambassador
> British Embassy Berlin
> 9th September 2003

Example: after

> Ladies and **Germs**, please **don't make yourself at home** in the British Embassy tonight, **you are not welcome**. **Shame you came**. Likewise **it's a pity** the Deutsch-Britische Gesellschaft had to go and organize this event.
>
> I **doubt** many of you will have heard of the Gesellschaft. **Quite some time** after the war, 4 years in fact, a group of citizens from Düsseldorf decided **there was no need** for their **interference** in reconstructing the relationship between Germany and Britain. **They failed** to organize a single conference anywhere which might have brought together German and British parliamentarians, academics and opinion-formers...

Clearly you will also invert the speaker's message. Don't worry about that *when doing this exercise* – the aim here is to practise reformulation alone. The fact that these exercises do not faithfully reflect what you'll actually do when working as an interpreter, or that they might actually be fun to do, will in no way detract from their usefulness.

Source: also Gile 1995: 212

D.62 Change the grammar, leave the meaning

Aim: to practise grammatical (as opposed to lexical) reformulation.
You will need: a speech transcript, later a speech.

Rework the grammatical structure of sentences without changing their meaning. There is almost no limit to what parts of speech can be changed, but a few examples are in the box below.

Examples of grammatical reformulation		
All of these examples work in both directions		
Noun to verb	there was no agreement	failed to agree
Adjective to verb	they're eligible	they can be, they may be
Double inversion	finite	not boundless
	we're keeping an open mind	nothing has been ruled out
Compound nouns	a way of collecting data	a data collection method
Indicative to passive	they drafted a report	a report was drafted

There are several variations of this exercise, in order of difficulty: you can work from a speech transcript and write your new version; you can use a speech transcript and 'sight-translate' it to arrive at your version; alternatively, get someone to read (or better, give a spoken version of) the speech and paraphrase that. Each time reformulate in the same language as the original, which should be one of your active languages.

To start with you should try to paraphrase only one part of speech, for example make indicative verbs passive as in the example overleaf. Then do the same with another. Slowly you'll find yourself able to make whichever of these changes is necessary to get yourself out of tricky situations while interpreting.

Example: before

> But I'd like to argue today that despite, or indeed because of, those doubts, Europe needs to work as hard as ever to strengthen its relationship with the US. Of course we all need to come to terms with the risks, and the much greater opportunities, of rapid growth in emerging markets in Asia and Latin America. But to do so at the cost of our relationship with the US would be a huge mistake.
>
> Speech by British Ambassador to Spain, Giles Paxman
> British-Hispanic Foundation's XV Annual Forum
> 18th November 2011

Example: after

> But the argument **to be made** today is that these doubts **require Europe** to work as hard as ever to make sure its relationship with the US is strengthened. The risks, opportunities, of emerging markets in Asia and Latin America **will have to be accepted**. But we'd be making a mistake if that was at the expense of our relationship with the US.

Source: Van Dam 1989: 174; Gile 1995: 212; Visson 1999: 18; Heine 2000: 215

D.63 Try extremes of register

Aim: to practise reformulating, saying the same thing in very different ways.
You will need: a speech.

Interpret not into the same register as the speaker, but into a different, extreme register instead. Interpret the same speech, for example, in very colloquial slang. Then interpret the same speech again in an over-the-top aristocratic drawl. You can also try to imitate different regional accents or certain types of people. Police officers or doctors also use a distinctive register in some languages.

There are several variations of this exercise, in order of difficulty: you can do this using a transcript and write your own version; or use a transcript and 'sight-translate' to arrive at your version; or get someone to read (or better, give a spoken version of) the speech and paraphrase that. Each time reformulate in the same language as the original, which should be one of your active languages.

Example: before

> Ladies and Gentlemen, a very warm welcome to the British Embassy this evening. Many thanks to you all for coming. And many thanks to the Deutsch-Britische Gesellschaft for organising this evening.
> The Gesellschaft hardly needs an introduction. Only four years after the war, in 1949, a group of Düsseldorf citizens decided that they needed to help reconstruct the relationship between Germany and Britain. They started a series of conferences in Königswinter to bring together German and British parliamentarians, academics and opinion-formers...
>
> British Ambassador, British Embassy, Berlin
> 9th September 2003

Example: lower register

> Hi **folks**, welcome to the British Embassy tonight. Thanks to everyone for **coming along**. And **a big 'thank you'** to the Deutsch-Britische Gesellschaft for putting on this **bash**.
> The Gesellschaft you all know. In '49, just 4 years after the war, **some guys** from Düsseldorf sat down and **came up with the idea** of rebuilding the ties between Blighty and Germany. They **kicked off** with a set of talks in Königswinter, **the idea being** to get German and British MPs, intellectuals and **media folk** to sit down together at one table...

Example: higher register

> Good evening Ladies and Gentlemen. Let me **express my great pleasure** at **being able to welcome** you here tonight. Let me also express **my gratitude** to the Deutsch-Britische Gesellschaft for hosting us this evening.
> The Gesellschaft **hardly requires introduction**. A mere four years after World War II, in 1949, a **league of gentlemen hailing** from Düsseldorf **determined to** reforge the relationship between Germany and the United Kingdom.
> They **convened** a series of symposia in Königswinter which would reunite German and British **parliamentarians**, **men of letters** and opinion-formers.

Source: Gillies 2001: 83; Mikkelson 2000: 82

D.64 Summarize drastically

Aim: to practise summarizing.
You will need: a speech extract.

Example: before

> Ladies and Gentlemen, a very warm welcome to the British Embassy this evening. Many thanks to you all for coming. And many thanks to the Deutsch-Britische Gesellschaft for organising this evening.
> The Gesellschaft hardly needs an introduction. Only four years after the war, in 1949, a group of Düsseldorf citizens decided that they needed to help reconstruct the relationship between Germany and Britain. They started a series of conferences in Königswinter to bring together German and British parliamentarians, academics and opinion-formers...
>
> British Ambassador, British Embassy, Berlin
> 9th September 2003

Example: after

> Welcome. Thank you for coming and thank you to the organizers, the Deutsch-Britische Gesellschaft, who you'll all know.
> Just after the war they began rebuilding relations between our two countries by organizing conferences to be attended by influential Germans and Britons...

Each time reformulate in the same language as the original, which should be one of your active languages. When you're comfortable doing that, try summarizing from one language into another.

Source: also Gile 1995: 212; Visson 1999: 126; Mikkelson 2000: 82

D.65 Add redundancies

Aim: to practise filling gaps without changing the message.
You will need: a speech, a list of redundant phrases.

When interpreting, add as many redundancies as possible. That is to say, fill out your version of the speech with expressions that add nothing to the text.

This exercise will help you recognize what is and isn't redundant in a speech by focusing your attention on the redundancies. It will also give you a useful coping strategy, because these same redundant expressions can also be inserted into your interpreting performance when you need a bit of time to think, or when you're not sure where the speaker is going with his point.

Example: before

> Ladies and Gentlemen, a very warm welcome to the British Embassy this evening. Many thanks to you all for coming. And many thanks to the Deutsch-Britische Gesellschaft for organising this evening.
>   The Gesellschaft hardly needs an introduction. Only four years after the war, in 1949, a group of Düsseldorf citizens decided that they needed to help reconstruct the relationship between Germany and Britain. They started a series of conferences in Königswinter to bring together German and British parliamentarians, academics and opinion-formers...
>
>   British Ambassador, British Embassy, Berlin
>   9th September 2003

Example: after

> Ladies and Gentlemen, **it is my pleasure to wish you all** a very warm welcome to the British Embassy on this **most special of** evenings. **For my part let me** thank you all for coming. **Let me also take the opportunity to** thank our friends at the Deutsch-Britische Gesellschaft **for going to the trouble of** organising this evening's **festivities**.
>   The Gesellschaft hardly needs an introduction, **as I'm sure you are all familiar with it. But allow me to briefly jog your memories. As I recall** it was only four years after the end of WWII, in 1949, when a group of Düsseldorf citizens decided that they needed to help reconstruct the relationship between Germany and Britain, **which was of course not at its best at that time.** They started a series of conferences, **if memory serves**, in Königswinter, **a place I have been fortunate enough to visit on several occasions**, to bring together German and British parliamentarians, academics and opinion-formers...

Source: also Gile 1995: 212; Mikkelson 2000: 82

D.66 Stock phrases

Aim: to familiarize yourself with frequently recurring expressions.
You will need: a speech to interpret, perhaps a list of prepared stock phrases.

Practise creating speeches made up almost entirely of 'stock phrases*' rather than any actual content. By doing this you will find that you develop an ability to find, and vary your use of, such phrases more easily.

Most of these phrases are repeated day in day out at international meetings and could be replaced with countless other synonymous phrases. The interpreter should not expend their energy on the translation of these phrases. Practising producing them, so that they come to mind very quickly when working, will leave more time for thinking about the really difficult stuff. They can also be inserted into your interpreting performance when you need a bit of time to think, or when you're not sure where the speaker is going with his or her point.

Example: before

> Ladies and Gentlemen, a very warm welcome to the British Embassy this evening. Many thanks to you all for coming. And many thanks to the Deutsch-Britische Gesellschaft for organising this evening.
>
> British Ambassador, British Embassy, Berlin
> 9th September 2003

Example: after

> Chairman, **I am much obliged** to you for giving me the **opportunity to take the floor** to **open proceedings. I shall be brief. For my part** there **are a couple of points** that I would like to **draw to colleagues' attention.** Firstly and **most importantly,** welcome to the British Embassy this evening. And many thanks to the Deutsch-Britische Gesellschaft for organising this evening.

D.67 Overuse a metaphor

Aim: to practise linguistic flexibility, practising interpreting the meaning, not only the words.
You will need: a speech.

Decide with colleagues on a type of metaphor and try to overuse it throughout a single speech. For example, sporting and nautical metaphors are two good choices: calm the waters, shots across bows, in the doldrums, shipshape, a loose cannon, embark, etc. The version of the speech you reproduce should, of course, still correspond to the sense of the original even though the original speaker has not indulged in the same way. The more common in everyday language the type of metaphor you choose, the easier this exercise will be.

This is best done only in your A language*, as you risk serious mistakes or a very odd sort of language version if you try it in a B language*. Practising working at your linguistic extremes in this way will make *normal* interpreting seem easier.

Example: before

Ladies and Gentlemen, a very warm welcome to the British Embassy this evening. Many thanks to you all for coming. And many thanks to the Deutsch-Britische Gesellschaft for organising this evening.

The Gesellschaft hardly needs an introduction. Only four years after the war, in 1949, a group of Düsseldorf citizens decided that they needed to help reconstruct the relationship between Germany and Britain. They started a series of conferences in Königswinter to bring together German and British parliamentarians, academics and opinion-formers...

British Ambassador, British Embassy, Berlin
9th September 2003

Example: after

Good evening **crew** and **welcome aboard**. Thank you all for **pushing the boat out** with us this evening. A **hearty** thanks also to the Deutsch-Britische Gesellschaft for this evening's **shindig**.

The Gesellschaft is a familiar **craft**. **Launched** four years after the war, in 1949, when a group of Düsseldorfers set out to **refit** the relationship between Germany and Britain. They **floated** the idea of a **raft** of conferences in Königswinter to bring together the **captains** of German and British academia, media and the political world...

D.68 Make salami 2

Aim: to practise grammatical (as opposed to lexical) reformulation, avoid unfinished sentences.
You will need: a speech to interpret.

The name of this exercise encourages us to slice up our sentences as salami is sliced – into lots of smaller bits. It's also sometimes called 'chunking'.

Systematically transform all long sentences, and sentences with clauses into two, or more, separate sentences. This is a very useful tool for the interpreter for at least two reasons. Firstly, speakers sometimes get lost in their own complex syntax, but the interpreter cannot allow themselves to get lost with them. Keeping sentences short like this will help you to keep an overview of what you're saying and where your version is going. Secondly, this technique can help you eliminate the scourge that is the unfinished sentence. If your sentences are shorter, then you have a better chance of finishing them, and finishing them correctly.

Example: before

> The closeness of the UK's relationship with the US is no secret. But Britain's relationship with our European neighbours is now so interlinked, be it in trade, in security, or in foreign policy, that the reality, unsurprisingly, is that the British government and our civil servants spend much more time thinking about European issues than about transatlantic ones – and that was before the Euro crisis! Moreover, I am convinced that our closeness to Europe and influence in decision taking bodies in Europe, is one of the key reasons why the US regards the UK as more than just another middling power.
>
> British Ambassador to Spain
> Giles Paxman
> British-Hispanic Foundation's XV Annual Forum
> 18th November 2011

Example: after

> The closeness of the UK's relationship with the US is no secret. But Britain's relationship with our European neighbours is now very interlinked. This goes for trade, security, and foreign policy. As a result the British government and our civil servants spend much more time thinking about European issues than about transatlantic ones. They did so even before the Euro crisis! What is my opinion? The UK is close to Europe. And it influences decision-taking bodies in Europe. This is one of the key reasons why the US regards the UK as more than just another middling power.

Source: also Van Dam 1989: 174; Gile 1995: 212; Jones 1998: 91; Heine 2000: 215; Szabó 2003: 150; Nolan 2005: 55

D.69 Shuffle information items

Aim: to practise syntactic reformulation.
You will need: a speech.

Just because the speaker puts things in a certain order does not mean that the interpreter must always follow the same order. Indeed, in some cases the interpreter should, or must, change the order to make sense or be stylistically correct. (For example, in German sentences tend to follow the order Time, Manner, Place. English does not.)

While interpreting, practise changing the order of elements in the clause: i.e. practise holding individual words or pieces of information (remembering them) and working them back into your version (saying them) much later. For example, a date can very easily be switched from first to last in a sentence.

Example

> **before**
> It was in August 1987 when he originally took office as chairman and to fill an unexpired term on the Board.
>
> **after**
> He originally took office as chairman and to fill an unexpired term on the Board **in August 1987**.
>
> Michael H. Moskow
> Fairmont, Illinois
> May 2003

D.70 Shuffle chunks of the sentence

Aim: to practise syntactic reformulation.
You will need: a speech.

Just because the speaker puts things in a certain order does not mean that the interpreter must always follow the same order. Indeed, in some cases the interpreter should, or must, change the order to make sense or be stylistically correct.

It may seem a little daunting at first, but changing the order of the clauses or phrases in a sentence without changing its meaning is not so much more difficult than moving a single piece of information, like a date, around in the sentence. If you understand a clause as a single item it will not be any more difficult to hold in your short-term memory than a date or a name etc. So look out for clauses and phrases that you can treat as single items and then try moving them around in your version of the speech.

Example: before

> The closeness of the UK's relationship with the US is no secret. But Britain's relationship with our European neighbours is now so interlinked, be it in trade, in security, or in foreign policy, that the reality, unsurprisingly, is that the British government and our civil servants spend much more time thinking about European issues than about transatlantic ones – and that was before the Euro crisis! Moreover, I am convinced that our closeness to Europe and influence in decision taking bodies in Europe, is one of the key reasons why the US regards the UK as more than just another middling power.
>
> British Ambassador to Spain, Giles Paxman
> British-Hispanic Foundation's XV Annual Forum
> 18th November 2011

Example: after

> **It's no secret** that UK's relationship with the US is a close one. **Be it in trade, in security, or in foreign policy,** Britain's relationship with our European neighbours is now so interlinked, that the reality, unsurprisingly, is that, **even before the crisis,** the British government and our civil servants spent much more time thinking about European issues than about transatlantic ones. Moreover, I am convinced that **the US regards the UK as more than just another middling power** because of our closeness to Europe and influence in decision taking bodies in Europe.

D.71 Correct with a thesaurus

Aim: to practise working through reformulation problems.
You will need: a speech recording.

Interpret the same speech twice. After the first attempt and before the second, spend a moment trying to solve any reformulation problems you had first time round and/or think about the words and expressions you used the first time that weren't ideal. Use a thesaurus and see if you can come up with anything better.

The artificial nature of the task is outweighed by the value of the exercise. By redoing the same speech you reduce the intellectual burden of doing it the second time, thus allowing you to concentrate on reformulation. Also you'll find that the solutions you find in the thesaurus and successfully use second time around will stick in your mind and come back to you when interpreting in the future.

D.72 Do it again

Aim: to practise working through reformulation problems.
You will need: a speech recording.

Interpret the same speech twice. Try the second attempt immediately after the first. Because you've already heard the speech once you should have a little more mental capacity to solve reformulation problems second time around.

Source: Van Dam 1989: 169

D.73 Give it a thorough going over

Aim: to monitor and correct your reformulation without time pressure.
You will need: a voice recorder, a speech.

Record yourself interpreting and listen to it sentence by sentence, paragraph by paragraph. As you go through your version, reword it (in the same language as the recorded interpretation) into a version you might have expected to hear from an articulate native speaker giving their own speech. What are the differences? Could you have applied what you now know to your interpretation? Try it.

You'll find that the solutions you arrive at here will stick in your mind and come back to you when interpreting in the future.

D.74 Make a transcript of your work

Aim: to monitor and correct your reformulation without time pressure.
You will need: a voice recorder, a speech.

Record your interpreting work and then write out, word for word, what you said. How would you improve it if you had to do it again?

Our assessment of written language is often more rigorous than that of the spoken language. As such, any expressions or formulations that are less than ideal will stand out here. Correct them yourself. You'll find that the solutions you arrive at here will stick in your mind and come back to you when interpreting in the future. You can also ask a native speaker to check your corrections.

Example

Your interpreted version	Your own correction	Native-speaker correction
However, the Rhine valley is the location for US military bases, military camps ever since the second World War and all you can see around these camps are concrete walls and wire fences, which is the reason why the people living in the area are so mad about this.	However, since the second World War, we see US military bases there. The bases are surrounded with concrete walls and barbed-wire fences. And all this infuriates local residents.	However, since the second World War, there have been US military bases there. The bases are surrounded by concrete walls and barbed-wire fences. And all this infuriates local residents.

D.75 Teacher demonstration

Aim: to see a professional performance as a point of reference.
You will need: a professional interpreter, a speech.

Get a professional interpreter, most likely your teacher, to give you a demonstration of their simultaneous interpreting. It will be a good example of how to reformulate a speech relatively freely, relative that is to most student interpreters, without losing the original meaning. In this way you'll get an idea of how much reformulation is the right amount of reformulation.

Source: Altman 1989: 237

D.76 Paraphrase when reading aloud

Aim: to practise reformulation.
You will need: a speech transcript.

Read aloud the text of a speech and as you go along, replace some of the words and expressions without changing the meaning of the text.

Source: Mikkelson 2000: 82

D.77 Replace cognates*

Aim: to practise reformulation, avoiding language interference*.
You will need: a similar language pair.

Sight-translate, or interpret, a speech from one language into a fairly closely related one   for example, EN-FR, DE-NL, IT-ES, IT-FR. Replace all the cognates (words that share the same root) with alternatives. For example, when interpreting the French 'commencer', 'véhicule', 'considérer' into English don't use the English words 'commence', 'vehicle', 'consider' but instead deliberately avoid them and use words like 'start', 'means of transport' and 'think'.

Source: Lomb 2008: 82

D.78 Use cognates*

Aim: to practise reformulation, avoiding language interference*.
You will need: a language pair including one romance language.

When interpreting between two closely related languages – for example, EN-FR, DE-NL, IT-ES, IT-FR – use as many cognates (words that share the same root) as you can. Record your interpreting and then listen to the result. How does your language sound with too many cognates? (If you're working into your A language* you'll be able to answer this question yourself. If you're working into a B language, ask a native speaker for their opinion). Cognates are often the 'easy' answer when we are interpreting, but that doesn't mean they are the best answer!

This exercise will make you aware of your tendency to literal translation and of the effects of language interference*.

D.79 Improvizing synonyms

Aim: to eliminate overuse of certain expressions, find synonyms for them.
You will need: a list of expressions that you overuse when interpreting.

Agree with your group in advance which expressions or words you overuse when you are interpreting. For example, 'think', 'problem', 'say', 'suggest'.
   Improvize a speech of two minutes on a subject volunteered by a colleague. As you improvize you avoid saying any of these words. The other members of the group referee and stop you if you say one. Then the next person tries the same. This exercise trains you to paraphrase and find synonyms under time pressure.

Source: also Szabó 2003: 162

D.80 Use Plan B

Aim: to force yourself to find alternative ways of expressing ideas.
You will need: a speech to interpret, a cool head.

While interpreting, deliberately don't use a word or expression that you've already thought of – instead, find a synonym. Repeat this process throughout a speech you're interpreting. This exercise will mirror those situations when it's the wrong word or expression that initially comes to mind in the booth and you really do need to find something else. It's also good practice for stretching your ability to find solutions quickly.

Source: Gillies 2001:84

D.81 Mnemonic activation* 3

Aim: to activate* recall of generic terms.
You will need: at least one other person, several lists of similar items.

One person offers a list of items, the others must offer a generic term for the end of the list.

Example 1

Lecturer: eagles, hawks, falcons, kites, ospreys, buzzards…

Students: eagles, hawks **and other birds of prey.**

Example 2

> Lecturer: prescriptions, dental treatment, sight tests, vouchers for glasses...
>
> Students: dental treatment **and other free Social Security benefits**.

Source: Ballester and Jimenez 1991: 240; Gran 1995: 157

D.82 Mnemonic activation* 4

Aim: to activate* recall of synonymous terms.
You will need: at least one other person, several lists of similar items.

One person offers a list of items, the others must offer synonyms.

Example 1

> Trainer: environment
>
> Students: ecology, atmosphere, the air we breathe, our natural surroundings, our medium...

Example 2

> Trainer: Mrs. Thatcher
>
> Students: the former British Prime Minister, the former British Premier, The Iron Lady, Mr. Major's predecessor, Mr. Gonzalez' former counterpart, Britain's longest-governing Prime Minister.

This exercise can be played as a game in a group of three or more, with each person taking it in turn to produce a synonym. The exercise activates linguistic reflexes (synonyms, antonyms, lexical structures) and basic strategies for interpreting – defining or describing when the exact word escapes us.

Source: Ballester and Jimenez 1991: 240; Ilg 1978: 79; Lomb 2008: 125

Self-monitoring

Whether working in consecutive mode or simultaneous, an interpreter has to check or monitor their own output while they are interpreting. This is another task to add to the long list of things the interpreter must do while interpreting. The exercises below seek to isolate the monitoring task or focus it on specific elements of your work.

D.83 Listen to other students' work

Aim: to practise assessing interpreting performances.
You will need: another student interpreter.

One of the simplest ways to train your ability to listen to, and monitor, your own interpreting performance is to listen to, and assess, those of your fellow students. Always listen with particular criteria in mind – for example, is the delivery good, do the main points make sense, is the language register appropriate? And try to listen only for one or two of these criteria, and not always all of them at once.

D.84 Post-it notes

Aim: to remind yourself of issues for which you need to monitor your performance.
You will need: a post-it note or a big felt-tip pen, a list of interpreting technique issues you wish to address.

Before you start interpreting (in consecutive or simultaneous modes), take a moment to think about which parts of your interpreting you need to work on (and therefore monitor most closely). Alternatively, ask a teacher or fellow student to suggest something. Pick one thing and write a single word that represents that issue on a post-it note, or with a big felt-tip on a piece of paper, and place it somewhere unavoidably visible to you while you're interpreting (for example on the console or the booth window). If you say 'umm' and 'err' a lot, you might just write 'ERR' on the post-it. If you suffer from language interference* you might write 'Reformulate!'.

When you're interpreting your mind is far too busy to think, for more than the first few seconds of the speech you're interpreting, about the technique issues that you valiantly swore to tackle today. This note will remind you every few seconds, without any additional strain on your mental capacity. Now you try to correct the problem throughout the speech you're interpreting.

D.85 Keep a logbook 3

Aim: to track progress over time and draw attention to recurring technique issues.
You will need: a small notebook.

Record the comments made about your interpreting performances by teachers and your fellow students. The first step to solving problems is to be aware of them. Keeping a record is the only sure way of remembering and comparing your performances over the year or two of your course.

Make a distinction between vocabulary and interpreting technique issues. Items of vocabulary tend to come up very rarely, and are therefore less useful per item. Technique issues will recur with greater regularity and are thus much more useful to you. One suggestion would be to note technique related comments from the front and vocab from the back of the same book. Alternatively you could keep a book for each. As time goes by you can flick through the pad seeing how the same problems recur, or what progress is being made (as comments noted change over time). It can also be used in the booth to remind you of certain 'dos' and 'don'ts'.
Source: also Sainz 1993: 139; Gillies 2001: 68; Sherwood-Gabrielson *et al* 2008: 224

D.86 Record your work

Aim: to keep a record of performances and problems and track progress.
You will need: a voice recorder, a notebook.

Record all your interpreting work! And listen to at least some of it each week. And then correct it!

Memory is not always reliable. After class or practice we might 'forget' things we like to hear less about our interpreting and remember only things we like to hear. In this way your subconscious might stop you dealing with a technique problem for quite some time. Recording yourself whenever you work will add a little more pressure and motivation to succeed. Practising with no apparent pressure on, you can let down your guard and relax. Interpreters should never do this while working.

D.87 Give it a thorough going over

Aim: to monitor and correct your reformulation without time pressure.
You will need: a voice recorder, a speech.

Record yourself interpreting and listen to it sentence by sentence, paragraph by paragraph. As you go, reword it (in the same language as the taped interpretation) into a version you might have expected to hear from an articulate native speaker giving their own speech. What are the grammatical, idiomatical, intonational and structural differences? Could you have applied what you now know to your interpretation? Try to.

You'll find that the solutions you arrive at here will stick in your mind and come back to you when interpreting in the future.

D.88 Record and transcribe

Aim: to isolate the self-monitoring skill, create awareness of what you've said while interpreting.
You will need: voice recorder, a native speaker.

You will be much more critical of your performance when reading a written version of it than you would be if (indeed when) you were speaking. Consequently you will notice more linguistic errors if interpreting into a B language*, and technique problems when working into your own language, for example unfinished sentences, excessive self-correction, umm-ing and err-ing, unconvincing intonation etc. In the example below you can see that the interpreter has spotted and made a self-correction, an unnecessary joining of two sentences with 'and', as well as some overly colloquial idiom.

Example

Your first version	*Your own correction*
However, the Rhine valley is the location for US military **bases, military camps** ever since the second World War **and** all you can see around these camps are concrete walls and wire fences, which is the reason why the people living in the area are **so mad about this.**	However, since the second World War, **we see** US military bases there. The bases are surrounded with concrete walls and barbed-wire fences. All this infuriates local residents.

D.89 Confer with colleagues

Aim: to reflect on your own performance.
You will need: a few minutes with colleagues after each interpreted speech.

When you leave the booth after doing a simultaneous, take a couple of minutes to discuss with the other students who were interpreting what was difficult about the speech and where and why you had difficulties. Sharing experience in this way can be a learning experience.

Source: Moser-Mercer

D.90 Shadow* a bad speaker

Aim: to familiarize yourself with possible delivery problems and practise correcting them.
You will need: a speech recording of a poor speaker.

Shadow a speech that has a large number of delivery problems (ie. frequent restarts, umm-ing and err-ing, self-correction etc.). Eliminate the same shortcomings in your version. Once you've corrected another speaker's flaws you'll be less likely to make the same mistakes yourself later.

Source: Kalina, 2000: 180

Stress management

Tensing your body, grimacing and clenching your fists will not help you concentrate.[2]

Seleskovitch and Lederer 1989: 20

There are countless ways to deal with, and prevent, stress that have nothing particularly to do with interpreting: sport, yoga, breathing techniques, meditation, going on holiday etc. They will work, or not work, on interpreters in the same way that they do on any non-interpreters. So if stress is a real problem for you, please also research these techniques elsewhere, or even consult a medical specialist. It's not my intention to list them all here (which would take up several books) or to suggest medical expertise that I don't have.

What I have listed here are (1) exercises that practise interpreting skills but are also sufficiently light-hearted to take a bit of the pressure off; and (2) exercises that I have seen used with success on interpreters or interpreting students. This is in no way an exhaustive list of stress-relieving exercises.

Having a bit of fun while interpreting may show you that, as Seleskovitch says above, being stressed doesn't actually help. And the fact that exercises are fun should not mean that they are unsuitable for the classroom. Fun can be a very positive factor when you are practising. We don't have to be unhappy to interpret well! And if you can recreate the feeling you had while interpreting and having fun when you are interpreting for real, you may well learn something important about managing your stress.

D.91 Dubbing 2

Aim: to deverbalize, have fun.
You will need: a video recording of part of a soap opera all students are familiar with, or where the plot-line is obvious.

This exercise can be a great ice-breaker, or a bit of fun to wind down after a stressful day.

Play a short extract of the recording to the group. Everyone listens. Now assign a character to each member of the group and play the recording again, this time with the sound muted. Each member of the group must now recreate and speak their part of the dialogue as faithfully as possible.

In a variation of this exercise, skip the first stage – don't watch the extract with the sound audible – and go straight into an improvisation of the dialogue.

Source: Szabó 2003: 90; Nolan 2005: 39

D.92 Re-enact a comedy sketch

Aim: to practise intonation patterns in a relaxed environment.
You will need: a film recording of a great comedy sketch.

Find a filmed recording of a comedy sketch and a transcript of it – the better-known and funnier the better. The sketch should involve 2–4 people and not be longer than 3–4 minutes. You can use part of a longer sketch as well, of course. Assign one role to each member of your group. Together, watch the sketch several times, making sure you know why it's funny. Now rehearse the sketch together, repeating the script and imitating the intonation and body language of the actors/comedians in the original. Give yourselves 30–60 minutes to rehearse and then perform the sketch for other colleagues. If they laugh, you've done a good job. You'll probably laugh either way, and that's good stress prevention.

Some British examples of the type of sketch that is well-suited to this are: *Monty Python*'s 'The Four Yorkshiremen'; *Not the Nine O'clock News*, 'Python Worshippers'; and John Bird and John Fortune, 'Subprime'.

D.93 Put your feet up

Aim: to practise interpreting in a relaxed environment/posture.
You will need: a speech, possibly a comfortable chair.

Instead of recreating a stressful environment, try interpreting in the most relaxed position you can come up with, both in consecutive and simultaneous interpreting. Exaggerate! This should counterbalance the unnaturally tense posture that most (student) interpreters have when working. It will also demonstrate that the working of the brain is not enhanced by being huddled over the microphone, eyes closed, grasping the desk so tightly that your fingers go white.

Put your feet up, lean back, chill out. It's only an exercise!

D.94 Stand on a chair

Aim: to practise working when you're the centre of attention.
You will need: a largish room, several other people.

This exercise is most obviously suited to consecutive, but it can be done in simultaneous 'chuchotage' as well.
  Try giving your interpretation from atop a chair. This position will make you feel a little more exposed, a little more the centre of attention. Classrooms tend to be much smaller, and often quieter, cosier and less intimidating, than the rooms and spaces in which interpreters really do consecutive. This exercise creates a little more stress so that *normal* interpreting later feels less stressful.

Source: Fox

D.95 Stand in a corner

Aim: to recreate a professional type of environment to work in.
You will need: a largish room, at least one other person.

This exercise is most obviously suited to consecutive, but it can be done in simultaneous 'chuchotage' as well.
  Try moving as far away in the room from your practice partners as you can and interpreting from there. In this way you are forced to project your voice further than you normally would.
  Classrooms tend to be much smaller, and often quieter, cosier and less intimidating than the rooms and spaces in which interpreters really do consecutive. This exercise mimics the atmosphere of real-life consecutive and creates a little more stress so that *normal* interpreting later feels less stressful.

D.96 Dress-up Friday

Aim: to recreate the professional environment (and stress) of real-life interpreting.
You will need: at least five other people, a set of smart clothes.

In some countries companies allow their staff to come to work dressed more casually than normal on Fridays, or once a month, in a tradition that's called 'dress-down Friday'. As students you won't be dressed that smartly for class, so every month recreate a professional atmosphere by arranging to all come into practice in your work (smart) clothes. Perhaps you could also arrange for a larger number of people to practise together in a larger room, to make the atmosphere a little different from your normal classes, more like the professional reality of interpreting. If your school organises mock-conferences for interpreting students, these are an ideal opportunity to 'dress up'.
  This exercise mimics the atmosphere of real-life consecutive and creates a little more stress so that *normal* interpreting later feels less stressful.

D.97 Blind drawing

Aim: to demonstrate the need for, and practise, precision of expression.
You will need: a map, diagram or the like, one other person.

This exercise will work with pretty much any picture, but start with a map, a diagram of a machine or a geographical feature. One person can see the diagram, the other cannot. The person who can see the diagram describes it in their B language* to the other person, who must try to recreate the diagram by drawing what they hear.

You might initially get something very different to the original diagram, but you'll soon learn to express with considerable accuracy all of the 'information' contained in the picture. In the meantime you might find it quite funny! This is also useful because interpreters should not assume that their listeners have understood what the speaker meant, just because they have said the same thing as the speaker.

Source: Nolan 2005: 298

D.98 Face massage

Aim: to improve diction and relax the face and parts of the body involved in speaking.
You will need: space to stretch your arms.

Massage your face, the underside of your jaw and the jaw muscles. Pull on your lips. Scrunch the face together and then stretch it apart. Pull funny faces (gurn)! Pull the hands down the front of your face, pulling your mouth open, relaxing the lower jaw and making a 'ha' sound as you do it.

A lot of tension resides in the face that can affect the quality of your voice and your stress levels.

Source: Mühle

D.99 Aahhh!

Aim: to relax.
You will need: space to stretch your arms.

Breathe deeply, raising your arms above your head, then let the arms, shoulders, head and chest fall, exhaling to the sound 'aahh'. Repeat five times.

Source: Mühle

D.100 Virtual travel

Aim: to relax.
You will need: a comfy chair or bit of floor clean enough to lie on.

Sit down, sit back and close your eyes. Imagine something particularly pleasant and calming for you. For example, that you are lying in a hammock by a beach somewhere warm and quiet. Look around the imaginary scene, take in all the detail, enjoy the calm. Listen to the quiet, perhaps the sound of the waves. Feel how comfy you are in your hammock.

You may not even realize that you are tense or stressed until you try an exercise like this that takes you back to a more relaxed state. Studying interpreting can be a full-on experience and it's important to take some time out (virtual or otherwise) to relax.

Source: Mühle

D.101 Shoulder release

Aim: to relax the shoulders and neck.
You will need: a quiet darkened room.

Arm weight release: standing on one spot, feet the width of your hips apart, let your arms hang heavily from relaxed shoulders. By just moving your body, get your arms swinging like a bored child. You should feel the arms slapping against your body. Feel how heavy your arms are.

Shoulder release swing: swing one arm backwards and forwards while bobbing the knees to help the momentum of the swing. Then, still with knees bobbing, let the arm wheel round in a full circle (the knees bob down with every downward movement of the arm). Keep the joints relaxed. See if you can let the elbow skim past your ear. This should feel effortless. (Any discomfort or pain, stop and move on to the next stage.)

Weight release exercise: lean your weight onto one leg with your head tilted to the same side, ear suspended over the tip of the shoulder as if you were listening to the floor. Let the arm on that side hang free of the body, setting it to swing like a pendulum. Once the movement has come to a finish, close your eyes and feel the weight of the arm hanging. Then follow the stages below. Imagine...

the fingers	getting heavier and dropping heavily away from the hand
the hand	getting heavier and dropping heavily away from the lower arm
the lower arm	getting heavier and dropping heavily away from the upper arm
the upper arm	getting heavier and dropping heavily away from the shoulder
the shoulder	getting heavier and dropping heavily away from the head and neck.

You may feel tingling as the blood supply is increased – this is natural. Now straighten the spine slowly without lifting the shoulder. Feel the weight of the shoulder hanging from the spine and the arm hanging from your shoulder. Check in a mirror to compare one side to the other, to see how much your shoulder has released.

Repeat the exercise on the other side.

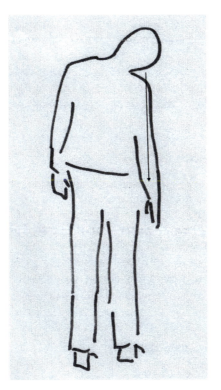

Source: Gudgeon

D.102 Auto-suggestion

Aim: to relax a tense body.
You will need: enough space to lie down.

If you are lucky enough to have a quiet corner available to you, with enough space to lie down flat on the floor, this relaxation technique can be very effective. And it only takes around five to ten minutes.

Lie down on your back and close your eyes. Take a couple of deep breaths. You are going to repeat mentally the following expressions and visualize the parts of the body described.

I relax the feet, I relax the feet. The feet are relaxed. I relax the ankles and calves, I relax the ankles and calves. The ankles and calves are relaxed. I relax the knees and thighs, I relax the knees and thighs. The knees and thighs are relaxed.

Continue with the same pattern through the rest of the body, including the hips and buttocks, the abdomen, the chest, the lower back, the upper back, the hands and arms, the shoulders, the neck and throat, the jaw and tongue, the lips and cheeks, the eyes and eyelids, the temples and forehead, the scalp and head.

You may fall asleep at some stage during this process. That's already a good thing, because it means you relaxed enough to fall asleep. If you practise regularly you will remain awake while your body sleeps. The relaxation in this case is even more thorough.

You can buy audio recordings of someone else speaking these instructions, which makes for an even more effective relaxation. This technique is closely related to a type of yogic meditation called yoga nidra for which recordings are also widely available.

D.103 Sight translation* with a time limit

Aim: to practise fluent delivery and voice project under pressure.
You will need: a stop watch and timer, a text to sight translate.

Start by sight translating a text as per usual, timing how long it takes. Now sight translate the same text again but set the timer for two-thirds of the time you took for your first effort. Try to finish sight translating the text within that time limit.

Compete with other students to see who can do the quickest version. But if you're doing this as a stress management exercise, don't take it too seriously!

Source: Van Hoof 1962: 115

D.104 Improvisation exercise 1

Aim: to think and speak clearly under time pressure.
You will need: an audience of at least one other person.

Improvise a speech of two minutes on a subject volunteered by a colleague. As you improvise you should be thinking ahead to your next sentence/paragraph or the rest of the speech so that the speech remains fluent. This mirrors the split attention that the interpreter achieves when working.

The other members of the group referee and stop you if you hesitate, repeat yourself or stop making sense. The game-like and competitive nature of this exercise makes it good fun, and therefore makes being under pressure fun.

D.105 Improvisation exercise 2

Aim: to think and speak clearly under time pressure.
You will need: an audience of at least one other person.

Improvise a speech of 2 minutes on a subject volunteered by a colleague. As you improvise you should be thinking ahead to your next sentence/paragraph or the rest of the speech so that the speech remains fluent.

As you speak the other person periodically shows cards with keywords on them. The person speaking must think ahead in order to incorporate the word/idea coherently into the improvised speech. This mirrors the split attention that the interpreter achieves when working.

The other members of the group referee and stop you if you hesitate, repeat yourself or stop making sense. The game-like and competitive nature of this exercise makes it good fun, and therefore makes being under pressure fun.

D.106 Say the opposite

Aim: to practise reformulating.
You will need: speech extracts.

Invert the meaning of a text, in the same language. There are several variations of this exercise; in order of difficulty: you can do this using a transcript and write your own version; or use a transcript and 'sight translate' to arrive at your version; or get someone to read (or better, give a spoken version of) the speech and paraphrase that. Each time, reformulate in the same language as the original, which should be one of your active languages.

All of this is likely to be quite funny, so don't take it too seriously. Enjoy, have a laugh. Interpreting doesn't have to be only about stressing out.

Example: before

Ladies and Gentlemen, a very warm welcome to the British Embassy this evening. Many thanks to you all for coming. And many thanks to the Deutsch-Britische Gesellschaft for organising this evening.

The Gesellschaft hardly needs an introduction. Only four years after the war, in 1949, a group of Düsseldorf citizens decided that they needed to help reconstruct the relationship between Germany and Britain. They started a series of conferences in Königswinter to bring together German and British parliamentarians, academics and opinion-formers...

British Ambassador
British Embassy, Berlin
9th September 2003

Example: after

> Ladies and **Germs**, please **don't make yourself at home** in the British
> Embassy tonight, **you are not welcome. Shame you came.** Likewise
> **it's a pity** the Deutsch-Britische Gesellschaft had to go and organise
> this event.
>   I **doubt** many of you will have heard of the Gesellschaft. **Quite some
> time** after the war, 4 years in fact, a group of citizens from Düsseldorf
> decided **there was no need** for their **interference** in reconstructing the
> relationship between Germany and Britain. **They failed** to organise a
> single conference anywhere which might have brought together German
> and British parliamentarians, academics and opinion-formers...

The fact that these exercises do not faithfully reflect what you'll actually do when
working as an interpreter, or that they might actually be fun to do, will in no way
detract from their usefulness.

Source: also Gile 1995: 212

D.107 Try extremes of register

Aim: to practise reformulating, saying the same thing in very different ways.
You will need: a speech.

Interpret, not into the same register as the speaker, but into a different, extreme
register instead. Interpret the same speech, for example, in very colloquial slang.
Then interpret the same speech again in an over-the-top aristocratic drawl. You
can also try to imitate different regional accents or certain types of people. With a
bit of imagination this exercise can be very entertaining. Have a bit of fun with it!

Example: original

> Ladies and Gentlemen, a very warm welcome to the British Embassy
> this evening. Many thanks to you all for coming. And many thanks to the
> Deutsch-Britische Gesellschaft for organising this evening.
>   The Gesellschaft hardly needs an introduction. Only four years after
> the war, in 1949, a group of Düsseldorf citizens decided that they needed
> to help reconstruct the relationship between Germany and Britain. They
> started a series of conferences in Königswinter to bring together German
> and British parliamentarians, academics and opinion-formers...
>
> British Ambassador, British Embassy, Berlin
> September 2003

Example: lower register

> Hi **folks**, welcome to the British Embassy tonight. Thanks to everyone for **coming along**. And **a big 'thank you'** to the Deutsch-Britische Gesellschaft for putting on this **bash**.
>   The Gesellschaft you all know. In '49, just 4 years after the war, **some guys** from Düsseldorf sat down and **came up with the idea** of rebuilding the ties between Blighty and Germany. They **kicked off** with a set of talks in Königswinter, **the idea being** to get German and British MP's, intellectuals and **media folk** to sit down together at one table…

Example: higher register

> Good evening Ladies and Gentlemen. Let me **express my great pleasure** at being able to welcome you here tonight. Let me also **express my gratitude** to the Deutsch-Britische Gesellschaft for hosting us this evening.
>   The Gesellschaft hardly **requires** introduction. A mere four years after World War II, in 1949, a **league of gentlemen hailing** from Düsseldorf **determined that they should** reforge the relationship between Germany and the United Kingdom. **They convened a series of symposia** in Königswinter which would reunite German and British parliamentarians, men of letters and opinion-formers.

Source: Mikkelson 2000: 82, Gillies 2001: 83

D.108 Overuse a metaphor

Aim: to make interpreting fun and funny, practising interpreting the meaning, not only the words.
You will need: a speech.

Decide with colleagues on a type of metaphor and try to overuse it throughout a single speech. For example, sporting and nautical metaphors are two good choices: calm the waters, shots across bows, in the doldrums, shipshape, a loose cannon, embark, etc. The version of the speech you reproduce should, of course, still correspond to the sense of the original, even though the original speaker has not indulged in the same way. The more common the type of metaphor you choose is in everyday language, the easier this exercise will be.

You don't need to be too strict about the meaning of the original if you are using this exercise as part of your stress management work. Allow yourself to have a laugh doing it.

Example: before

> Ladies and Gentlemen, a very warm welcome to the British Embassy this evening. Many thanks to you all for coming. And many thanks to the Deutsch-Britische Gesellschaft for organising this evening.
>
> The Gesellschaft hardly needs an introduction. Only four years after the war, in 1949, a group of Düsseldorf citizens decided that they needed to help reconstruct the relationship between Germany and Britain. They started a series of conferences in Königswinter to bring together German and British parliamentarians, academics and opinion-formers...
>
> British Ambassador
> British Embassy, Berlin
> 9th September 2003

Example: after

> Good evening **crew** and **welcome aboard**. Thank you all for **pushing the boat out** with us this evening. A **hearty** thanks also to the Deutsch-Britische Gesellschaft for this evening's **shindig**.
>
> The Gesellschaft is a familiar **craft**. **Launched** four years after the war, in 1949, when a group of Düsseldorfers set out to **refit** the relationship between Germany and Britain. They **floated** the idea of a **raft** of conferences in Königswinter to bring together the **captains** of German and British academia, media and the political world...

Notes

1 Gerver 1974; Gile 1987.
2 'Ce n'est pas en adoptant une attitude physique, traits crispés et poings serrés, que l'on obtient un effet de concentration.' Translation from the French by Andrew Gillies.

Glossary

A language According to AIIC an A language is the interpreter's native language (or another language strictly equivalent to a native language), into which the interpreter works from all her or his other languages in both modes of interpretation, simultaneous and consecutive. (www.aiic.net)

Activate You may have seen a word, expression or phrase several times but never actually used it yourself. The first time you try to use it will require considerably more intellectual effort than subsequent times. By deliberately using it a few times you will move that word, expression or phrase from your passive knowledge to your active knowledge and from then on it will be more rapidly available to you for active use (until, or unless, it drifts back into your passive knowledge through disuse).

Active language A language into which an interpreter interprets. All interpreters have one active language, many have two. Only very few have more than two. An active language should be at least comparable in standard to a university-educated native-speaker's level.

B Language According to AIIC a B language is a language other than the interpreter's native language, of which they have a perfect command and into which they work from one or more of their other languages. Some interpreters work into a B language in only one of the two modes of interpretation. (www.aiic.net)

C Language According to AIIC a C language is a language of which the interpreter has a complete understanding and from which they work. (www.aiic.net)

Cloze (test) A cloze test is an exercise consisting of a portion of text from which certain words have been removed. The object of the exercise is then to replace the missing words.

Cognates Words in different languages derived from a single language or language form, e.g. Konstellation (DE), constellation (FR), constellation (EN).

Décalage Also called 'time lag' or Ear-Voice Span. It is the time difference between when the speaker says a thing and the moment the interpreter reproduces that thing in the target language.

Delivery How you speak, rather than what you say. Your public speaking skills.

Deverbalization A technique that has been fundamental to the teaching of interpreting, particularly in the Parisian schools, over the last 40 years. Initially described and taught by Seleskovitch, it consists in understanding and/or visualizing the content of what one is hearing and producing a target-language version based on that understanding or visual image, rather than based on the words used in the source-language version.

Ear-Voice span See **Décalage**.

Idea When referring to part of a speech, in this book 'idea' will mean the smallest 'parts of the message' (Thiéry 1981: 110), that is to say, Subject, Verb (and often Object) groups (Gillies 2005: 35). In other words, a unit of the speech that tells you 'who does what'.

    In other books you will find the term 'idea' used to mean the major points of a speech (corresponding almost to paragraphs or groups of paragraphs), and in yet others to mean the underlying meaning of an expression, rather than the words that go to make it up (so 'bored' for 'twiddling his thumbs').

Interference Sometimes called calque, from the French, interference is the inappropriate use in the target language of structures and words from the source language.

Internalize Carry out an activity with a degree of automation, that is to say without giving it our full attention. This level of competence in a skill is usually achieved through repeated practise of the skill in question over several months.

Links Links signal the way the speaker wants the listener to relate what is about to be said to what has been said before (Baker 1992: 190). They are sometimes also called logical links, conjunctions, link words or connectors.

Passive language A language from which an interpreter interprets. Also known as a C language, see above.

Sight translation To give an oral rendition in one language of a text written in another as you read that text for the first time, simultaneously so to speak.

Shadowing Listening to a speaker and repeating word for word what they say.

Source language The language from which you are translating/interpreting.

Stock phrases Also known as pat phrases. Standard expressions that come up repeatedly in political discourse and which are no more than synonyms for other, more common expressions; e.g. I'm much obliged (thank you); to my mind (I think) etc.

Target language The language into which you are translating/interpreting.

Time lag See **Décalage**

Unit of meaning Small sections of discourse that have a meaning in context for someone wishing to understand. The suggestion being that it's not worth starting to interpret until you have heard at least a unit of meaning. 'Units of meaning are the synthesis of a number of words present in short-term memory associating with previous cognitive experiences or recollections' (Lederer 1978: 330).

Bibliography

Marked in bold are those texts that will be of most interest and use to students of conference interpreting.

Alexieva, B. (1992) 'The optimum text in simultaneous interpreting: a cognitive approach to interpreter training', in Dollerup, C. and Loddegaard, A. (eds) (1992), *Teaching Translation and Interpreting – Training, Talent and Experience*, Amsterdam: Benjamins, pp. 221–31

Alexieva, B. (1994) 'On teaching note-taking in consecutive interpreting', in Dollerup, C. and Lindegaard, A. (eds) (1994), *Teaching Translation and Interpreting 2. Insights, Aims, Visions*, Amsterdam: Benjamins, pp. 199–210.

Altman, J. (1989) 'The role of tutor demonstration in teaching interpreting', in Gran, L. and Dodds, J. (eds) (1989), *The Theoretical and Practical Aspects of Teaching Conference Interpreting*, Udine: Campanotto Editore, pp. 237–40.

Baker, M. (1992) *In Other Words*, London: Routledge.

Ballester, A. and Jimenez, C. (1992) 'Approaches to the teaching of interpreting: mnemonic and analytic strategies', in Dollerup, C. and Loddegaard, A. (eds) (1992), *Teaching Translation and Interpreting – Training, Talent and Experience*, Amsterdam: Benjamins, pp. 237–44.

Bartram, M. and Walton, R. (1991) *Correction – a positive approach to language mistakes*, Brighton: Language Teaching Publications.

Bryson, B. (1990) *Mother Tongue*, London: Penguin.

Collins-Robert (1995) *Collins-Robert French Dictionary*, 4th edn, London: HarperCollins.

Daniels, P., *Magic Memory Language Method*, website, www.200words-a-day.com/learn-spanish.html (accessed 1 June 2012).

De Clarens, J. (1973) 'L'expression', in *ELA* 12, Oct–Dec, 124–6.

Déjean Le Féal, K. (1976) 'Le perfectionnement linguistique', in *ELA* (24), Oct–Dec, 42–51.

Déjean Le Féal, K. (1981) 'L'enseignement des méthodes d'interprétation et de la traduction', in Delisle, J. (ed.), *L'enseignement de l'interprétation et la traduction simultanée*, Ottawa: University of Ottawa Press, pp. 79–90.

Déjean Le Féal, K. (1997) 'Simultaneous interpretation with "training wheels"', *Meta* 42(4), 616–62.

Delisle, J. (ed.) (1981) *L'enseignement de l'interprétation et la traduction simultanée*, Ottawa: University of Ottawa Press.

Dollerup, C. and Appel, V. (eds) (1996) *Teaching Translation and Interpreting 3*, Amsterdam: Benjamins.

268   *Bibliography*

Dollerup, C. and Lindegaard, A. (eds) (1994) *Teaching Translation and Interpreting 2. Insights, Aims, Visions*, Amsterdam: Benjamins.

Dollerup, C. and Loddegaard, A. (eds) (1992) *Teaching Translation and Interpreting – Training, Talent and Experience*, Amsterdam: Benjamins.

EMCI (2002) *Teaching Simultaneous Interpretation into a 'B' language*, Paris: EMCI. Online. Available: www.emcinterpreting.org/repository/pdf/EMCI-TeachingSimultaneousInto B-vol1.pdf (accessed 1 August 2012).

Falbo, C. (1995) 'Interprétation consécutive et exercices préparatoires.' *The Interpreters' Newsletter* 6, 87–91.

Gelfert, H-D. (2005) *Was ist Deutsch?*, München: Verlag C. H. Beck.

Gerver, D. (1974) 'Simultaneous listening and speaking and retention of prose', *Quarterly Journal of Experimental Psychology* 26. 337–42.

Gerver D. and Sinaiko, H.W. (1978) *Language Interpretation and Communication*, New York: Plenum Press.

Gethin, A. and Gunnemark, E.V. (1996) *The Art and Science of Learning Languages*, Oxford: Intellect.

Gile, D. (1985) 'L'interprétation et la connaissance des langues', *Meta* 30(4), 320–31.

Gile, D. (1987) 'Les exercices d'interprétation et la dégradation du français: une étude de cas', *Meta* 32(4).

Gile, D. (1995) *Basic Concepts and Models for Interpreter and Translator Training*, Amsterdam: Benjamins.

Gillies, A. (2001) *Conference Interpreting: A Students' Companion*, 1st edn, Cracow: Tertium.

Gillies, A. (2004) *Conference Interpreting: A New Students' Companion*, Cracow: Tertium.

Gillies, A. (2005) **Note-taking for Consecutive Interpreting**, Manchester: St Jerome.

Gran, L. (1995) 'In-training development', in Moser-Mercer, B., Ozeroff, A. and Kralova, J. (eds), *Translator's Strategies and Creativity*, Benjamins: Amsterdam.

Gran, L. and Dodds, J. (eds) (1989), *The Theoretical and Practical Aspects of Teaching Conference Interpreting*, Udine: Campanotto Editore.

Guichot de Fortis, C. (2009) **A Few Thoughts on 'B' Languages**. Online. Available http://interpreters.free.fr/language/BlanguagesDEFORTIS.htm (accessed 14 August 2012).

Harmer, J. (1990) *The Practice of English Language Teaching*, New York: Longman.

Hartzell, J. (ed.) (1998) *Ocenia Tłumaczenia Ustnego – materiały konferencji naukowej*, OBSP: Łódź.

Heine, M. (2000) '**Effektives selbststudium – schluessel zum erfolg in der dolmetscherausbildung**', in Kalina, S., Buhl, S. and Arbogast, G. (eds), *Dolmetschen: Theorie – Praxis – Didaktik*, St. Ingbert: Roehriger UniVerlag, pp. 213–29.

Herbert, J. (1952) *Le manuel de l'interprète*, Geneva: Georg.

Hey, J. (2006) *Die Kunst des Sprechens*, Mainz: Schott.

Ilg, G. (1978) 'L'apprentissage de l'interprétation simultanée. De 1 'allemand vers le français', *Parallèles* 1, *Cahiers de l'ETI*, University of Geneva.

Interpreters and Conference Interpreting Forum (2010) comment thread. Online. Available: http://interpreters.freeforums.org/index.php (accessed 1 June 2010).

Interpreter's Launchpad (2012). Online. Available: www.interprenaut.com (accessed 10 August 2012).

Jones, R. (1998) **Conference Interpreting Explained**, 2nd edn, Manchester: St Jerome.

Kalina, S. (1992) 'Discourse Processing and Interpreting Strategies – an approach to the teaching of interpreting', in Dollerup, C. and Loddegard, A. (eds), *Teaching Translation and Interpreting – Training, Talent and Experience*, Amsterdam: Benjamins, pp. 251–8.

Kalina, S. (1998) *Strategische Prozesse beim Dolmetschen: Theoretische Grundlagen, empirische Fallstudien, didaktische Konsequenzen*, Tübingen: G. Narr Verlag.

Kalina, S. (2000) 'Zu den Grundlagen einer Didaktik des Dolmetschens', in Kalina, S., Buhl, S. and Arbogast, G. (eds) (2000), *Dolmetschen: Theorie – Praxis – Didaktik*, St. Ingbert: Roehriger UniVerlag. pp. 161–189.

Kalina, S., Buhl, S. and Arbogast, G. (eds) (2000) *Dolmetschen: Theorie – Praxis – Didaktik*, St. Ingbert: Roehriger UniVerlag.

Kesselman-Turkel, J. and Peterson F. (1982) *Note-taking Made Easy*, Madison: University of Wisconsin Press.

Kornakov, P. (2000) 'Five principles and five skills for training interpreters', *Meta* 45(2), 241–8.

Krawutschke, P. (ed.) (1989) *Translator and Interpreter Training and Foreign Language Pedagogy*, State University of New York.

Kremer, B. (2005) 'Réflexions d'un praticien sur une étape de la formation des interprètes de conférence: approche méthodologique et pédagogique', *Meta* 50, 785–94.

Kurz, I. (1992) 'Shadowing exercises in interpreter training', in Dollerup, C. and Loddegard, A. (eds) (1992), *Teaching Translation and Interpreting – Training, Talent and Experience*, Amsterdam: Benjamins, pp. 245–50.

Lakoff, G. and Johnson, M. (1980) *Metaphors We Live By*, University of Chicago Press.

Lambert, S. (1989) 'Information processing among conference interpreters', in Gran, L. and Dodds, J. (eds) (1989), *The Theoretical and Practical Aspects of Teaching Conference Interpreting*, Udine: Campanotto Editore. pp. 83–91.

Lambert, S. and Moser-Mercer, B. (eds) (1994) *Bridging the Gap*, Amsterdam: Benjamins.

Lederer, M. (1978) 'Simultaneous interpreting – units of meaning and other features', in Gerver, D. and Sinaiko, H.W. (1978), *Language Interpretation and Communication*, New York: Plenum Press, pp. 323–32.

Lederer, M. (2001) *Interpréter pour traduire*, Paris: Didier Érudition.

Lederer, M. (2003) *The Interpretative Model* (English translation of *La traduction aujourd'hui – le modèle interprétif* (1994), Hachette), Manchester: St Jerome.

Lewis, M. and Wilberg, P. (1990) *Business English: An Individualised Learning Programme*, Brighton: Language Teaching Publications.

Lewis, M. (1986) *The English Verb*, Brighton: Language Teaching Publications.

Lewis, M. (1993) *The Lexical Approach*, Brighton: Language Teaching Publications.

Lewis, M. (2000) *Teaching Collocation*, London: Heinle Cengage Learning.

Linklater, K. (2006) *Freeing the Natural Voice*, London: Nick Hern Books.

Lomb, K. (2008) (English edition) Polyglot – How I Learn Languages, Berkeley: TESL-EJ. Available: http://tesl-ej.org/ej45/tesl-ej.ej45.fr1.pdf (accessed 1 August 2012).

Lorayne, H. (1958) *How to Develop a Superpowered Memory*, Preston: A.Thomas and Co.

Lorayne, H. and Lucas, J. (1974) *The Memory Book*, New York: Ballantine.

Makarova, V. (1994) 'Whose line is it anyway? Or teaching improvization in interpreting', in Dollerup, C. and Lindegaard, A, (eds) (1994), *Teaching Translation and Interpreting 2. Insights, Aims, Visions*, Amsterdam: Benjamins. pp. 207 10.

Margolis, R. and Bell, C. (1986) *Instructing for Results*, Minnesota: Pfeiffer and Co.

Marín, M. and Heffington, V. (2008) *Memorias del IV foro Nacional de Estudios en Lenguas*, Chetumal: Universidad de Quintana Roo.

Martin, A. and Padilla, P. (1989) 'Preparing students for scientific and technical conferences' in Gran, L. and Dodds, J. (eds), *The Theoretical and Practical Aspects of Teaching Conference Interpreting*, Udine: Campanotto Editore.

Mikkelson, H. (2000) *Introduction to Court Interpreting*, Manchester: St. Jerome.

Moeller, S. (2006) *Polskę da się lubić*, Poznań: Publikat.

Monacelli, C. (1999) *Messaggi in codice. Analisi del discorso e strategie per prenderne appunti*, Milan: FrancoAngeli.

Moser-Mercer, B. (1994) 'Aptitude tests of conference interpreting', in Lambert, S. and Moser-Mercer, B. (eds) (1994), *Bridging the Gap*, Amsterdam: Benjamins, pp. 57–68.

Moser-Mercer, B., Ozeroff, A. and Kralova J. (1995) *Translators' Strategies and Creativity*, Amsterdam: Benjamins.

Nadstoga, Z. (1989) 'Translator and interpreter training as part of teacher training at the Institute of English, UAM Poznan', in Krawutschke, P. (ed.), *Translator and Interpreter Training and Foreign Language Pedagogy*, State University of New York, pp. 109–18.

Namy, C. (1978) 'Reflections on the training of simultaneous interpreters: a metalinguistic approach', in Gerver D. and Sinaiko, H.W., *Language Interpretation and Communication*, New York: Plenum Press, pp. 25–33.

Nolan, J. (2005) *Interpretation: Techniques and Exercises*, Clevendon: Multilingual Matters.

Paxman, J. (1998) *The English*, London: Penguin.

Pergnier, M. and Lavault, E. (1995) *Comment perfectionner ses connaissances linguistiques*, ESIT (university published brochure).

Perlman, A. (1998) *Writing Great Speeches*, Boston: Allyn and Bacon.

Pöchhacker, F. (2004) *Introducing Interpreting Studies*, London: Routledge.

Rozan, J-F. (1956) ***La prise de notes en interprétation consécutive***, Genève: Georg.

Rozan, J-F. (2003) ***Note-taking in Consecutive Interpreting*** (English translation by A. Gillies of Rozan (1956), *La prise de notes en interprétation consécutive*), Cracow: Tertium.

Sainz, M-J. (1993) 'Student-centred corrections of translations', in Dollerup, C. and Lindegaard, A. (eds), *Teaching Translation and Interpreting 2. Insights, Aims, Visions*, Amsterdam: Benjamins, pp. 133–42.

Schjoldager, A. (1996) 'Assessment of simultaneous interpreting', in Dollerup, C. and Appel, V. (eds), *Teaching Translation and Interpreting 3*, Amsterdam: Benjamins, pp. 187–96.

Schweda-Nicholson, N. (1985) 'Consecutive interpretation training: videotapes in the classroom', *Meta* 30, 148–54.

Seleskovitch, D. (1968) *L'interprète dans les conférences internationales*, Paris: Minard Lettres modernes.

Seleskovitch, D. and Lederer M. (1989) *Pedagogie raisonnée de l'interprétation*, 2nd edn, Paris: Didier Erudition.

Seleskovitch, D. and Lederer M. (1995) *A Systematic Approach to Teaching Interpretation* (English translation by J. Harmer of Seleskovitch, D. and Lederer M. (1989), *Pedagogie raisonnée de l'interprétation*), 1st edn, The Registry of Interpreters for the Deaf.

Setton R. (2008) 'Progression in SI training', in *Forum* 6:2, pp. 173–93, Seoul.

Sherwood-Gabrielson, P., Newington, V. and Swabey, L. (2008) *Consecutive Interpreting: An Instructor's Manual*, University of Minnesota.

Szabó, C. (2003) *Interpreting: From Preparation to Performance. Recipes for Practitioners and Teachers*, Budapest: British Council.

Taylor-Bouladon, V. (2001) *Conference Interpreting – Principles and Practice*, Adelaide: Crawford.

Thiéry, C. (1981) 'L'enseignement de la prise de notes en interprétation consecutive: un faux problème?', in Delisle, J. (ed.) *L'enseignement de l'interprétation et de la traduction – de la theorie a la pedagogie*. Cahiers de traductologie 4, Ottawa: 99–112.

Tryuk, M. (2002) 'Le perfectionnement linguistique pour les interprètes vers la langue B', in *Teaching Simultaneous Interpretation into a 'B' Language*, Paris: EMCI.

Van Dam, I. (1989) 'Strategies of Simultaneous Interpretation' in Gran, L. and Dodds, J. (eds), *The Theoretical and Practical Aspects of Teaching Conference Interpreting*, Udine: Campanotto Editore, pp. 167–76.

Van Hoof, H. (1962) *Théorie et pratique de l'interprétation*, Munich: Hueber.

Visson, L. (1999) *From Russian into English – An Introduction to Simultaneous Interpretation*, 2nd edn, Newburyport: Focus Publishing.

Walker, David, 2005, *Dekalog*, at Interpreter Training Resources. Online. Available: http://interpreters.free.fr/language/dekalog.htm (accessed 1 June 2012).

Weber, W. (1989) 'Improved ways of teaching consecutive interpretation', in Gran, L. and Dodds, J. (eds), *The Theoretical and Practical Aspects of Teaching Conference Interpreting*, Udine: Campanotto Editore, pp. 161–6.

Zalka, I. (1989) 'The teaching of lexical items in Consecutive Interpretation', in Gran, L. and Dodds, J. (eds), *The Theoretical and Practical Aspects of Teaching Conference Interpreting*, Udine: Campanotto Editore, pp. 185–7.

Zanier Visintin, A. (2008) 'Pedagogic translation as a skill-enhancing tool', in *Memorias del IV foro Nacional de Estudios en Lenguas*, Universidad de Quintana Roo, pp. 460–8.

Interpreter trainers

(quoted as the unpublished source of exercises)

Béziat, Catherine, ISIT
Borg, Astrid, ISIT
Brehm, Beate, European Parliament
Carsten, Svetlana, Leeds
Fox, Brian, European Commission
Getan Bornn, Jesus, ESIT and ISIT
Gudgeon, Ailsa, Voice coach, London
Llewellyn-Smith, Sophie, Leeds
Moser-Mercer, Barbara, ETI
Mühle, Hans-Werner, Heidelberg
Poger, Julia
Walker, Karin, Cologne FHK
Walker, David, European Parliament
Woodman, Nick, European Parliament

Index

A.23	Prepare speeches in consecutive note form	Practice	Practice material	transcript	one
A.24	Prepare technical speeches	Practice	Practice material	texts, transcript	one
A.25	Read around your subject	Practice	Preparation	texts	one
A.26	News round-up	Practice	Preparation	media	group
A.27	News round-up presentation	Practice	Preparation	media	group
A.28	Pool your resources	Practice	Preparation	media	group
A.29	Brainstorm	Practice	Preparation	–	group
A.30	Brainstorm without a pen	Practice	Preparation	–	group
A.31	Improvise from prepared information	Practice	Preparation	media	group
A.32	Read around both sides of the argument	Practice	Preparation	media	one
A.33	Create a debating society	Practice	Preparation	spoken	group
A.34	Know thy speaker 1	Practice	Preparation	media	one
A.35	Know thy speaker 2	Practice	Preparation	media, spoken	one
A.36	Work with real documents	Practice	Preparation	texts	one
A.37	Sight translation	Practice	Preparation	texts	one
A.38	Focus on technique issues	Practice	Feedback	any	one
A.39	Structure your feedback	Practice	Feedback	any	pairs
A.40	Be positive	Practice	Feedback	any	pairs
A.41	Be disciplined about time management	Practice	Feedback	spoken	group
A.42	Use a feedback template	Practice	Feedback	spoken	pair
A.43	Write feedback down	Practice	Feedback	spoken	one
A.44	Keep a logbook 1	Practice	Feedback	any	one
A.45	Record your work	Practice	Feedback	spoken	one
A.46	Analyze problems encountered	Practice	Feedback	any	one
A.47	Use Post-it notes	Practice	Feedback	spoken	one
A.48	Rehearse	Practice	Feedback	spoken	one
A.49	Collect solutions	Practice	Feedback	any	one
A.50	Look for learning strategies	Practice	Feedback	internet	one
B.1	News round-up	Language	General Knowledge	media	group
B.2	News round-up presentation	Language	General Knowledge	media	group
B.3	Question the implicit knowledge in newspaper articles	Language	General Knowledge	media	one
B.4	Swot up from school books	Language	General Knowledge	books	one

B.5	Read specialist magazines	Language	General Knowledge	media	one
B.6	Prepare technical speeches	Language	General Knowledge	media	one
B.7	Understand rather than translate	Language	General Knowledge	internet	one
B.8	Wiki-parallels	Language	General Knowledge	internet	one
B.9	Research your speaker's people	Language	General Knowledge	books	one
B.10	Trivial Pursuit	Language	General Knowledge	–	group
B.11	Read books	Language	General Knowledge	books	one
B.12	The picture you can't see	Language	General Knowledge	media	pairs
B.13	Word association	Language	General Knowledge	–	group
B.14	Acronym testing	Language	General Knowledge	–	group
B.15	General knowledge collocation	Language	General Knowledge		group
B.16	Re-introducing context	Language	General Knowledge	media	pairs
B.17	What's in a name?	Language	General Knowledge	–	one
B.18	Get the news in multiple formats	Language	Passive language skills	media	one
B.19	Read different papers	Language	Passive language skills	media	one
B.20	Reading for register	Language	Passive language skills	media	one
B.21	Read specialist magazines	Language	Passive language skills	media	one
B.22	Copy out what you've read	Language	Passive language skills	media	one
B.23	Read about your language(s)	Language	Passive language skills	books	one
B.24	Make friends with dictionaries	Language	Passive language skills	books	one
B.25	Use Wikipedia as a multi-lingual dictionary	Language	Passive language skills	internet	one
B.26	Listen to talk radio	Language	Passive language skills	radio	one
B.27	Watch popular TV	Language	Passive language skills	TV, internet	one
B.28	Use the internet in other languages	Language	Passive language skills	internet	one
B.29	Change your settings to 'other language'	Language	Passive language skills	internet	one

B.30	Listen to pop music and read the lyrics	Language	Passive language skills	internet	one
B.31	Use your school's facilities	Language	Passive language skills	any	one
B.32	What's on!	Language	Passive language skills	media	one
B.33	A change is as good as a rest	Language	Passive language skills	any	one
B.34	Write in your language(s)	Language	Active language skills	–	one
B.35	Become an watchful reader	Language	Active language skills	media	one
B.36	Create topic files	Language	Active language skills	media	one
B.37	Parallel texts	Language	Active language skills	media	one
B.38	Sight translation* to activate* new language	Language	Active language skills	texts	one
B.39	The language of death	Language	Active language skills	transcript	one
B.40	Parallel texts for political standpoint	Language	Active language skills	media	one
B.41	Magic Bag	Language	Active language skills	–	group
B.42	Use concordance software	Language	Active language skills	internet	one
Bb.43	Activating grammatical structures	Language	Active language skills	transcript	one
B.44	Vocabulary ball	Language	Active language skills	–	group
B.45	Talk to native speakers	Language	Active language skills	–	pairs
B.46	Talk to yourself – internal monologue	Language	Active language skills	spoken	one
B.47	Listen to yourself live	Language	Active language skills	spoken	one
B.48	Record yourself 1	Language	Active language skills	spoken	one
B.49	Record and transcribe	Language	Active language skills	spoken	one
B.50	Record yourself 2	Language	Active language skills	spoken	one
B.51	Your favourite mistakes	Language	Active language skills	spoken	one
B.52	Reading aloud	Language	Active language skills	transcript	one
B.53	Total reading	Language	Active language skills	media, transcript	one
B.54	Total listening	Language	Active language skills	transcript	one

B.55	Inversion of form	Language	Active language skills	spoken	one
B.56	Shadowing	Language	Active language skills	spoken	one
B.57	Paraphrasing	Language	Active language skills	spoken	one
B.58	Paraphrase a single sentence	Language	Active language skills	text	one
B.59	Semantic dictation	Language	Active language skills	spoken	pairs
B.60	Blind drawing	Language	Active language skills	spoken	pairs
B.61	Learn by heart 1	Language	Active language skills	transcript, media	one
B.62	Learn by heart 2	Language	Active language skills	transcript	one
B.63	Write and learn speeches	Language	Active language skills	–	one
B.64	Create a debating society	Language	Active language skills	–	
B.65	Impersonate	Language	Active language skills	Internet	one
B.66	Poems and songs	Language	Active language skills	internet	one
B.67	Re-enact comedy sketches	Language	Active language skills	internet	
B.68	Recording vocabulary	Language	Active language skills	any	one
B.69	Collect vocab in collocation	Language	Active language skills	any	one
B.70	Create a collocation dictionary	Language	Active language skills	any	one
B.71	Become a label spotter	Language	Active language skills	–	one
B.72	Look up only what crops up (several times)	Language	Active language skills	books	one
B.73	Use Google images as a picture dictionary	Language	Active language skills	internet	one
B.74	Wiki-parallels	Language	Active language skills	internet	one
B.75	Read and record interesting terms	Language	Active language skills	any	One
B.76	Stock expressions	Language	Active language skills	transcript	One
B.77	The rise and fall of the synonym	Language	Active language skills	media	One
B.78	Crosswords	Language	Active language skills	–	One
B.79	Link memory	Language	Active language skills	–	One

C.30	Speech summaries 1	Consecutive	Analysis	spoken	pairs
C.31	Counting on your fingers	Consecutive	Analysis	spoken	pairs
C.32	Speech summaries 2	Consecutive	Analysis	spoken	pairs
C.33	Speech summaries 3	Consecutive	Analysis	spoken	pairs
C.34	Speech summaries 4	Consecutive	Analysis	spoken	pairs
C.35	Structured speeches 1	Consecutive	Analysis	spoken	pairs
C.36	Five point speeches	Consecutive	Analysis	spoken	pairs
C.37	Interpret film plots	Consecutive	Analysis	spoken	pairs
C.38	Monolingual interpreting	Consecutive	Analysis	spoken	pairs
C.39	Chop up into sections	Consecutive	Analysis	transcript	pairs
C.40	Jigsaw puzzle	Consecutive	Analysis	transcript	pairs
C.41	Spoken jigsaw puzzle	Consecutive	Analysis	transcript	group
C.42	Identify the skeleton of meaning	Consecutive	Analysis	transcript	one
C.43	Redaction	Consecutive	Analysis	transcript	one
C.44	Introduction to structure maps	Consecutive	Analysis	transcript	one
C.45	Create structure maps	Consecutive	Analysis	transcript	one
C.46	Mind Maps	Consecutive	Analysis	spoken	one
C.47	Notes on a single page	Consecutive	Analysis	–	one
C.48	Le fil rouge	Consecutive	Analysis	spoken	pairs
C.49	Identify ideas*	Consecutive	Analysis	transcript	one
C.50	Highlight the links*	Consecutive	Analysis	transcript	one
C.51	Ideas* and Links* – introduction to note structure	Consecutive	Analysis	transcript	one
C.52	Note only the links*	Consecutive	Analysis	transcript	one
C.53	Hands up if you hear a link	Consecutive	Analysis	spoken	group
C.54	Give note-taking structure to a text	Consecutive	Analysis	transcript	one
C.55	Create information hierarchies	Consecutive	Analysis	media	one
C.56	Connective exercises	Consecutive	Analysis	–	group
C.57	Re-introducing context	Consecutive	Analysis	media	pairs
C.58	Uncover the implicit	Consecutive	Analysis	media	one
C.59	Semantic Network Activation* 1	Consecutive	Analysis	transcript	pairs
C.60	Semantic Network Activation* 2	Consecutive	Analysis	transcript	pairs
C.61	Note-taking from lectures	Consecutive	Analysis	spoken	one
C.62	Note-taking with time lag	Consecutive	Analysis	spoken	pairs
C.63	Semantic dictation	Consecutive	Analysis	spoken	pairs
C.64	Take notes after the speech	Consecutive	Analysis	spoken	pairs
C.65	Take notes but don't use them	Consecutive	Analysis	spoken	pairs

C.66	Analyze how speeches are written	Consecutive	Analysis	transcripts	one
C.67	Learn to write speeches	Consecutive	Analysis	–	one
C.68	Recreate real meetings	Consecutive	Analysis	–	group
C.69	Work with real documents	Consecutive	Analysis	texts	group
C.70	Remembering sentences	Consecutive	Memory and recall	spoken	group
C.71	Rucksack packing exercise 1	Consecutive	Memory and recall	spoken	group
C.72	Rucksack packing exercise 2	Consecutive	Memory and recall	spoken	group
C.73	Info-Chain	Consecutive	Memory and recall	spoken	group
C.74	Liaison interpreting	Consecutive	Memory and recall	spoken	group
C.75	Recreate the news	Consecutive	Memory and recall	TV	one
C.76	Interpret from a picture	Consecutive	Memory and recall	spoken	group
C.77	Interpret from a picture you can't see	Consecutive	Memory and recall	spoken	group
C.78	Interpret film plots	Consecutive	Memory and recall	spoken	pairs
C.79	Tell a story	Consecutive	Memory and recall	spoken	pairs
C.80	Interpret fairytales	Consecutive	Memory and recall	spoken	pairs
C.81	Visualization	Consecutive	Memory and recall	spoken	pairs
C.82	Memory Linking	Consecutive	Memory and recall	–	one
C.83	Visual memory linking	Consecutive	Memory and recall	spoken	pairs
C.84	Location linking technique	Consecutive	Memory and recall	–	one
C.85	Structured speeches 2	Consecutive	Memory and recall	spoken	group
C.86	Counting on your fingers	Consecutive	Memory and recall	spoken	pairs
C.87	Deliberately don't note something	Consecutive	Memory and recall	spoken	pairs
C.88	Note left-handed	Consecutive	Memory and recall	spoken	one
C.89	Highlight and hide	Consecutive	Memory and recall	transcript	one
C.90	Brainstorm without a pen	Consecutive	Memory and recall	–	group

C.91	News round-up presentation without notes	Consecutive	Memory and recall	media	group
C.92	Improvize from prepared information	Consecutive	Memory and recall	media	group
C.93	Take notes after the speech	Consecutive	Memory and recall	spoken	pairs
C.94	Take notes but don't use them	Consecutive	Memory and recall	spoken	pairs
C.95	Word association	Consecutive	Memory and recall	–	group
C.96	Acronym testing	Consecutive	Memory and recall	–	group
C.97	Numbers and names speeches	Consecutive	Memory and recall	spoken	pairs
C.98	Mnemonic activation* 1	Consecutive	Memory and recall	–	pairs
C.99	Mnemonic activation* 2	Consecutive	Memory and recall	–	pairs
C.100	Ideas* and Links* – introduction to note structure	Consecutive	Note-taking	transcript	one
C.101	Give note-taking structure to a text	Consecutive	Note-taking	transcript	one
C.102	Monolingual interpreting	Consecutive	Note-taking	transcript, spoken	pairs
C.103	One word per paragraph	Consecutive	Note-taking	transcript, spoken	one
C.104	Note left-handed	Consecutive	Note-taking	spoken	one
C.105	Five point speeches	Consecutive	Note-taking	spoken	pairs
C.106	Semantic Network Activation* 1	Consecutive	Note-taking	–	pairs
C.107	Semantic Network Activation* 2	Consecutive	Note-taking	–	pairs
C.108	Take notes after the speech	Consecutive	Note-taking	spoken	one
C.109	Keep on keeping on	Consecutive	Note-taking	–	one
C.110	Take notes from transcript and slow speeches	Consecutive	Note-taking	transcript, spoken	one
C.111	Prepare speeches in consecutive note form	Consecutive	Note-taking	transcript	one
C.112	Practise diagonal notes	Consecutive	Note-taking	transcript	one
C.113	Divide the page in two	Consecutive	Note-taking	–	one
C.114	Highlight margin items	Consecutive	Note-taking	transcript	one
C.115	Note link and one word only	Consecutive	Note-taking	transcript	one
C.116	Noting less	Consecutive	Note-taking	transcript, spoken	one

C.117	Try different equipment	Consecutive	Note-taking	–	one
C.118	Rewrite your notes	Consecutive	Note-taking	–	one
C.119	Telescoping	Consecutive	Note-taking	–	one
C.120	Compare notes	Consecutive	Note-taking	–	pairs
C.121	Practise your structure and symbols	Consecutive	Note-taking	transcript	one
C.122	Reading your notes days later	Consecutive	Note-taking	–	one
C.123	Practise noting names	Consecutive	Note-taking	spoken	pairs
C.124	Take notes standing	Consecutive	Note-taking	–	one
C.125	Note only in target language	Consecutive	Reformulation	spoken	one
C.126	Do the same speech twice	Consecutive	Reformulation	spoken	one
C.127	Record your interpreting	Consecutive	Reformulation	spoken	one
C.128	Consec from consec	Consecutive	Reformulation	spoken	group
C.129	Film or record yourself	Consecutive	Self-monitoring	spoken	one
C.130	Referee each others' work	Consecutive	Self-monitoring	spoken	group
C.131	Improvization exercise 1	Consecutive	Split attention	spoken	group
C.132	Improvization exercise 2	Consecutive	Split attention	spoken	group
C.133	Improvization exercise 3	Consecutive	Split attention	spoken	group
C.134	Interpret from a picture you can't see	Consecutive	Split attention	spoken	group
C.135	Shadow and write	Consecutive	Split attention	spoken	one
C.136	One word per paragraph	Consecutive	Split attention	spoken	one
C.137	Take notes from slow speeches	Consecutive	Split attention	spoken	pairs
C.138	Note-taking with time lag	Consecutive	Split attention	spoken	one
C.139	Note-reading according to Jones	Consecutive	Split attention	transcript	one
C.140	Double note-taking	Consecutive	Split attention	spoken	one
D.1	Do consecutive from simultaneous	Simultaneous	Delivery	spoken	group
D.2	Inverted conference	Simultaneous	Delivery	spoken	group
D.3	Whispering	Simultaneous	Delivery	spoken	group
D.4	Do it again	Simultaneous	Delivery	spoken	pairs
D.5	Shadow* a bad speaker	Simultaneous	Delivery	spoken	one
D.6	Turn the volume down	Simultaneous	Delivery	spoken	one
D.7	Improvization exercise 1	Simultaneous	Split attention	spoken	group
D.8	Improvization exercise 2	Simultaneous	Split attention	spoken	group
D.9	Two words at a time	Simultaneous	Split attention	spoken	pairs
D.10	Two questions at a time 1	Simultaneous	Split attention	spoken	pairs
D.11	Two questions at a time 2	Simultaneous	Split attention	spoken	pairs
D.12	Listen and count	Simultaneous	Split attention	spoken	one
D.13	Listen and do sums	Simultaneous	Split attention	spoken	one
D.14	Sight translation* – one sentence at a time	Simultaneous	Split attention	texts	pairs

D.15	Sight translation*	Simultaneous	Split attention	texts	pairs
D.16	Interpret in slow motion	Simultaneous	Split attention	spoken	one
D.17	Interpret silently	Simultaneous	Split attention	spoken	one
D.18	Listen first, interpret second time	Simultaneous	Split attention	spoken	one
D.19	Consecutive first	Simultaneous	Split attention	spoken	pairs
D.20	Reported interpreting	Simultaneous	Split attention	spoken	pairs
D.21	Number plates	Simultaneous	Split attention	–	one
D.22	Read and listen	Simultaneous	Split attention	transcript, spoken	one
D.23	Spotting meaningful chunks	Simultaneous	Time lag	spoken	one
D.24	Maximise your time lag*	Simultaneous	Time lag	spoken	one
D.25	Minimize your time lag*	Simultaneous	Time lag	spoken	one
D.26	Vary your time lag*	Simultaneous	Time lag	spoken	pairs
D.27	Make salami	Simultaneous	Time lag	spoken	one
D.28	Shuffle the sentence	Simultaneous	Time lag	spoken	one
D.29	Shuffle the clauses	Simultaneous	Time lag	spoken	one
D.30	Time lag* with numbers only	Simultaneous	Time lag	spoken	pairs
D.31	Analyze how speeches are written	Simultaneous	Anticipation	books, transcript	one
D.32	Learn to write speeches	Simultaneous	Anticipation	books	one
D.33	Give structured speeches 1	Simultaneous	Anticipation	spoken	pairs
D.34	What comes next	Simultaneous	Anticipation	transcript	pairs
D.35	What comes next 2	Simultaneous	Anticipation	transcript	one
D.36	What comes next 3	Simultaneous	Anticipation	transcript	one
D.37	Cloze exercise	Simultaneous	Anticipation	transcript	one
D.38	Highlight and anticipate	Simultaneous	Anticipation	transcript	one
D.39	Torn newspapers	Simultaneous	Anticipation	media	one
D.40	Fill in the blanks	Simultaneous	Anticipation	spoken	pairs
D.41	Shadow and eliminate interference	Simultaneous	Anticipation	spoken	pairs
D.42	Do it again	Simultaneous	Anticipation	spoken	pairs
D.43	Written translation	Simultaneous	Reformulation	texts	one
D.44	Read translations	Simultaneous	Reformulation	texts	one
D.45	Group translation	Simultaneous	Reformulation	texts	group
D.46	Keep a logbook 2	Simultaneous	Reformulation	–	one
D.47	Parallel texts	Simultaneous	Reformulation	media	one
D.48	Parallel texts for political standpoint	Simultaneous	Reformulation	media	one
D.49	Multiple paraphrasing	Simultaneous	Reformulation	texts	group
D.50	Paraphrase (in same language)	Simultaneous	Reformulation	transcript	one
D.51	Deverbalization 1	Simultaneous	Reformulation	transcript	one
D.52	Deverbalization 2	Simultaneous	Reformulation	media	one

D.53	Reverbalization	Simultaneous	Reformulation	spoken	one
D.54	Dubbing	Simultaneous	Reformulation	TV	group
D.55	Improvization exercise	Simultaneous	Reformulation	spoken	group
D.56	Interpret from a picture	Simultaneous	Reformulation	spoken	group
D.57	Interpret from a picture you can't see	Simultaneous	Reformulation	spoken	group
D.58	Describe a photo	Simultaneous	Reformulation	spoken	pairs
D.59	Sight paraphrasing	Simultaneous	Reformulation	transcript	pairs
D.60	Monolingual interpreting	Simultaneous	Reformulation	spoken	pairs
D.61	Say the opposite	Simultaneous	Reformulation	transcript, spoken	one
D.62	Change the grammar, leave the meaning	Simultaneous	Reformulation	transcript, spoken	one
D.63	Try extremes of register	Simultaneous	Reformulation	spoken	one
D.64	Summarize drastically	Simultaneous	Reformulation	spoken	one
D.65	Add redundancies	Simultaneous	Reformulation	spoken	one
D.66	Stock phrases	Simultaneous	Reformulation	spoken	one
D.67	Overuse a metaphor	Simultaneous	Reformulation	spoken	group
D.68	Make salami	Simultaneous	Reformulation	spoken	one
D.69	Shuffle information items	Simultaneous	Reformulation	spoken	one
D.70	Shuffle chunks of the sentence	Simultaneous	Reformulation	spoken	one
D.71	Correct with a thesaurus	Simultaneous	Reformulation	spoken	one
D.72	Do it again	Simultaneous	Reformulation	spoken	one
D.73	Give it a thorough going over	Simultaneous	Reformulation	spoken	one
D.74	Make a transcript of your work	Simultaneous	Reformulation	spoken	one
D.75	Teacher Demonstration	Simultaneous	Reformulation	spoken	group
D.76	Paraphrase when reading aloud	Simultaneous	Reformulation	transcript	one
D.77	Replace cognates*	Simultaneous	Reformulation	transcript, spoken	one
D.78	Use cognates*	Simultaneous	Reformulation	transcript, spoken	one
D.79	Improvizing synonyms	Simultaneous	Reformulation	spoken	one
D.80	Use Plan 'B'	Simultaneous	Reformulation	spoken	one
D.81	Mnemonic activation* 1	Simultaneous	Reformulation	–	pairs
D.82	Mnemonic activation* 2	Simultaneous	Reformulation	–	pairs
D.83	Listen to other students' work	Simultaneous	Self-monitoring	spoken	group
D.84	Post-it notes	Simultaneous	Self-monitoring	–	one
D.85	Keep a logbook	Simultaneous	Self-monitoring	–	one
D.86	Record your work	Simultaneous	Self-monitoring	–	one
D.87	Give it a thorough going over	Simultaneous	Self-monitoring	–	one
D.88	Record and transcribe	Simultaneous	Self-monitoring	spoken	one
D.89	Confer with colleagues	Simultaneous	Self-monitoring	spoken	group

D.90	Shadow* a bad speaker	Simultaneous	Self-monitoring	spoken	
D.91	Dubbing	Simultaneous	Stress management	spoken	group
D.92	Re-enact a comedy sketch	Simultaneous	Stress management	spoken	group
D.93	Put your feet up	Simultaneous	Stress management	spoken	
D.94	Stand on a chair	Simultaneous	Stress management	spoken	
D.95	Stand in a corner	Simultaneous	Stress management	spoken	group
D.96	Dress-up Friday	Simultaneous	Stress management	–	group
D.97	Blind drawing	Simultaneous	Stress management	–	pairs
D.98	Face massage	Simultaneous	Stress management	–	one
D.99	Aahh	Simultaneous	Stress management	–	one
D.100	Virtual travel	Simultaneous	Stress management	–	one
D.101	Shoulder melting	Simultaneous	Stress management	–	one
D.102	Auto-suggestion	Simultaneous	Stress management	–	one
D.103	Sight Translation* with a time limit	Simultaneous	Stress management	texts	pairs
D.104	Improvization exercise 1	Simultaneous	Stress management	spoken	group
D.105	Improvization exercise 2	Simultaneous	Stress management	spoken	group
D.106	Say the opposite	Simultaneous	Stress management	spoken	group
D.107	Try extremes of register	Simultaneous	Stress management	spoken	group
D.108	Overuse a metaphor	Simultaneous	Stress management	spoken	group